M000247964

Field Marshal Viscount Edmund H. H. Allenby
of Megiddo and Felixstowe, GCB, GCMG.

▼ A patrol of Australian Light Horse leaves camp near Alexandria in early 1916. Note cavalier plumes and goggles attached to the hatbands. The sergeant riding in the foreground has the special canvas and bamboo cavalry stretcher strapped to the rifle bucket and saddle (next to his right arm).

David L. Bullock

ALLENBY'S WAR

The Palestine-Arabian Campaigns, 1916–1918

BLANDFORD PRESS

LONDON NEW YORK SYDNEY

In Memoriam Gladys (Finch) Flint

First published in Great Britain
in 1988 by Blandford Press, Artillery
House, Artillery Row, London
SW1P 1RT.

Distributed in the USA by Sterling
Publishing Co. Inc., 2 Park Avenue,
New York, NY 10016.

Distributed in Australia by
Capricorn Link (Australia) Pty. Ltd.,
P.O. Box 665, Lane Cove,
New South Wales 2066, Australia.

© David Bullock, 1988
All rights reserved. No part of this
book may be reproduced or
transmitted in any form or by any
means electronic or mechanical
including photocopying recording or
any information storage and
retrieval system without permission
in writing from the Publisher.

British Library Cataloguing in
Publication Data:
Bullock, David
Allenby's war: the Palestine-Arabian
campaigns, 1916–1918
1. World War, 1914–1918 –
Campaigns – Arab countries
I. Title
940.4'15   D568.4

ISBN 0-7137-1869-2

The illustrations in this book have
been collected from many sources,
and vary in quality owing to the
variety of circumstances under
which they were taken and
preserved. As a result, certain of the
illustrations are not of the standard
to be expected from the best of
today's equipment, materials and
techniques. They are nevertheless
included for their inherent
information value, to provide an
authentic visual coverage of the
subject.

Designed by DAG Publications Ltd.
Designed by David Gibbons; edited
by Michael Burns; typeset by
Typesetters (Birmingham) Ltd.,
camerawork by M&E Graphics,
North Fambridge, Essex; printed
and bound in Great Britain by
Richard Clay Ltd, Chichester,
Sussex.

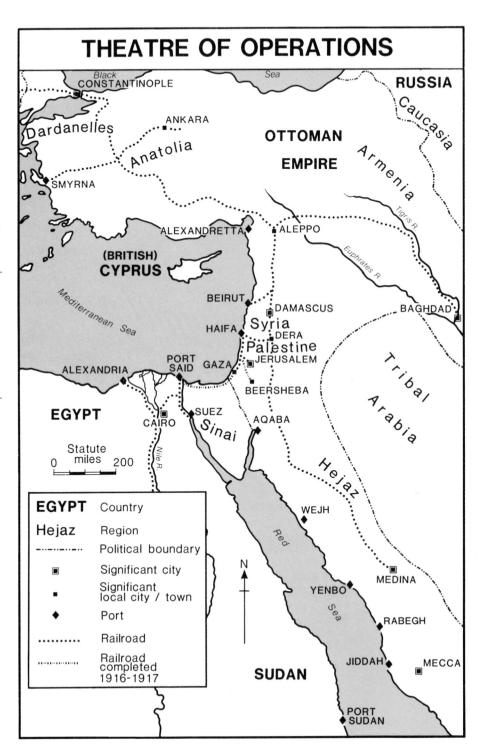

THEATRE OF OPERATIONS

Statute miles
0   200

EGYPT   Country
Hejaz   Region
--·--·--   Political boundary
▣   Significant city
▪   Significant
           local city / town
◆   Port
·········· Railroad
·····⋯⋯·   Railroad
           completed
           1916-1917

CONTENTS

MAPS

⊠	British General Headquarters, or GHQ
C*	Turkish General Headquarters, or GHQ
xxx / 21	British Corps Headquarters and number
xxxx / 8	Turkish Army Headquarters and number
⊠	British Infantry
◻	British Cavalry
⊠	Turkish Infantry
▨	Turkish Cavalry
54	Unit Number
xxxx	Army size unit or HQ
xxx	Corps size unit or HQ
xx	Division size unit
x	Brigade size unit
III	Regiment size unit
II	Battalion size unit
△	EEF cavalry screen
▲	Turk cavalry screen
⚔	Arab raid
⚔	Turkish surrender
→	Thrust
– – –	Army boundary
------→	Detachments position
–·–··–	Border
+++++	Railroad
⛴	British Naval Force
AC	Asia Corps
AMD	Australian Mounted Division
ANA	Arab Northern Army
ANZMD	Anzac Mounted Division
CCB	Caucasian Cavalry Brigade
20CC	20th Cavalry Corps
CF	Composite Force
DMC	Desert Mounted Corps
EEF	Egyptian Expeditionary Force
ICB	Imperial Camel Brigade
IMD	Imperial Mounted Division
ISCB	Imperial Service Cavalry Brigade
LH	(Australian) Light Horse
NZMR	New Zealand Mounted Rifles
YMD	Yeomanry Mounted Division

Right: Turkish cavalry crossing a Jordan ford, probably the Caucasian Cavalry Brigade.

PREFACE

FEW locales can excite the adventurous Western reader as the exotic East, and no other setting can command the historical and spiritual presence of the Holy Land of the Christian, Moslem, and Jew. Unfolding against this majestic backdrop, the 1916–1918 Palestine–Arabian Campaigns may unavoidably be called a Crusade . . . the 'Last Crusade'. From General Sir Edmund Allenby we may, perhaps, receive an impression of a modern Richard the Lionheart, and in his cavalry the resurrection of the knights of renown. From the legendary Lawrence of Arabia and his bodyguard of 'Forty Thieves' we may imagine the heights of romance and derring-do. And in this reverie we might not be far from the truth, for reality is sometimes more incredible than fiction, and these were great men.

The events of the Palestine–Arabian Campaigns have seldom been considered as as the coordinated allied effort they were. From 1916–1918 the Egyptian Expeditionary Force and the leaders of the Arab Revolt sought, by common cause, to defeat the Ottoman Empire by force of arms. Few perhaps appreciate that the Arab Revolt would have been stillborn without British supply and gold, and without the presentation of the Egyptian Expeditionary Force front in Palestine. Conversely, few Western readers, and even regular veterans of the Palestine Front, may be aware of the pervasive extent of Arab influence and, indeed, the considerable almost 'unseen' hand which so greatly eased their burden of campaign by the distraction of Turkish manpower, resource, and national will. For this reason the Arabs have received a naturally proportionate share of this book. Similarly, Arab personalities are perhaps more 'personalised' than their Egyptian Expeditionary Force counterparts. My apologia is that personalities, as in any feudalistic or tribal structure, are more important in their particular expression of war.

Although this book has primarily a 'Western', English-speaking orientation, I have attempted to present the German–Turkish point of view wherever possible. Analysis of the 'other side' is important to demonstrate that even though the campaigns were the most outstanding Allied theatre success of World War One, the victory was not a walk-over and the 'other side' were valiant soldiers. As for the ANZACs, they were magnificent, and after Gallipoli, nothing else would have been expected. It would be hard to imagine a finer breed of man to fight on Palestine's fields than the light horseman of the outback mounted on his country-bred waler.

The maps in this text have been researched and adapted from official records provided by intelligence sources shortly after the war. Dates are expressed 'European style', that is – 1/12/16 means first December 1916. These maps portray more order of battle and operations than is usual because, armed with such data, the discerning strategist will acquire a much clearer picture of the Palestine–Arabian Campaigns.

I have tried to be consistent with spellings transliterated from the original Arabic and Turkish. There have been so many past haphazard derivations that probably no 'scientific' attempt at consistency could today undo the inexhaustible supply of variation or obtain universal acceptance. Sadly, Lawrence in his writings contributed to the confusion almost with pleasure; as a lesser mortal, I will hide behind his robes in meek apology.

ACKNOWLEDGEMENTS

MY first thanks must go to Claire (Grainger) Carlton for taking my crudely drawn (sketches) and transforming them into proper maps. Repeatedly, she rearranged them to suit my changing whim, all on the barest expense account, and sometimes perhaps against her better cartographical judgment. If there is honour here it is unreservedly hers, a mistake – it is mine. And, if taxing the wife were not enough, I taxed the husband as well . . . thanks to Richard Carlton for unstinting personal assistance during my last months on England's shore.

I must acknowledge over the years as a 'Yank at Oxford' the inspirations of several individuals. For historical companionship, John and Monica Pocock, Ralph Lloyd-Jones, Dr Ted Herbert, the distinguished body of the Victorian Military Society, Jeff and Janet Burn, and the noble Nicholas Volkov-Mouromtsoff.

On the other side of the pond, I must thank Mayor Mike Carr for the many chats in military history, especially during those long months in the wilds of Africa, and Bill Thomas and Mark and Harold Grotjahn for their many partnerships and mutual travels. And above all, for any imaginative or historical merit herein, gratitude to my parents, Terry and Elaine Bullock.

I am indebted to the Imperial War Museum and its professional staff, and to Jane Carmichael, its Keeper of Photographs, for her high sense of cooperative fair-play. I include the following citation of this hallmark museum:

> The bulk of the photographs in this book are drawn from the substantial archive of the Imperial War Museum, London. Members of the public are welcome to consult the collection in the Department's Visitors' Room and help with research is also given by post. Copy prints are available for a small fee.

Also of assistance was Colonel M. B. Haycock, CBE, TD, DL, Chairman of the Warwickshire Yeomanry Museum Trust, whose archival and photo displays were most interesting. Instrumental for my research was the Oxford Bodleian Library and the London Public Records Office. Thanks to Major D. Baxter, DL, curator of the Museum of the Northamptonshire Regiment where I came across John F. Brown, grandson of Colonel John Brown. Late in 1917 a Turkish shell hurled the elder John Brown from a window at the defence of Wilhelma. Had the explosion been inches nearer there might have been no younger John Brown nor the applicable photos enclosed. My acknowledgements carry the below citation:

> Colonel (later General Sir) John Brown led the 4th Battalion of the Northamptonshire Regiment from May 1916 through the devastating attacks on Gaza and the much admired defence of Wilhelma – 'A model of what an offensive defensive should be' (Maj. Gen. Sir S. W. Hare) – until ill health forced his repatriation to England in April 1918. 'I have known the Battalion now for three years and all that time they have never done anything but the very best. I have seen their work both in bad times and in good and I could not wish to see a better Battalion or one better commanded.' (Maj. Gen. Sir S. W. Hare, 1919).

I have been unable to locate, if such still exists, any copyright owner of the photos I have taken from a copy of Lowell Thomas' exciting book *With Lawrence in Arabia*, published by Hutchinson and Co., Ltd circa 1921.

David L. Bullock, 1987

PICTURE CREDITS

All photographs are reproduced by courtesy of the Imperial War Museum except for the following: Australian War Memorial, pages 21, 98 (bottom), 113, 122, 132 (top); Bodleian Library, pages 92, 94 (bottom), 96 (bottom), 105 (bottom), 132 (bottom), 138; Bruce Robertson Collection, pages 32, 33 (top), 63, 69, 96 (top), 102 (top), 115 (top) 132; Bundesarchiv, pages 43 (top), 70; John F. Brown Collection, pages 20, 25 (top), 60, 121 (bottom), 139; National Army Museum, page 24; Warwickshire Yeomanry Museum, pages 27, 33 (bottom), 43 (bottom left), 78, 101 (top); *With Lawrence in Arabia* (Hutchinson, London, c.1921), pages 38, 39, 40, 58, 84, 111, 150.

Right: Turkish marines on the march.

PROLOGUE

IN August, 1914, the belligerents of Europe waltzed in the anticipation of a short and glorious war. Not since Napoleon had mainland Europe engaged in armed conflict lasting beyond a few weeks duration. War was the science of training and maneuver, and the sabres of the *arme blanche* and the bayonets of the *offensive à outrance* had yet to be soaked in the stalemated blood of history's first total war.

The 'Guns of August' which shattered the Concert of Europe staked the powers of the Triple Entente — Britain, Russia, and France — against the might of Wilhelmine Germany and its ally Austria–Hungary. After breathtaking opening moves, the Germans crushed Russia's offensive at Tannenberg, and were themselves halted by the French on the Marne. The war machine's momentum slowed. With the decimation of the first tide and the depletion of the stocks of war, autumn leaves fell as all sides paused for breath, then dug-in. Few, even then, forsaw the magnitude of this new war which dropped as a meteor into the centre of a placid sea and rippled outward from Europe's madness onto the calm of distant shores.

In 1914, Egypt was a political anomaly caught between two worlds threatening to pull her into the general conflict. Egypt's unfortunate position was as host to the Suez Canal. When the Canal had opened in 1869, Britain had immediately recognised its invaluable line of communication to India and to the eastern colonial possessions. The Canal's integrity became a cornerstone of Imperial policy, resulting in an embroilment in Egyptian affairs from 1882–1898. The successful conclusion of the Protective Power's operations left Britain's Consul General premier in Egyptian foreign policy and defence. Ironically, Egypt's nominal head of state was still the Sultan of Turkey who had the additional significance, as Caliph, of heading the Moslem world.

This irony led to a political farce. Britain, though at war with Germany and Austria-Hungary, was officially unable to expel enemy diplomats and agents from Egypt. Turkey was still neutral and such a dismissal on her technically sovereign soil would have provoked a diplomatic incident. As it was, Turkey's position of armed neutrality was becoming increasingly suspect from all quarters as Germany's heavy courtship increased.

The question of Turkish neutrality was of paramount interest to the *Chargé d' Affaires*, Sir Milne Cheetham, to Major-General Byng commanding the Force in Egypt, and to General Sir Reginald Wingate, Governor-General of the Sudan and Sirdar of the Egyptian Army. Rumours of sabotage were afloat and 70,000 Turkish nationals were residing in Egypt. On Egypt's western border the Senussi Moslems were in revolt against colonial Italy, still neutral in the European arena. To the south, the Sudan had only been pacified in recent years. To the east, German officers were reported supervising Turkish road building in Palestine. It was a ring of potential trouble, especially if Turkey broke neutrality and the Caliph called the faithful to Holy War.

Despite concern for the Canal, Britain's own security came first. Lord Herbert Kitchener embarked from Egypt in early August having been promoted Secretary of State for War. Soon after, Byng left for Britain, leaving Lieutenant-General Sir John Maxwell in charge of the Force in Egypt. Maxwell's fame at the Battle of Omdurman had been enhanced by a command of the Force in Egypt from 1908–12.

A series of troop embarkations, disembarkations, and transfers progressed throughout autumn as troops from India arrived in Egypt and were sent on to the battle-grounds of France. The Force in Egypt was kept balanced with a curious formula against the perceived threat in the Middle East, as opposed to the more certain menace on the Western Front.

As the weeks went on, this perception of threat in the Middle East resulted in the imminence of armed clash. Germany desired the reinforcement of a Turkish force with its assets aptly aimed at British possessions. Enver Pasha, Turkey's practical head of state as the leader of the 'Young Turks', desired his country to enter the foray on the winning side. Germany could already exert a strong lever on Turkey's decision by the method of its exported arms, loans, engineering, and extensive diplomatic contact. Further, German martial prestige was high, and in the 1914 scenario, seemingly triumphant. Enver was in no doubt as to his choice. It only remained for him and collusive German elements to drag Turkey by degrees into the flames of war.

Within Turkey, Enver's path was eased by the British contract cancellation on 3 August of two dreadnoughts she had been building for Turkey at the Armstrong-Whitworth shipyards in Britain. Even though compensation was tendered in lieu of delivery the Turkish public outcry was prolific – for the construction funds had been donated by popular subscription.

Capitalising on this seeming slap to Turkish national pride, the Germans returned their battle cruiser *Goeben* to its pre-war anchorage at Constantinople, along with the German cruiser *Breslau*, in cooperative violation of Turkish neutrality on 11 August. In response to diplomatic protest the German crews humourously donned Turkish fezzes and announced the ships purchased by the Turkish government. Three days later the British Naval Mission in Constantinople was handed its walking papers.

Alarmed, on 18 August the Entente Powers turned the other cheek and jointly declared the guarantee of Turkish security in exchange for fastidious neutrality. It was not known – indeed, it was a secret from much of the Turkish government – that Enver and the German Ambassador, von Wangenheim, had already concluded a treaty of armed cooperation. Over the next three months Turkey began a general mobilisation.

The final straw was laid when the German and Turkish crews of the *Goeben* and *Hamidieh* bombarded Russian ports in the Crimea on 27 October. Three days later the ambassadors of Britain, Russia and France had terminated all official business.

The Middle East was at war.

Left: Turkish (Anatolian) infantry taking a rest from marching. Note protective goggles.

Right: Turkish lancers on parade by troops with commanding staff in the foreground. At least one German officer is discernible in tropical uniform in the second rank of staff (fourth from left). A brigade was composed of two or three regiments with four field squadrons and one reinforcement depot squadron each. Brigade strength was intended to be from 1,400 to 2,000 sabres with 12 machine guns and eight horse artillery pieces. Before the First World War, however, many ethnic Arab and Kurdish cavalry units had been disbanded from suspect political loyalty so that the Turkish formations in the Palestine–Arabian Campaigns were fortunate to see half this establishment.

PART 1
GAMBIT
August 1914 to December 1915

THE 'SICK MAN' AND THE GERMAN PHYSICIAN

FROM the foundation of the Ottoman dynasty in AD 1299 to the destruction of the Byzantine Empire at Constantinople in 1453, the Turks had displayed a knack for administration and a zeal for conquest. The historical impetus of the Ottoman Turk carried him across Central Asia, the Middle East, North Africa, and into the Balkans. This successor to the Arab Empire absorbed Arab culture while adopting, then heading, the Moslem experience. Twice this dynamic new power rapped sternly at Vienna's gates, threatening the subjugation of Christendom.

Yet, from the highwater of 1683, the Ottoman Empire slipped into a slow but steady state of historical decline. The emergence of Russia and Austria as expansionist powers rolled back the Turkish frontiers, while the impulse of the nineteenth-century Industrial Revolution accentuated the reality of internal decay. Rising nationalism among Ottoman subject peoples and foreign encroachment under the colonial auspice beset the 'Sick Man of Europe' as a disease which atrophied the Turkish limbs to leave an uncertain trunk. Three wars were fought with Russia before the breaking of the twentieth century.

This power vacuum, inevitably produced by the decline of empire, left Europe entangled in searching for solutions to the 'Eastern Question', and Turkey in the need of finding a friend. Britain's record had been too vacillating and self-interested for amity, for 'Perfidious Albion' had regularly supported Turkey to hinder Russian aims, yet had as often supported Ottoman national aspirants throughout the 1800s. Too often the British press had been wont to decry the occasional Turkish massacre of an unruly subject people. By 1907, when Britain and France entered into the Triple Entente with Turkey's traditional enemy, Russia, the choices for allies among the great powers were dwindling. And Wilhelmine Germany was anxious that this be so.

From the 1888 ascension of Kaiser Wilhelm II to the German throne there was no secret of Germany's overtures to the Ottoman Empire. Six years earlier, a military mission had been established in Constantinople under General Colmar von der Goltz. The Kaiser visited Sultan Abdul Hamid, the 'Damned', on two state occasions in 1889 and 1898, recognising him as Caliph of Islam's 300 million subjects. Wilhelm spoke of friendship, and ceremoniously laid the foundation stone of the German hospice in Jerusalem. To a moribund state, the attentions of the vital new German Empire were flattering.

Deed surmounted word. Economics and military assistance went hand-in-hand with diplomatic contact. The Deutsche Bank advanced credits, the lauded 'Berlin to Baghdad' railway was put under construction, and shipping, communications, and medical relief work began. Such aid was not altruistic; the Ottoman Empire sat astride the hub of three continents – Europe, Asia, and Africa. Its Dardanelles Straits were as strategically significant to Russia as was the

◄
Kaiser Wilhelm II in German uniform with *pickelhaube*, Sultan Mohammed V of Turkey (white glove upraised), and Enver Pasha (seated front, facing backwards) in the state carriage in Constantinople under cavalry escort. Enver has given the Sultan seating precedence for decorum, when in reality, Enver's dictatorial power had reduced the Sultanate to a nonentity.

Suez Canal to Great Britain. If Turkey physically dominated the Straits, she was in position to physically threaten the Canal. And her spiritual leadership of Islam, through the unified position of Sultan and Caliph, was a potentially poised dagger aimed at the heart of Britain's colonial administration of Moslem territory.

During Baron Field Marshal von Bieberstein's tenure as ambassador in Constantinople the 'Young Turk' Revolution of 1908 erupted in a bloodless coup against Sultan Abdul Hamid, who was officially deposed the following year. The 'Young Turks', or the Party of Union and Progress, sought to reverse the Turkish decline and to constitute a new Turkey under a competent and nationalistic government. The 1876 Constitution was reinstated, and Mohammed V, an aged non-entity, was raised as titular Sultan.

The real power of the Revolution was in the hands of the top four Cabinet members of the Committee of Young Turks: Enver, at 27 years old, the Minister of War; Djemal, aged 36, Minister of Marine; Djavid, Minister of Finance; and Talaat, aged 34, Minister of the Interior. Both Enver and Djemal had been trained at the Turkish War College. Enver had additionally been Military Attaché in Berlin where he had acquired definite Germanophile tendencies. In the next years the Committee increasingly fell under the spell of Enver's immense if egotistical personality. And German influence enlarged with him.

Turkey's new rulers were soon challenged by a series of conflicts. In 1911, Italy attacked Turkish garrisons in Tripoli (modern Libya). The First Balkan War commenced in October, 1912, with Greece, Serbia, Bulgaria, and Montenegro pouncing on the remnant of the Turkish domain in Europe. The state of Albania emerged from this liberated land in 1913. Only a month after the peace the Second Balkan War broke out, Turkey seizing the chance to expand her *desmesne* around Adrianople in her last corner of Southeastern Europe.

In 1912, Baron von Wangenheim succeeded as German ambassador, nicknamed, for his forceful personality, the 'Cuirassier Diplomat'. Turkey's experience in the Balkan Wars had not been happy: too many men, horses, and war materials had been lost. More than ever a sympathetic and revitalising ally was needed. This support came, in 1913, in the manner of the German military mission led by General Liman von Sanders and 70 officer personnel. Its application would increase Turkish dependence on German equipment, methodology, and expertise.

Early in 1914, the Kaiser promoted von Sanders to general of cavalry. As German officers were by contract accorded one rank higher in Turkish service, this elevated von Sanders to Field Marshal. Simultaneously, he was appointed Inspector-General of the Turkish Army. In his autobiography, *Five Years in Turkey*, von Sanders rendered a critical account of Turkish conditions, citing a 'mental depression' among the officers of 1st Corps near the capital, and a general disregard for the common soldier everywhere. The General Staff College and training centres taught 'an excess of theory', while practical terrain exercises were neglected, which resulted in an overall lack of operative judgment.

▲ Kaiser Wilhelm II dressed as a Turkish Field Marshal during his state visit to Constantinople, 16 October 1917. The Kaiser paid similar official state visits in 1889 and 1898. Taken to heart was Napoleon's rhetorical comment: 'Who is to have Constantinople? That is always the crux of the problem.'

▲ A Turkish Volunteer Regiment on parade in high fezzes with reed flutes (foreground). Officers in regular infantry uniform and 'enverieh' caps ride behind the platoons on horses. Rear platoons have rifles. On paper, a Turkish division of three regiments of three battalions each stood at 8–9,000 rifles, including 12 machine guns, and from 24–36 pieces of artillery. Few divisions ever saw this establishment, the divisions in the Palestine–Arabian Campaigns rarely exceeding even one-third of this intended rifle strength.

Cooking arrangements were irregular in service and unsanitary in practice, as were barracks, and even official buildings. There were no barrack baths nor any airing procedures. To the German, matters were devoid of a 'sense of order and cleanliness and diligence'. In the prevailing circumstances these observations were hardly surprising, for many senior Turkish officers considered it beneath their dignity to attend to such detail!

During his inspections efforts were made to keep certain unpleasantries in the closet. In hospitals, the most critically ill were kept away from view under lock and key, while on parade the weak and poorly trained soldiers were hidden. As if from a scripted comedy, the scarcity of Turkish uniform was concealed by rotating the same inspected uniforms upon different soldiers at different inspection sites. Von Sanders soon learned to conduct no-notice inspections . . .

Of particular interest was the condition of the cavalry. Many mounts were suffering from farcy contracted during the Balkan Wars. The horses were small by European standards and Turkish training had emphasised the role of mounted infantry rather than the vaunted 'shock' action of European cavalry still enamoured with the chivalric tradition. Sadly, Turkey maintained only a small proportion of cavalry because many Arab and Kurdish units had been disbanded due to political unreliability.

For military purposes, Turkey was divided between four Army Inspectorates or Fronts, with General Headquarters at the political capital of Constantinople.

Front	Headquarters
European	Constantinople
Caucasian	Erzinjan
Mesopotamian	Baghdad
Palestine-Arabian	Damascus

The number of corps attached to each Front varied with the current strategic emphasis, while the usual number of divisions allotted to a corps was three. In August, 1914, Turkey possessed 36 understrength divisions, each consisting of three regiments, each of three battalions.[1] One million men were liable for military service, and 200,000 men and 10,000 officers were serving with the peacetime colours. Eventually, Turkey would mobilise another 34 divisions, and a total of 2,700,000 men. Because of desertion and heavy losses in some units, however, there were never more than 43 divisions in simultaneous action during World War 1, nor more than a ration strength of 650,000 in action at a given time.[2]

German influence sat at a high level within this military machine. Enver Pasha, as Minister of War, was preeminent, despite theoretical parliamentary checks guaranteed by the Constitution. Enver headed the Superior Military Council with his right hand position occupied by von der Goltz – the original military mission emissary sent out in 1882.

It remained for the trial of battle to pass verdict on its craft.

Recruitment in the Turkish Army

The foot soldier is the national common denominator in war. His assessment is as revealing as any textbook study of national theory or strategy. Without him the country and the general does not wage war, and only *through* him can a war be won. Military service in the Turkish Army began with a compulsory two-year active duty assignment followed by 16 years in the active reserves. From this impressive pool was in reality subtracted a rulebook of exemptions and loopholes. Nevertheless, from a peacetime standing army of 210,000 in August, 1914, the Turkish ration strength under arms had expanded to 1,000,000 by the late autumn.

Overall, leadership was below general European standards, and was particularly so when compared with the more advanced industrialised countries. Officers came from two distinct groups: those from formal military schools and those from the ranks — most of whom lacked rudimentary communication skills. Under German guidance and staff improvements prior to World War 1, this latter category was diminishing until mass mobilisation reintroduced destabilising numbers.

Two broad geographical areas were recruiting grounds for the Turkish Army. Anatolia was the traditional Ottoman homeland, bordered in the north, west, and southwest by the Black and Mediterranean Seas, in the northeast by the district of Armenia, and in the southeast by the Taurus Mountains which separated Anatolia from the occupied Arab lands. In Anatolia resided the pride of Turkish martial pursuit: stolid peasant stock, brave in the attack and stubborn in the defence. If his marksmanship was notably poor, yet his artillery was well served, and he could record infantry marches often comparable to that expected of European cavalry. Recurrently the butt of an officer's ill-humour and the victim of corrupt supply and inefficient transport, the Anatolian suffered with hardiness to exist in conditions proven detrimental to European health and morale.

South of the Taurus and the Armenian province were the lands of the ethnic Arab, long subjugated by Ottoman rule yet united by common religion. Alexander Aaronsohn, a Syrian Jew who was drafted into the Turkish Army in 1914–15, offered a vivid portrait of recruitment and training in his brief memoirs, *With the Turks in Palestine*.

Turkish standards of acceptance in the ethnic Arab region were low. Evasion of service was rife and inductees would imbibe compounds to create artificial sores and sickness, or resort to minor mutilations in order to be released. Officers familiar with such evasion were seen to beat offenders with sometimes fatal results for the genuinely sick.

Upon registration for service, Aaronsohn and other draftees were given no time in which to conclude personal affairs, but were force-marched in civilian clothes to the nearest garrison town at Saffèd. As no commissary arrangements were provided en route, those with pocket money spent it for food, while those without learned to steal, their pilferage increasing in daring under the accepting eyes of their officers.

At camp, reveille began at 0500 hours and training continued until nightfall. Drill progressed in lots of 50 men, supervised by an NCO graduate from the military schools of Constantinople or Damascus, or when one was not available, by a senior private. German military drill was in force in autumn, 1914, but it was the root of confusion, especially with voice commands, as older ways were not so quickly forgotten, nor new translations so easily understood. Target practice was rare because of an ammunition shortage. Similarly frugal were Government meals, which were usually of boiled rice ministered in tin wash basins, in quantities deemed sufficient for ten men.

Months into the War, Turkish military authorities began systematically disarming Christian and Jewish soldiers and began conscripting them into labour battalions. Their loyalty had become increasingly suspect as had, to a lesser degree, Turkey's ethnic Arab subjects.

These problems were traditional to the Turks and were not by themselves conclusive. The main challenge to Turkish arms was whether the rank and file could meet the technical skill necessary to handle complex weaponry and whether they could preserve a high sense of morale and staying power in the clash of modern war.

▶ Each Turkish infantry division nominally possessed a field gun regiment comprised of two or three artillery battalions. A battalion had three batteries of four field guns each. Additionally, a corps of three infantry divisions was delegated two mountain artillery battalions and a howitzer battalion of six-piece batteries. Two horse artillery batteries were to complement the usual corps cavalry brigade. In reality, Turkish artillery was far below paper establishment.

2

THE SUEZ GAMBIT

AS Britain's ambassador sailed from Constantinople with his papers, the East Lancashire Division marched through Cairo in a show of force. On 2 November Egypt was placed under martial law and declared a Protectorate. Consistent with the change of territorial status, the title of the chief British representative was converted from Consul General to High Commissioner – Sir Henry McMahon assuming those reins in person early in January, 1915. Sensibly, opportunity was taken to depose the current Egyptian Khedive who was absent in Constantinople on a pro-Turkish mission. Prince Hussein Kamel Pasha superseded him and was further elevated with the title of Sultan – ostensibly as a political counterpoise to Turkey's Sultan Mohammed V.

In the pre-war press, Germany had spoken of the Suez Canal as Britain's 'jugular'. Intelligence indicators pointed to a major Turkish thrust against this sensitive artery, which stretched for 100 miles from Port Said on the Mediterranean Sea in the north, to Suez on the Red Sea in the south. The Canal rested in desert 30 miles from the fertile Nile Delta, and was variously 65–100 yards wide and 34 feet deep.

The water supply of the Canal was dependent upon the Sweet Water Canal and the confluent railroad which branched north and south at Ismalia. Ismalia was thus the water, rail, and geographical centre for the Suez Canal, earmarking the town as the strategic axis of an enemy advance. However, since the capture or damage of *any* part of the Canal would negate its functional purpose, it was the whole length which required protection. Fortunately, 29 miles of the Canal had been constructed through natural lakes, which provided a more serious obstacle, and in December British engineers inundated low-lying areas north of Qantara and around Port Said to enhance this.

No Canal roads as yet existed, but the water supply was adequate and the railroad was in parallel communication along its extent. On the eastern bank, posts and bridgeheads were established with sandbags and barbed wire, the largest of these being opposite Ismailia. The Canal Zone was divided into three military sectors: Sector One in the south from Suez to Deversoir; Sector Two continuing in the centre to El Ferdan, and Sector Three continuing in the north to Port Said.

The total manpower assets of General Maxwell's Force in Egypt were 70,000 by January, 1915. These troops reflected a diverse degree of training and cohesion. The 42nd Division was in garrison at Cairo and throughout the Delta, while posted with General Wilson's command on the Canal were the 10th and 11th Indian Divisions with four batteries of artillery, the colourful princely contingents of the Indian Imperial Service Cavalry Brigade, and the Bikanir Camel Corps. Besides some Yeomanry (cavalry) formations there were the Australian and New Zealand units, or ANZACs. The

▲ General Sir John Maxwell, commander of the Force in Egypt, November, 1914.

Right: Djemal Pasha (left on white horse), Minister of Marine and commander of 4th Army. Djemal was one of the founders of the Young Turk Revolution. On the right is Nussrat Bey, his *aide de camp*, and in the centre a Turkish naval officer.

▶

Australians had arrived in December with an infantry division and a light horse brigade; the New Zealanders with 2,500 mounted rifles, 5,000 infantry, and one field artillery brigade.

General Wilson's Indian Divisions and support troops in the Canal Zone totalled 30,000 and were composed of entirely Indian battalions – that is – without the usual British battalion complement per each of a division's three brigades. Wilson's overall weakness in artillery was augmented by Allied ships: from the British the *Swiftsure, Clio, Minerva, Himalaya, Ocean* and *Hardinge*, and from the French the *Requin, Prosperine*, and *D'Entrecasteaux*.

For air support, chiefly in a reconnaissance mode, an assortment of aeroplanes was collected at the new aerodrome at Ismailia and the landing strip at Qantara. Captain Massey, of the 29th Punjabis, had flown out from India with three Maurice Farman Pusher aircraft, which were soon increased by two Maurice Farmans, and a BE 2a from the Indian Flying School at Sitapur, India. Alongside two Henri Farmans purchased from an Italian firm in Cairo, this menagerie would become No. 30 Squadron, RFC, later that spring.[1]

A similar Allied enterprise was commanded by Lieutenant de Vaisseau l'Escaille. Flying reconnaissance from the decks of the converted seaplane carriers *Doris* and *Anne*, seven French 80-horse-power Nieuports, with French pilots and British observers, cooperated with Massey's aerial detachment to ascertain Turkish intentions. Although Massey's depth of surveillance was limited to only a 45-mile radius, between his detachment flights and those of the more mobile-based French seaplanes, enough intelligence was gathered to conclude the main Turkish offensive would fall against Sector Two, central Canal Zone.

Turkish Preparations

The original planning for the Turkish Suez offensive began as far back as August, 1914. Under the vision of Djemal Pasha, Minister of Marine, and newly appointed commander of 4th Army, the plan was transformed from a simple military attack to a politico-military operation aimed at the capture of the Suez Canal, the fomentation of Egyptian rebellion, and the severance of that country from British administration.

Djemal Pasha Kuchuk, commander of 8th Corps, was put in charge of technical detail with the Bavarian Colonel Kress von Kressenstein as his chief of staff. The German Military Mission detached extra advisory officers including Colonel von Frankenburg-Proschlitz as chief of staff to Djemal Pasha's 4th Army.

Any offensive plan must consider the parameters of actual force projection. The construction of roads was just getting underway in 4th Army's zone of control – Syria and Palestine. The railroad was the critical factor in supply and reinforcement determination for Palestine–Egyptian operations, and 4th Army's main strategic source was situated opposite the capitol at Haidar Pasha, a distant 1,275 miles. It was a serpentine journey over two mountain ranges, with halts at incomplete tunnels to hike on foot, further train changes, due to three gauges of track, (standard, one metre, and 1.05 metre), and potential end-run congestion after Riyaq, possibly resulting in a 250-mile march to the front.

The Suez Expeditionary Force would march with an insecure right flank, namely, its vulnerability to the Allied Mediterranean fleets, but beyond coastal bombardment the threat was not serious. Palestine had historically never been successfully invaded by sea. Of greater concern was the Sinai Desert, through which the Turks must pass before attacking an entrenched position. In order to handle the logistics of a mandatory leap-frog advance in stages, a special 'Desert Line of Communications Inspectorate' was instituted. This organisation established supply and hospital depots 15–20 miles apart, from the starting base at Beersheba through the heart of the Sinai. Main depot headquarters were set up, near the coast at El Arish and near the Sinai centre at Kalaat-ul-Nahl, which would act as the prime drawing points for the forward troops as well as bases for friendly Arab irregulars cooperating on both flanks of the central force. Artesian wells were sunk, and dykes fabricated to contain the unusually heavy and welcome rainstorms predicted that winter.

An independent Line of Communication Inspectorate was also founded in Jerusalem as a collection and forwarding base for the 8th Corps spearhead. Eleven thousand camels were massed as beasts of burden. The Herculean task of supply was additionally reduced by the introduction of a 'desert ration' composed of a one kilogram daily allocation per man of biscuits, olives, and dates, as well as the equivalent water measure of a Turkish gourd.

Djemal Pasha left his 4th Army headquarters in Damascus to march with the First Echelon from Beersheba on 14 January 1915. While the 27th (Arab) Division remained in Beersheba in reserve, the Second Echelon was to follow Djemal a day behind. Full of heart, they sang the Turkish tune 'The Red Flag Flies over Cairo' as they marched at night to obscure their numbers and direction from enemy eyes. The order of battle for 8th Corps is listed below. Including supports and reserves, the Suez Expeditionary Force did not exceed 25,000 men.[2]

First Echelon

25th Division, 23rd/27th Composite Regiment, one cavalry regiment, four Camel Corps squadrons, 1,500 Arab volunteers, six engineer companies, five field gun batteries, two mountain gun batteries, one 15cm howitzer battery, and telegraph, pontoon and hospital personnel for a total of 12,642 men, 968 horses, 12,000 camels, and 328 oxen.

Second Echelon

10th Division, divisional artillery, one cavalry squadron and auxiliary units.

The Assault

The Suez Expeditionary Force had only the two winter months in which to cross the Sinai and complete its mission objectives at the Canal. Only because of the advantageous rains that year was such a large assemblage able to effect such a desert crossing. More critically, the final water reservoir was 30 miles from attack positions, a limitation allowing only part of the Expedition to spar at the Canal for four days before securing additional water sources.

By strict necessity, then, Djemal Pasha was intending to make a surprise crossing, to grab Ismailia, and to inspire an Egyptian revolt within nature's schedule. Ismailia would be secured with 6,000 men while 10th Division would widen the bridgehead and 8th Division could reinforce the main column from Palestine. As the attack and subsequent development was going in, feint thrusts from the flanks would theoretically keep the British in suspense.

But by 1 February, the British were in no suspense concerning three of Djemal's columns, totalling 13,500. Aerial reconnaissance was all too clearly filling in the picture. Then, nature took a hand and cloaked the next day in a sandstorm of darkness.

The gale swept through the night and early morning of 3 February. From their positions, the Indian sentries scanned the inhospitable murk, faces screened underneath their puggarees, and rifle breeches wrapped in rags. South of Tussum Post at 0325 hours first contact was made. As the howling wind calmed to the illumination of the full moon, dark masses of pontoons, rafts, and infantry appeared, stretching for a mile-and-a-half along the east bank. Under the leadership of Captain von dem Hagen, the gloomy apparition slithered down the gully banks toward the water.

The Indian soldiers of Sector Two commenced rapid firing. Pontoon after raft was holed and sunk, only three

THE SUEZ GAMBIT
FEBRUARY, 1915

Mediterranean Sea
Port Said
Romani
SINAI
Qantara
Sand and Scrub
Dunes
Ismailia
Ferry Post
8th Corps
Jifjaffa
Deversoir
Great Bitter Lake
N
Suez

0 10 20
Miles
Gulf of Suez

Main Turk attack
Turk feints
Suez Canal

Above: Nieuport Monoplane Seaplane ascending in defence of the Suez Canal, 1915.

Right: Men of the Hong Kong and Singapore Battery defending the Suez Canal.

craft reaching the opposite bank where a determined counterattack swept up the intruders. The first probe had been a failure.

At dawn a general assault was launched at Tussum Post then spread north to Serapeum Post. Wherever the Turks gained niches, the Indian infantry countercharged under the supporting guns of the French Navy. By mid-morning the Turkish heavy howitzer battery had damaged the British ship *Hardinge* but the Turks had been repulsed. As desultory counter fire continued into the afternoon, the 7th and 8th Battalions of Australian infantry were transferred to Ismailia in anticipation of further action.

But that night the Turks retired in orderly fashion, leaving nests of snipers behind to retard a pursuit which never came. Both flank feints had failed to achieve their purposes through lack of supporting weight. A month after setting out, the Turkish 8th Corps Suez Expeditionary Force was back in Beersheba. While Turkish historians admitted losing 1,400 soldiers, the Canal's Indian defenders had lost only a tenth of that figure. The failure was a disappointment to Djemal who had offered grants of money and pensions to the families of the killed and disabled as well as government-built homes should Egypt to be conquered.[3] Nor was his reputation enhanced by grandiose promises withered by reality. Turkish morale in Syria and Palestine backlashed as the premature announcement of victory was withdrawn.

The Suez gambit did not entirely fail. British anxiety for the Canal's security reached a fever pitch. Troops slated for Western Front transfer had been retained in theatre. Perhaps most significantly of all, Allied attention had been diverted from a very auspicious offensive option at the Dardanelles and thereby delayed the Gallipoli landings to a later ill-fated date and conclusion.

1915

On 20 February Britain and France bombarded the Turkish forts in the Dardanelles Straits and Egypt became the base for General Sir Ian Hamilton's Mediterranean Expeditionary Force. From 25 April to 6 August landings were phased onto the Gallipoli Peninsula. The frustration and bloodied check at Gallipoli are legendary. By early January of 1916 the engaged forces had been withdrawn — most for recuperation in Egypt.

During this time Egypt acted not only as supply base for these operations, but when Bulgaria entered the war against the Allies, Egypt played host for the 'Levant Base' as well. The Levant Base existed to assist allied Serbia against the aggression of the Central Powers in the Balkans. Simultaneously, Egypt was burdened with the training and dispatching of Indian troops to the Western Front.

The year 1915 saw the Force in Egypt engaged in brush war operations either directly, or in a supporting capacity. Troops were forwarded to halt the moves of Turkish regulars in Aden and Mesopotamia, and against Turkish incited rebellions in the western Sudan and on the western Egyptian border. The Force in Egypt also assisted Allied plans known as the 'Alexandria Project'. This scheme was a massive amphibious landing option in the Gulf of Alexandretta which, if successful, could have offered the prospect of severing the communications of Turkish armies in Syria, Palestine, and Mesopotamia. Exploitation could have lead to a linking with allied Russian forces in the Caucasus. The plans were attractive, so attractive as to be seriously mooted several times throughout the war, but never attractive enough for the risk of authorisation.

Anxiety on the Palestine–Egyptian frontier was maintained through the actions of von Kressenstein, the real mastermind behind the bid for Suez. Von Kressenstein had been placed in charge of the 'Desert Force' of three battalions, two mountain batteries, and a camel squadron with which he cleverly harassed the border. Threats of sabotage were directed against the Canal itself.

Meanwhile, the 'Desert Line of Communications Inspectorate' hardened the string of supply depots and Djemal Pasha impressed 50,000 labourers into road improvements and extensions throughout Syria and Palestine. By November, the Turkish railroad had reached Beersheba and plans for a second offensive against the Canal were already in progress.

If the British had been affected by the vagaries of 1915, so the fortunes of their Turkish opposites waxed and waned. From 4th Army, Djemal lost three divisions to Gallipoli and a fourth to Mesopotamia, leaving him with 12 battalions, the majority of which were the less reliable ethnic Arab. On the negative ledger, the Turks had begun 1915 badly. With Napoleonesque vision, Enver Pasha had conceived of a winter campaign against the Russian Caucasian Army. The outcome was the rout and destruction of the Turkish 3rd Army at Sarikamish in one of the most decisive defeats of World War 1. On the positive ledger, Turkish mobilisation was increasing to fill the vacancies and Bulgaria had become a co-belligerent, thus allowing German war munitions rail access through its territory to reach Turkey. Turkish arms had won the duel at Gallipoli. In November, 6th Army had halted General Townshend's Mesopotamian advance at Csestiphon and had put the British under siege at Kut-al-Amara.

By year's end, General Maxwell's Force in Egypt had diminished in technical competence from the incessant siphoning of his command to support the multitude of flashpoints, as well as the Western Front. Most of his 60,000 men were in temporary training formations or awaiting embarkation. As the Turkish legions were released from their victorious Hellespont, the foremost question in Maxwell's mind was how many of these Gallipoli veterans would be directed against the Canal?

◀ A study in triangles – a British encampment at the Great Pyramid.

▼ German service pattern pontoons riddled during the defence of the Suez Canal, February, 1915. The pontoons were constructed of galvanised iron and held 20 personnel. Rafts 15 by 12 feet of wooden framework filled with empty kerosene cans were also used.

PART 2
THE PREPARATION
January 1916 to June 1917

'The desert, till then almost destitute of human habitation, showed the successive marks of our advance in the shape of strong positions firmly entrenched and protected by hundreds of miles of barbed wire, of standing camps where troops could shelter in comfortable huts, of tanks and reservoirs, of railway stations and sidings, of aerodromes and of signal stations and wireless installations, by all of which the desert was subdued and made habitable, and adequate lines of communication established between the advancing troops and their ever-receding base.'

– General Sir Archibald Murray

Below: Machine gun section on pack-horses of the 2nd Light Horse Brigade.

A. LOGISTICS CONQUERS NATURE
THE SINAI, 1916–1917

LOGISTICS FLOW CHART   NOVEMBER, 1916

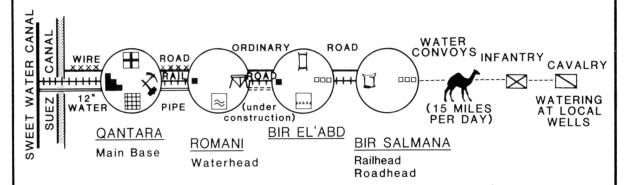

✚	Hospital
◼	Main Depot
▪	Sub Depot
▦	Filtration Plant
⚒	Rail Repairs
≈	500,000 Gallon Water Reservoir
┄	500,000 Gallon Water Reservoir under construction
▽	Stand Pipes to fill Rail Cars
☐☐☐	Water Tanks
⊓	Replenishment Points
⊓	Casualty Clearing Station

TRANSPORT CORPS ANIMAL EFFICIENCY (weights in pounds)			
ANIMAL	LOAD CAPACITY	DAILY WATERINGS	DAILY FEED
Camel	400	Once	24
Horse	310	Twice	20
Mule Argentine	300	Twice	20
Mule Indian	200	Twice	16

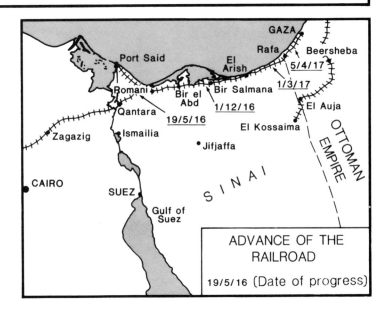

ADVANCE OF THE RAILROAD

19/5/16 (Date of progress)

LOGISTICS CONQUER NATURE

IN principle, the Force in Egypt was to protect the Suez Canal, yet early in 1916 it appeared to the British public as if the Canal were protecting the Force in Egypt.[1] In November, 1915, Lord Kitchener, in his capacity of Secretary of State for War, had condemned the defence scheme as putting the Canal in jeopardy. Responding to a December assessment, the War Office approved a three-line plan to be set out along roughly parallel lines.

At 11,000 yards east of the Canal the first line would deny the enemy artillery range. The second line, at 6,500 yards, would refuse the enemy effective artillery range and serious observation. The third line, or last ditch, was on the Canal itself with the familiar post and bridgehead system. Pursuant to the plan, Maxwell took stock. Colonel Wright was appointed over the engineering services, which also included general communications and water supply. Colonel Grant was put over military engineering and railroad communications, with Sir George Macauley over internal railway services. Major-General Sir H. V. Cox acted as Maxwell's liaison in the oversight of tasks.

The sector water supply was almost exclusively dependent upon an ancillary body of water known as the Sweet Water Canal. This Canal was piped from Cairo to Ismailia where it forked north and south along the course of the Suez Canal. The fresh water was processed through a filtration system of plants on the west bank, and pumped into reservoirs on the east bank. From these standing 50,000 gallon capacity reservoirs the water was piped to auxiliary tanks in the forward areas.

From Zagazig to Ismailia the railway was doubled and roads were extended and improved. Pre-existing ferries were supplemented by floating bridges. Ten thousand workers were hired for the January reformations, and out of the pressing need for regular labour sprung an impressive organisation which became the common denominator upon which British engineering miracles were based.

This denominator was the Egyptian Labour Corps or ELC, which expanded from a concept of 500 workers that January to a pool of 185,782 volunteers by June, 1917. Contracts were renewable quarterly so that only a portion of the force was engaged in a given period. For sake of efficiency the ELC ran as a paramilitary establishment of 600-man companies with a camp headquarters employing 1,200–1,800 men, and a branch headquarters employing approximately 10,000. Alexandria was the administrative headquarters with a form of basic training at Hadra Camp.

Work was hard and pay low, except for significant ration and commissary benefits which extended to wives if the husband was disabled. The ELC uniform consisted of khaki shorts and a smock with 'ELC' in red letters on the chest; headdress, boots, overcoat, and underclothes were additionally provided during inclement weather. At the end of a term the garments were disinfected and redistributed. Few men — because of the intensity of labour — served successive quarters.

It would be easy in the summary of colourful campaigns to forget that such bodies of native men laid the necessary ground work upon which General Allenby's later victories were based. The ELC hammered rails, built roads, connected water pipes and loaded freight. These tasks and more were performed under conditions thought dangerous to European health, and to a local standard superior to what might have been achieved by imported labour.

An outgrowth of the ELC was the Camel Transport Corps which, by June 1917, passed 28,305 drivers and attendants and 33,594 camels through its ranks. Formed into 17 companies, variously labelled 'A' through 'R', each company hosted approximately 2,000 camels. The camel was the age-old ship of the desert, and the Ministry of the Interior was responsible for its purchase. The finest camel on the market was the Arabian, but the war had shut off this supply. Of the remaining eight types (the Sudanese, Somali, Upper Egyptian, Western Desert, Delta Heavy, Indian, Egyptian female, and the Algerian), the Delta Heavy was found superior. Their carriage capacity was 350 pounds. Size, acclimatisation, age, and health were important purchase criteria: unfortunately, half of all Egyptian camels were infected with mange.

The influx of various camel breeds with their corresponding sizes and carriage capacities played havoc with military guidelines. Standardisation of saddlery was a nightmare and the insufficient quantity of native saddles was made even more inadequate from their fragility to quartermaster-laden stores. Finally, a special type of anglicised saddle was produced and shipped from Manchester.

Native drivers served on six-month contracts while British officers were selected from men experienced in local language and native custom. Despite the thrill of a ride, as opposed to their foot-slogging ELC counterparts, Camel Transport Corps personnel were not envied . . . in the course of the year, 380 were put in the hospital from camel bite, while 70 actually lost limbs!

Administrative Reshuffling

Water and changes of command roll downhill, and the reshuffling along the Western Front at the end of 1915 reached Egypt in the new year. General Maxwell was not only bogged down in internal Egyptian affairs, but was enmeshed in a brush war with the Senussi tribesmen along Egypt's Western Desert. Lieutenant-General Sir Archibald Murray had been longing to escape the political confines as Chief of the Imperial General Staff in England. Murray succeeded in being shipped out to Egypt to supplement

Maxwell by taking charge of the troops evacuating Gallipoli into the Canal Zone. Murray's organisational vehicle was the staff of the Mediterranean Expeditionary Force Head-quarters, while behind him, General Sir William Robertson filled the vacancy of 'CIGS'. France's General Sarrail soon after assumed command of the Allied front in the Balkans, thus relieving Murray of that technical responsibility.

From 9 January to 10 March Murray and Maxwell shared command responsibilities until Maxwell was recalled to England and the Mediterranean Expeditionary Force and the Force in Egypt were united under Murray's single com-mand. The new command was termed the Egyptian Expeditionary Force or 'EEF'. Shortly afterward the defunct concept of the Levant Base became administratively extinct.

Murray, however, was not to fare so lightly. With the clean-up and unity of command functions came a burden from the War Committee. Murray's EEF was to consider itself 'The Imperial Strategic Reserve'. This simply meant that as the Western Front was recognised as Britain's main defence, the EEF was to lick the Gallipoli evacuees into shape along with the new arrivals, then hold them for dispatch when requested. Egypt would retain ·only what troops were required for the security of itself and the Suez Canal. As compensation, the Committee promised to supply all materials to get the divisions onto a proper war footing.

By June, Murray had surrendered 10 of his 14 recently trained and reorganised divisions: nine to France (including five ANZAC divisions), and one to Mesopotamia. Only four territorial infantry divisions – the 42nd (East Lancashire), the 52nd (Lowland), the 53rd (Welsh), and the 54th (East Anglian) remained.

Murray was fortunate to possess a splendid mounted arm. The majority of his British cavalry were Yeomanry, raised on a territorial basis from the English countryside, dating in concept from the Napoleonic Wars. One excep-tional unit was formed in March, 1916 from the flower of Commonwealth chivalry. This unit was the ANZAC Mounted Division under Major-General H. G. Chauvel. It represented a fusion of the 1st, 2nd, and 3rd Australian Light Horse Brigades and the New Zealand Mounted Rifle Brigade.

Many of the ANZAC troopers had given up their horses for the trench at Gallipoli, and returning to their old Egyptian training camp at Zeitun, were happily reunited with their steeds. Most of the mounts had themselves been trans-ported from the South Pacific with their owners so that man and beast knew the drill when subjected to the new riding familiarisation tests. Nevertheless, slow learners were reacquainted in the onerous 'Detail Squadron' run by each regiment.

The New Zealand Mounted Rifle Brigade comprised three regiments (the Auckland, Wellington, and Canterbury Regiments) with three squadrons per regiment, each regiment named after its recruiting ground. Attached to the Brigade was the Machine Gun Squadron (a regimental amalgamation of sections to concentrate firepower), the Signal Troop, the Mounted Field Ambulance, the Mobile Veterinary Section, and a British Royal Horse Artillery

▲ General Sir Archibald Murray had served with distinction in field commands in Zululand and South Africa and, by 1915, had risen to the Army's senior staff position as Chief of the Imperial General Staff. Anxious to end his career in an independent field capacity, he obtained the command of the Mediterranean Expeditionary Force in January, 1916. Adept at administration and organisation, Murray laid many of the foundations basic to General Allenby's successful campaigns, but his conduct of field operations became a disappointment.

battery. The compliment of each regiment was nominally 24 officers, 499 men, and 616 horses.

Another extraordinary mobile unit was the Imperial Camel Corps, the inception of which began under Lieu-tenant-Colonel Leslie Smith in the last weeks of Maxwell's command. The idea was that four or five companies would form a battalion of approximately 830 men and 1,000 camels. The 1st, 3rd, and 4th Battalions were composed of ANZACs, the 2nd Battalion of British Yeomanry. Eventually, 18 companies would be raised: ten Australian, six British, and two New Zealand.

Each battalion was commanded by a lieutenant-colonel, each company by a major or captain, and each of the four sections of a company by a lieutenant. Headquarters, medical, quartermaster, and veterinary staffs were attached to the battalion, with one Lewis gun section to a company. Brigaded for overall corps use were Indian mountain guns, heavy Vickers machine guns, and the usual proviso of sapper and signal support.

It was a happy and fortunate formation as time after time was to prove in the Sinai, the Western Desert, and even in a later long-distance raid through northern Arabia. The Corps could move 40 miles per day and go for nearly five days

DESERT NAVY

Depicted in the photo is a Bikanir camel soldier on loan to the EEF from a prince of the Scinde Desert, India. The camel is a one-humped dromedary well-suited to the inhospitable clime. The hump is a reserve of fat, the size of which varies with its availability of food. The camel's stomach has several compartments, each able to store approximately two gallons of pasty food and water. The soles of its feet (which have two toes) as well as portions of limb joints and chest, are naturally calloused to protect against environmental thorns, abrasions, and the hot sand. Long eyelashes, thick eyelids and narrow, closable nostrils provide an internal shelter to counter the elements, particularly sandstorms.

Able to drink 30 gallons of liquid at one watering, camels can go for six days without a drink. Kitted out in Imperial Camel Brigade 'regular' fashion, a camel could transport a 450 lb burden 30 miles per day for several weeks. Such statistics made them the virtual navy of the desert.

For the cavalryman, camels were initially an unchivalric proposition. They bit and side-kicked viciously, spat a green cud, had obnoxious rutting habits and, stubborn by nature, were immovable when they had sunk to their knees in defiance. Camels roared when mounted by 'regular' troopers in groups. Both mounting and riding them was like the 'forward and back' roll of a sea-wave in motion. Camels at a gallop were hell on

the rider, but six miles per hour was discovered to be a most satisfactory pace for all. As some cameliers lamented:

Once you join the Camels you're smellful and coarse men:
Goodbye to the swank of the Kiwi Light Horsemen,
All plumed and booted and spurred.

Hogue

After trials, a genuine affection grew up between some troopers and their new-found steeds. Frank Reid recalled one camelier using the forelegs of his camel as a pillow. Captain Inchbald owned a succession of camels known as Pharoah, Mark Antony, Pompey, Tommy, Mick, and Mrs. —, after a great aunt. An armada of camels served not only the Imperial Camel Brigade, and the Bikanir Camel Corps, but the Egyptian Camel Corps, the Camel Transport Corps, and the Arab Revolt. In the end an informal barrack room ditty expressed the oddly sentimental relationship that had grown up between man and mount:

So its farewell now, old Hoosta, our paths diverge from here;
I have got to be a Horseman now and not a Camelier.
You were smellful, you were ugly. Now I've got a horse instead.
Still, you had the camel virtues, so I take back all I've said.

Hogue

◄ The Camel Transport Corps was an outgrowth of the Egyptian Labour Corps. The Corps eventually raised 17 companies of approximately 2,000 camels each. Drivers served renewable six month contracts. The zinc metal container (hung one to each camel side) is a *fanatis* which held from 10–12 Imperial gallons of water. This company is probably transporting water from a pumping station to soldiers in the forward area.

▲ The Camel

He's a quadruped of singular deportment,
With an air of injured innocence unique,
He stalks along without undue excitement,
In fact he's rather tardy; so to speak.
His pedicular extremities are padded,
And enable him to ambulate quite pert,
That sandy stretch of waste, which is suited to his taste,
The desert.

He bears up his back a huge lipoma,
We designate it vulgarly 'the hump',
And if, perchance, provided not with fodder,
Supports himself for years upon this lump;
His capacity for 'moyyah' is abnormal,
He's a deglutition envied by the worst,
Thirty gallons at a time, consummation most sublime —
'Some thirst!'

He is moderately docile in behaviour
And 'barraks' with an indecisive grace;
Takes up his load with supercilious hauteur,
Suggestive of indifference out of place;
On occasions he becomes a trifle fractious,
And displays an independence importune,
Blows bubbles, kicks and bites, and of his eyes he shows
    the whites,
'Magnoon.'

W.N.P.W., *Palestine News*, 1918 (Warwickshire Yeomanry Museum)

◄ The saddler's shop of the Camel Transport Corps displaying frames and pads under stages of repair. Precise fittings were a difficult science because of the eight camel breeds in use. The native standing to the right of the British Sergeant-Major (centre) is wearing the Camel Transport Corps smock with the letters 'CTC'.

without watering. The troopers themselves were planned to be self-contained during this period:

'. . . the *"Dhurra"* bag carrying five days grain for the camel, and a cylindrical five-gallon tank holding the rider's five days water supply. Food for five days, and spare clothing were carried in a canvas *"Pikau"* bag slung over the saddle. Strapped over all were blankets, overcoat, rifle, etc., the full weight carried being about 320 lb. including the man'.[2]

In the air, there was mobility of a different sort, the mobility of temporary aerial freedom as desert miles slipped away below without immediate concern for water or the trudge-weary weight of sand. Number 30 Squadron having been posted to Mesopotamia, it was replaced by 5th Wing Royal Flying Corps (RFC) under Lieutenant-Colonel Salmond. The 5th Wing headquarters were at Ismailia in February, 1916, with auxiliary aerodromes for Nos. 14 and 17 Squadrons (flying mostly BE 2c aircraft) at Heliopolis, Qantara, and Suez. At Abassia was the repair and supply 'X' aircraft park. The Qantara Flight of No. 14 Squadron was one of the most unique in history, for it was made self-sufficient by the augmentation of 80 camels for petrol transport, and a compliment of sand carts for the hauling of tents and spare parts.[3]

Reconnaissance and survey were the chief functions of the RFC in spring, 1916, despite some bombing and strafing attacks on forward Turkish posts. Reconnaissance was only possible to a distance of 100 miles, and this with the portage of extra petrol tanks. It was enough, however, for the RFC and the Topographical Section of Intelligence to formulate a series of squared 1:20,000 scale maps from which aerial observers could derive pinpoint references.

Additional air support was conferred by the East Indies and Egypt Seaplane Squadron, formed from ex-Gallipoli craft and carried by the *Ben-my-Chree, Anne, Raven*, and the *Empress* seaplane carriers. The first three ships provided throughout 1916–1917 photographic intelligence and bombing missions along the Syrian Coast and in support of the Arab Revolt. From May, 1916 the squadron was lead by Commander Sampson.

The strategic question was how this force would stack up against a second Turkish invasion. In February, Murray informed Robertson he considered it possible for a Turkish launch of a quarter of a million men. His assessment, of course, was excessive, not taking into account the proximity of the summer season (the 'time-out' season for desert campaigns) and the enemy logistical inability to project such a feat. Robertson returned a more realistic maximum of 100,000, and hindsight reveals this was the maximum considered by German and Turkish planners.

The appreciation Murray sent to Robertson judged the water site at El Arish on the eastern side of the Sinai was the best vantage point from which to defend Egypt. From El Arish Murray could break-up potential enemy bases in Palestine, or to menace the flank of any invading body pushing for the Canal. The first step in Murray's plan was the occupation of Qatiya, the western end of a series of oases spread east for 15 miles to Bir el Abd. Even though these oases held only brackish water, at a mere 25 miles from the

Canal they were the only possible final base from which a hostile attack could launch.

In mid-April, a broad gauge railway started at Qantara was in progress for Qatiya and was set to converge at the planned station of Romani, with a narrow track line under construction from Port Said. Brigadier Wiggin's 5th Mounted Brigade, consisting of the Warwickshire, and Worcestershire Yeomanry and the Gloucester Hussars, marched ahead of the rail on outpost and reconnaissance duty, being forced to leave behind their guns because of the heavy sand.

Keeping an alert eye on this extension of British ambition was the 'Desert Force' of the wily von Kressenstein. With six camel companies, 32nd Regiment, several 75mm guns, and ancillary assets totalling 3,655 men, he was carefully waiting his moment to strike.

At 0430 hours, coming suddenly out of the morning ground fog, the scorpion stung at Oghratina Oasis. From the outset, the Turkish infantry were within 50 yards of the post, firing at close quarters. The two squadrons of Worcestershires found they could only retreat by abandoning the Royal Engineers and so stayed in the hope of eventual relief which never came. After three hours half of the men were casualties and sand had clogged the rifles of many left standing. Surrounded, the post surrendered.

A similar scenario was played out at Qatiya Oasis to the southwest. One squadron each of the Worcestershire and Gloucester Hussars discovered, after skirmishing, that as the fog cleared, the Turks were surrounding the oasis. By 0945 hours a mountain gun assisted by enemy aircraft began lobbing shells into the vulnerable horse lines. By early afternoon, the Turks had edged to within 50 yards and soon after went in with the bayonet. Captain Wiggin and the horseholders were able to dash forward with the remainder of the unpanicked horses and about 80 troopers managed to mount up and shoot their way clear.

Turkish arms were parried at Dueidar Oasis by the 5th Royal Scots Fusiliers, then riposted by British aeroplanes. Two relieving cavalry columns which could have saved the other oases had been turned back by the 'Desert Force'.

The EEF had been taught a lesson in the danger of leaving isolated detachments too exposed. On 24 April, Major-General Chauvel established a strong camp at Romani, this time more watchful, stronger, and better prepared. A month later the railway arrived, bringing with it needed infantry and artillery.

Jacks of All Trades

In harsh environments, the path of military history is as much the conquest of the elements as it is the defeat of the enemy. Water was the most overriding factor in the Sinai Campaigns: east of the Canal each man was on a daily ration of one gallon for all purposes. Man drew his water in a variety of fashions from Mother Earth, both naturally, and by technology.

The most impressive feat was the 12-inch piping system from America, which had been escorted through the German submarine net. The Qantara waterworks mixed alum with the waters from the Sweet Water Canal, pumping the solution through filtered settling tanks. Then, the water was pumped underneath the Suez Canal into east bank reservoirs where it was chlorinated to make it *potable*, then it was pumped forward by stages. When the system was finally completed in spring, 1917, water was being transported through 17 stages from Romani to the men sieging Gaza on the Palestine frontier – 200 miles from its source on the banks of the Nile.[4]

A special relationship sprung up in the triangle of pipeline, railway and man. Pipe and rail assisted, and were dependent upon, each others progress. The railroad carried the pipes into position, then the water-giving pipeline succoured the construction progress of the railroad: man then returned life to both systems through his engineering. Due to this interdependence, cavalry and infantry were usually restricted to a day's march from railhead. Camels provided first-line transport and camel convoys replaced the usual divisional supply train because wheeled transport was impractical in the soft sand. Thus, the most brilliant strategic plan was slave to the plodding pace of the developing rail.

Mother Nature had visited brackish water on the Sinai. The farther one marched from the coast the more the alkaline quality of the water, when boiled, rendered a thoroughly salty cup of tea. Water 50 parts of salt per 100,000 was deemed drinkable for man and up to 150 parts for horses, assuming said horses had been acclimatised and the water chlorinated. The cavalry's Divisional Field Squadron concept made one troop of mounted engineers per brigade responsible for locating, testing, and classifying water as 'drinking water', 'horse water', or 'not fit for horses'.

'Hods', a type of small oasis, were dotted all over the Sinai, but because of indifferent standards of tribal maintenance these were found almost always polluted. On 21 July 1916 an order forbidding drink at desert wells was issued to the EEF and only allowed in certain emergency conditions and then after mixing two sulphate tablets per canteen.[5] The bottle-shaped, native-dug rain cisterns 20–30 feet below the surface were similarly categorised. Near the coast, bathing or animal water could be found a few feet underground with the installation of a sump.

Several innovations or 'tricks of the trade', so to speak, were adapted from Bedouin or Turkish practice, or from plain common sense, to defeat the vagaries of the desert clime. Instead of the Bedoiun gourd or skin suspended from a transport camel, the EEF adapted the *fanatis*, a zinc drum holding ten Imperial gallons, one to each camel side. This was an invaluable first-line asset for ferrying water from forward storage tanks into advanced positions.

It was discovered that cavalry could make a tiring 25-mile trek per day through the sand. When scouting for new water souces, mounted parties employed a 'spear point' drill or boring plant, consisting of a 'triangle, pulleys, large pipe in sections and weight.'[6] Including pumps it would be borne on a half limber or carried on the back of a pack animal, and was good at bringing up water at a depth of 20 feet.

A day's march for the artillery was even shorter, at about 15 miles at best promise. As wheels were useless, 'sand tyres', or an iron tyre, six to eight inches wide, were used

▲ The Egyptian Labour Corps laid the 12-inch water pipe (imported from the United States) across the length of the Sinai. Water was pumped through 17 stages over 200 miles to reach the EEF troops on the Palestine border.

▲ **The Wire Road**

'Tis a longish way to Sinai,
  Behind us there's miles of the trail
Coming up from the Base at Kantara
  The North Route replaced by the Rail;
And, beside it, 'cross leagues of the desert,
  By palm-grove, sand-dune, Bir and hod,
There's a long, snaky ribbon, far winding –
  The toil-saving thrice-bless'd Wire Road.

Rex Scott, *Palestine News*, 1918

but later scrapped for the 'pedrail'. Pedrails were strong blocks of foot-square wood two-and-a-half inches thick held on to a gun's tyres by chains. The British 18 pounder gun employed an eight-horse team with the pedrail.

For the wounded, sand sledges and the camel *cacolet* were implemented. The *cacolet* was a camel and canvas construction handy enough to take sitting or lying patients. In the spring of 1916, the Yeomanry equipped the camel with a shortened cavalry bamboo and canvas stretcher able to bear sitting cases.

The infantry also considered 15 miles a day a substantial march. Probably inspired, however ironically, by the Eskimo – a desert 'snowshoe' of wire frame attached to the boots was invented. It so prevented sinking as to inspire a larger arrangement – a virtual road of wire netting unrolled then pegged down. Infantry speed was doubled over this wire road, but as animals and vehicles tore the mesh, they were restricted access, being allowed to criss-cross only at selected gaps.

The 52nd (Lowland) Division was the first infantry into the Sinai, and being so honoured, it fell to their lot to lay the wire road. Colonel Anderson in the divisional history gives a poignant description of a brigade column en route across the desert:

'Bivouac has probably been left soon after sunrise, shelters having been struck in darkness, blankets rolled and loaded and breakfast taken before the sun is well above the horizon; battalion stores have been loaded, the battalion bivouac area cleaned and refuse burnt. The battalion marches with fours well spread out in width, but not in length, to minimize dust and allow free passage of air; all ranks are in shirt sleeves, the lower arms bare and the neck open; the drill jacket is strapped to the haversack or inside the pack, if the latter is being carried, but pack and

haversack were never worn together while we were on trek, one or other being left behind to be brought up later. The company commander is probably walking at the head or by the side of his company. At the rear of each company are its pack animals, carrying its Lewis guns and a proportion of ammunition. In rear of the battalion, though sometimes marching parallel with it, are the 1st line transport limbers and camels carrying ammunition, tools, water and cooking pots. The 2nd line transport, with blankets, stores, etc., is in rear of the brigade.'

In short, the total sum of the logistical conquest of natural obstacle was impressive, and continued to be so throughout the future campaigns. To subdue basically one triumphal avenue across the Sinai, the EEF had expended by early 1917:

'30,000,000 sandbags, 2,000,000 square feet of timber, 50,000 rolls of wire netting and 7,000 tons of barbed wire. In addition, 220 miles of macadamised roads were constructed, 359 miles of railway, and 300 miles of water-pipes.'[8]

'Who can the desert's strength subdue?
Pipe, Rail and Road.
Pipe to carry your drink to you;
Rail to speed your rations through;
Road to march on firm and true
Past bir and hod.'

– Crawsley Williams

4

SECOND STAKE

Romani

Shoulders galled by the braces,
  Knees that tremble and creak,
Sores in a hundred places,
  Scarcely the breath to speak;
Hark to the oaths we utter
  Husky and hoarse and low,
Dragging our weary footsteps
  After a fleeting foe.

We are the Mobile Column,
  Dirty and dour and dry,
Slogging it over the sand-hills
  Under a blazing sky;
Bending our backs to our burdens,
  Staggering four by four,
We are the Mobile Column,
  God, but we're tired and sore.

The Mobile Column: (by the late Captain W. F. Templeton, 4th RSF)

AS spring deepened toward the heat of summer, von Kressenstein managed to convince the Turkish High Command to go for the Canal ahead of their planned autumn schedule. It was a daring plan which ignored the usual slumberous summer inactivity of desert operations, yet a more careful one in objective. This time there would be no crossing, but an occupation of a portion of the east bank and the blocking of Canal traffic.

With Bulgaria's entry into the war, Allied Serbia was soon knocked out, and the Berlin to Baghdad Railway was finally able to function in one of its prewar aims – the through supply of military hardware to Turkey. German and Austrian reinforcements, modest – but of great technical benefit – were put in transit under the codename 'Pasha 1'.

By June, 1916, the Turkish Expeditionary Force had collected on the Sinai–Palestine frontier:

3rd (Anatolian) Division
27th (Arab) Division
Syrian Dromedary Corps (400 troopers)
Arab Irregular Horse
Composite Engineer Battalion
Pioneers (three companies)
3rd Regiment Mountain Artillery
5,000 camels and 1,750 horses for transport

The Expeditionary Force totalled 16,000 with probably only 10,000 combat troops. As it crossed the frontier in early July, it was accompanied by part of the technical arms of Pasha 1, and was marching in expectation of the remaining German reinforcements before clashing with Murray's EEF. In whole, Pasha 1 comprised:

German machine gun battalion, eight companies, 32 guns
Five sections, German anti-aircraft guns
60th Battalion Heavy Artillery (100mm, 150mm, 210mm calibre)
Two companies, German trench mortars
Two batteries, Austrian mountain howitzers
300th Flight Detachment (12 Fokker, Albatros, Aviatik)
Three railway companies

Two field hospitals
Wireless detachment
Mechanical transport companies

Murray had determined for his own advance to cross the northern Sinai where Allied naval supremacy would ensure a secure left flank and the possibility of cooperative supply and fire support. In order to deny any other route to the enemy, Light Horse, Yeomanry, engineers, and the Bikanir Camel Corps had sallied into the central Sinai in a spoiling raid of destruction against the water points used by the Turks the previous year. Von Kressenstein's options were thus mathematically reduced to recognisable proportions.

The EEF was in a state of readiness. General Lawrence's Sector Three forces included one brigade of the 53rd (Welsh) Division, the 52nd (Lowland) Division, and in rear echelon, the 42nd (East Lancashire). Thirty-six guns were in support. At Romani were the 1st and 2nd Light Horse Brigades with the New Zealand Mounted Rifles and 5th (Yeomanry) east of Qantara. On the far right the Imperial Camel Corps and 3rd Light Horse Brigade were in potential menace of von Kressenstein's left flank.

The EEF geographical position was anchored on its left by the Mediterranean and the immense Bardawil Lagoon. From the coast seven miles south, 18 redoubts had been sited on a line of sandhills, each redoubt built to hold 100 men and two machine guns. A high dune, Katib Gannit, marked the end of the hills and the start of the Wellington Ridge which ran west for miles. South of Katib Gannit and southeast of the Ridge were high, isolated sand dunes, the most prominent being Mt. Meredith (four miles south of Romani) and Mt. Royston (four miles southwest of Romani). In strategic position, then, the EEF was showing that of a large refused right flank.

But as the EEF waited assault, the Turks did a curious thing. Having sighted the British placement they halted for two weeks until the end of July. The German 300th Flight Detachment, with its faster aircraft, put pressure on the British aerial observance but they could not prevent it, nor the in-tandem reconnaissance in strength of the 1st and 2nd Light Horse Brigades.

Murray and his staff planners had wanted a fight at Romani, for they had prepared it, and were at least the numerical equal of their enemy, and the better potentially supplied and reinforced. Frustrated, they began considering an attack of their own when the enemy struck on the morning of 4 August. It was later learned von Kressenstein had only been awaiting the advent of his own heavy guns.

The clever von Kressenstein had taken advantage of the clockwork reconnaissance of the Light Horse, and in the dark evening of 3 August followed the retirement of the 2nd Light Horse Brigade with his Turkish infantry. The night was still with only 100 yards visibility through slight haze. Shortly after midnight the 1st Regiment discovered its picquets engaged, and by 0200 hours the Brigade pressed along the entire Mt. Meredith line by infantry closing within 50 yards. Before dawn, the Australians had been pushed back to the Wellington Ridge, and soon after — both the 1st and 2nd Regiments were forced to give further ground. Although fighting transpired all day, neither side was able to establish itself on the Ridge. The Turks effected gains near Mt. Royston, but their diversionary attacks — supported by their heavy artillery — failed to make any impression on the sandhill redoubts further north.

▼ Colonel Freiherr Kress von Kressenstein (tallest figure sixth from right) was born in 1870 of a noble Bavarian family with a soldiering tradition. In 1914 he was posted to the German Military Mission in Constantinople, first in artillery, then as chief-of-staff to Djemal Kuchuk's 8th Corps. The attack on the Canal was von Kressenstein's brainchild. In 1916 he commanded the Sinai 'Desert Force' and in 1917, the 8th Army. Depicted in the photograph are several German technical staff of 'Pasha I' in tropical and campaign uniforms. Flyers of the 300th Flight Detachment stand at far left, with mixed uniforms of Turkish staff officers interspersed (several of the Germans including von Kressenstein, sport the Turkish fez).

By dawn of 5 August the Turks had been ejected from their toeholds on Wellington Ridge, 1,500 of their infantry — who had been without water for 24 hours — surrendering in the process. Murray had waited for this moment of greatest Turkish commitment against his centre so that he could release his superior cavalry against the Turkish left. By conviction, he planned nothing short of capturing the entire enemy expedition.

Von Kressenstein's alert reactions, and the amazing marching capacity of the Turkish soldier, however, robbed Murray's show as the EEF counterblow hit heavy sand. Until 12 August, the Turkish Expeditionary Force gathered and rested at Bir el Abd, then rapidly fell back another 50 miles to the Palestine frontier.

Romani was a turning point in the Sinai–Palestine Campaigns: never again would the Suez Canal be threatened. The EEF took 4,000 prisoners and total casualties were estimated to equal half the Turkish expedition. Eager to play down Romani, the Turkish papers proclaimed the battle a victory, campaign medals being struck for the remembrance.

Chauvel's ANZAC Mounted Division would not forget: of the 1,100 EEF casualties they had sustained 87 per cent!

Long Range Reconnaissance

Von Kressenstein's retreat to El Arish fitted in with Murray's plans. Since February, Murray had been urging Robertson to obtain War Office approval for an EEF advance to El Arish as the best position from which to defend Egypt and the Canal. Near the coast, blessed with an abundance of water, and near the Turkish bases on the Palestine border, El Arish was the strategic pivot of the eastern Sinai. A friendly mobile garrison would be able to posture in both defensive and offensive roles — making insufferable any enemy attempt to circumvent it, or alternatively serving as a strike base from

General Murray established the Egyptian Expeditionary Force Headquarters at the Savoy Hotel in Cairo in 1916. The hotel also hosted the Arab Bureau, the intelligence headquarters of the Arab Revolt.

◀

which to break up enemy concentrations. Permission was granted for early winter.

Autumn, 1916 was consumed in administrative and logistical matters. Murray shifted his headquarters from Ismailia to Cairo to mastermind this larger picture, while Lieutenant General Sir Charles Dobell took charge of the 'Eastern Force' at Ismailia. Earlier in the war Dobell had commanded successful operations in the Cameroons, and recently − against the Senussi uprising in the Western Desert. 'Eastern Force' was the EEF sub-command responsible for the conduct of maneuvers toward El Arish.

Eastern Force's efforts took the shape of a series of long mounted probes, often of 45 miles length, into pro-Turkish tribal territory. While every attempt was made to close with the enemy or to 'cut out' his posts, all too often the 17 tribes (with a male population of 10,000) had already alerted the Turkish soldiers to escape.

Desert navigation was a feat in itself. Direct marching up and down the dunes was impossible so that perfect compass work and careful map plotting were required to correct the numerous deviations. The old telegraph line from Qantara to El Arish provided the most consistent navigational updates. The long range missions of Eastern Force from the bases of Romani or Et Maler are exemplified in the graph below:[1]

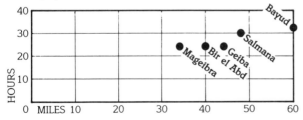

Murray's own logistical efforts were impressive. The pipeline had reached Romani and the filtration plant at Qantara was processing 600,000 gallons of water daily. The broad gauge railroad was proceding at 15 miles per month, the line handling a volume of 13 trains per day.

In December, David Lloyd-George became British Prime Minister. Lloyd-George embodied the 'Easterner' school of thought which believed that the comparison of bloody deadlock on the Western Front with the relative mobility in the East, and the potential of destroying Germany's weaker allies, demanded a greater emphasis in that theatre. The 'Easterners' were bitterly opposed by the 'Westerners' with their eternal theme of 'France first'. It would take Lloyd-George and his political allies some time to mobilise their strengths into the realistic, coherent, and sustainable eastern policy which would support General Allenby's campaigns.

Murray was encouraged by the War Office but was given to understand that he would largely have to make good with what he had. Murray was not without certain resources, for his ration strength was 150,000 British, 6,000 Indians, and 13,000 Egyptian Labour Corps. Determining to hold Sectors One and Two of the Canal lightly, he placed the bulk of his mobile forces into Sector Three, and specifically with Eastern Force.

With orders to capture the 1,600-man Turkish garrison in El Arish, General Sir Philip Chetwode was put in charge of Eastern Force's 'Desert Column', which consisted of the recently renamed Imperial Camel Brigade, the ANZAC Mounted Division, and the 42nd and 52nd Infantry Divisions with supports. After so much effort, the fall of El Arish was a denouement. In the end, von Kressenstein pulled in his tail to Rafa and Maghdaba, wary of the rumour of an amphibious landing. Days before Christmas, the Desert Column cavalry encountered the first green patches of cultivation on the Palestine frontier.

Throughout the Sinai crossing the value of the aeroplane in desert reconnaissance was verified. The 5th Wing, RFC had positioned its flights of No. 14 Squadron and the 1st Australian Flying Squadron at Qantara, Ismailia, and Port Said. The Germans, in their technically superior Fokkers and

▲ Trooper, horse, and tack of the Egyptian Police.

منائی عسکرلری الکلیز اسرا قزار ة اهلرت.

منائی عسکرلری الکلیز اسرا قزار کا هلرنه.

◀ Smokes aplenty! Two examples of the propaganda leaflets dropped in bundles from aircraft over enemy lines. The smiling centre figure is smoking a *hookah*, or 'hubble-bubble' while the gentleman at lower right adopts a 'wiser than thou, friend' attitude to his comrades still fighting.

Aviatiks, had based their 300th Flight Detachment out of El Arish. While they periodically bombed Port Said, the British bombed the German aerodrome in return. Aerial duels were few, almost by a mutual consensus of balance of power. The British had numerical superiority with their mostly BE 2c aerial fleet, while the Germans – in their faster aircraft, fitted with interupter gear (the machine-gun was synchronised to fire through the propellor for improved line of sight) – retained the qualitative edge.

During the year, the RFC entered into the propaganda game by dropping bundles of leaflets on the Turks and their Arab sympathisers. Printed in Turkish and Arabic, the leaflets depicted contented prisoners of war smoking, well-fed, and sporting engaging smiles of the sort becoming all too scarce among their erstwhile front-line comrades. Less to Teutonic appetite were allegations that the Germans were exploiters and if only the Turks would divest themselves of the German nuisance, the Allies would be on amiable terms.

As the Allied naval blockade tightened and the war stumbled on, the leaflets provoked Turkish commanders to extend the promise of the death penalty to all interested readers. Under those circumstances it is hardly surprising that the RFC witnessed local Arabs scrambling away from the leaflet bundles as if they were unexploded time bombs.

5

THE DESERT REVOLT

ON 5 June 1916 Sherif Hussein fired the opening shots of the Arab Revolt at Mecca while the Sherifian standard was unfurled in defiance at Medina . . . and so began the first step of a colourful quest to end 400 years of Turkish domination.

Arabia under the Ottoman Empire was an area two-and-a-half times the size of France and Imperial Germany combined, with less than six million inhabitants. At least half the poplace was nomadic or Bedouin, and town or hamlet dwellers constituted the other half. Only among the townsmen and the fertile regions – the ribbons of agriculture along the coast of the Hejaz and in the southwest highlands of Asir and Yemen – had Turkish influence made notable inroads.

A veneer of tribes had spread across this land-mass owing feudal-style allegiance to their particular chiefs who,

in their turn, gave nominal suzerainty to the Turkish dominion. Six great lords exerted extraordinary leverage. The Imam of Yemen was neutral in attitude, and enticed so by the presence of the Turkish 39th and 40th Divisions. The Idrissi of Asir was anti-Turkish in sentiment, but was similarly encouraged to neutrality by the occupation of the Turkish 21st Division. These garrisons and leaders, on the southern shores of the Red Sea, were so distant from practical lines of communication as to be effectively outside the pale of rebellion. Ibn Saud was likewise restricted, whose sect of fanatical *Wahabis* lived in the desolate center of the Arabian plateau.

The Turks had a genuine friend in Ibn Rashid of the Shammar Confederacy of north-central Arabia, from whom they purchased many of their transport camels. In northern

POLITICAL SPHERES

(NURI ES SHALAAN)

Damascus •Baghdad

ANAZEH

•Jerusalem

ARABIA

Aqaba BENI SAKR

HOWEITAT (IBN RASHID)

ATIYEH SHAMMAR

BILLI

JUHEINEH (IBN SAUD) WAHABIS

Medina

ATEIBEH

0   200   •Mecca   N

Miles

SUDAN

(IDRISSI)

BILLI Tribal Area
(IMAM) Leader
------ Boundary
• City

(IMAM)

ADEN

Red Sea

▲ Hussein ibn Ali, Sherif, Amir of Mecca, King of the Hejaz (1854–1931). As Keeper of the Holy Cities, his reputation transcended Ottoman boundaries to make him the only possible figure behind whom the Arabs could rally in opposition to the Turks. His sons, (from eldest down) Ali, Abdullah, Feisal, and Zeid, were his generals in a feudalistic tribal structure. Courteous and hospitable on one side, his was a shrewdly suspicious and obstinately iron-willed personality on the other.

Arabia-southern Syria, Nuri-es-Shalaan, the great Anazeh-Rualla lord, also seemed friendly. Situated directly under the heel of Turkish military administration, however, such seeming was the essence of survival. When the fruit ripened, Nuri-es-Shalaan would emerge as having one of the Revolt's best orchards.

By dint of geography, lineage, and personality, the only leader who could oppose the Turkish will and hope to nurture a credible revolt was Sherif Hussein ibn Ali. Hussein's immediate power base was the southern Hejaz which included the Holy Cities of Mecca and Medina. The Hejaz stretched from the base of the mountains of Asir, in the south, along the Red Sea ports of Jiddah, Rabegh, and Wejh, north to the southeast corner of the Sinai at Aqaba. Its loose interior boundary circumscribed the Hejaz Railway which led from its southern terminus at Medina north to Damascus and beyond.

The 65-year old Arab grandee, Sherif Hussein, had been born of substantive lineage. He was preeminent among the Ashraf (plural of Sherif) who claimed descent through the Prophet Mohammed's daughter Fatima, who was the wife of Ali, Islam's third Caliph. Pedigreed Ashraf are entered into the Register of Mecca, a custom reputed to date from the Prophet himself. The Register thus formed an aristocracy of religious significance – but which transcended into political privilege. As Hussein's family was deemed senior and himself the eldest son, he was acknowledged the 'Keeper of the Holy Places of Islam'.

Hussein therefore represented an alternative to the Caliph, or spiritual fount of Islam and his politico-religious power. In order to keep Hussein out of political harm's way, Sultan Abdul Hamid 'the Damned' (1876–1908) had taken him into 'protective custody' for 18 years at Constantinople. Abdul Hamid's optional insurance plan was to dump political rivals from his palace walls into the Bosporus inside

▼ Mecca, as portrayed by oblique photography in 1917. Violation of the most Holy City of Islam carried the death penalty for an unbeliever, so that the observer taking the photo was likely doing so with a curiosity prejudicial to the Amir of Mecca's directive not to overfly Holy Cities. Known in ancient times as *Macoraba*, Mecca is home of the black Kaaba Stone (centre foreground) which tradition ascribes was tossed from Heaven by the Angel Gabriel for Abraham. Two sets of intersecting hills make Mecca a cul-de-sac guarded by three overlooking forts.

weighted sacks. It cannot be surprising, then, that when the 1908 Young Turk Revolution took control that Hussein welcomed it as a political substitute. Out of gratitude for his spiritual endorsement, the Young Turks added 'Amir of Mecca' to Hussein's titles.

It was soon apparent, however, that the treatment of Arabs to second class status had survived the Revolution, and with a new twist of Turkish nationalism. Disenchantment crept in with the new era of repression against Arab language and custom. By 1914, secret societies had sprung up dedicated to the overthrow of Turkish hegemony from the Arab lands. The most important of these were *Al-Ahd*, or the Covenant, formed of Arab officers in the Turkish Army, and *Al Fatat*, or the Young Arab Society, embodying Moslem and Christian Arab officials and intellectuals.

These societies sought out the flavour of Hussein's political taste by envoy in early 1915. To his third son, Feisal, the Amir of Mecca delegated the task of testing the strength of the conspiratorial movements in return. Soon convinced of their depth and sincerity, Feisal joined Al Fatat in Damascus.

That spring, Djemal Pasha, a senior Young Turk leader and commander of 4th Army, discovered secret papers of negotiations between the underground societies and the French diplomat Monsieur Picot. In April, Djemal began his hangings of exposed Arab nationalists on the charge of treason. Djemal gave in to the psychological stupidity of having Feisal witness the executions, some of them his friends, *pour encourager les autres*. The obvious result, of course, was that inwardly Feisal vowed dire revenge. Outwardly, however, through covert communications, romantically secreted in cakes, sandals, and sword hilts by trusted family retainers, Feisal cautioned his father to await the outcome of British negotiations before casting the dice.

The British had known of Hussein's desire for an autonomous Hejaz since early 1914 when Hussein's second son, Abdullah, had arrived in Cairo on a private mission to see Lord Kitchener. A year later, the Foreign Office had sent out Sir Henry MacMahon as Egyptian High Commissioner with specific instructions to cultivate Hussein's friendship.

Throughout 1915, diplomatic contacts had played a waiting game for the moment of a mutually satisfactory union. Hussein desired an annual subsidy to replenish losses sustained by the war's restriction of pilgrims to the Holy Cities, as well as recognised 'Arab' independence over the vast Arab lands of the Ottoman Empire. Unfortunately, Britain was saddled with the poilitical demands of France which claimed special interests in Syria and Lebanon.

Out of this dalliance an extraordinary opportunity was missed. Al-Ahd had arranged a scheme whereby five Arab divisions would change hands as soon as the Allies landed at the Gulf of Alexandretta. At one daring stroke the Turks would be swept from Mecca to Aleppo, and out of a thousand miles of Arab land. With the unfortunate hindsight of history, however, the Allies landed instead at Gallipoli.

By spring, 1916, general terms of cooperation had been arranged. Intelligence revealed the assembly of a movable Turkish column in Damascus: destination Hejaz. The Turks were aware of unrest bubbling in the Hejaz, and possibly that the British Governor-General in the Sudan was shipping consignments of rifles across the Red Sea. Officially, the column was to escort the special German von Stotzingen Mission to Yemen where a wireless station was to open contact with German forces operating in East Africa.

Outwardly, relations between the Young Turk leaders and Feisal were cordial, and Enver and Djemal insisted on accompanying Feisal on his return by train to Mecca from Constantinople. In one of those whimsical twists of fate, upon their arrival at the Medina train station the Turkish leaders were entertained by a *razzia* of 5,000 galloping tribesmen who were discharging their rifles as if in celebration. Enver ironically commented on the largesse and enthusiasm of the 'welcome'. True to the unbreakable code of Arab hospitality, Feisal that night dined and slept his guests on the one hand while holding his tribesmen – who were making hands across throats gestures – at bay on the other. The next morning Feisal boarded Enver and Djemal on a train heading north and acted as escort to Damascus. Feisal pleaded it was but another example of Arab hospitable custom, but Enver and Djemal seemed wiser for their journey. The Hejaz was put under blockade, the mobile column collecting in Damascus was spurred on, and Feisal barely managed to disentangle himself from an extended stay.[1]

Feisal had just returned to Medina when the match touched powder.

Rebellion

In his youth, Hussein had explored the desert with the Bedouin in preference to the town, and had participated in the manly sport of raiding. His sons – from eldest down: Ali, Abdullah, Feisal, and Zeid – had been born during his palace captivity in Constantinople, so that when the 1908 Revolution came he sent them into the desert to learn the Bedouin ways and to efface the pristine manners of the Turkish court. His sons were now his principal officers within the tribal-feudal structure of the revolting Arab forces.

On 5 June 1916, Feisal and Ali raised the Sherifian standard of revolt at Medina and 30,000 tribesmen rallied to the call. As Feisal prepared to assault the Turkish garrison inside Medina's walls, Ali set off north to tear up the Hejaz

▶ Hussein's sons Abdullah (centre) and Ali (holding the Sherifian Standard). The flag is described by a red triangle superimposed on three horizontal stripes of (from top to bottom) black, green, and white. All three front-rank figures carry the curved dagger denoting the rank of Sherif.

Inset: The second most Holy City of Islam, Medina was the ancient city of *Yathrib*, where Prophet Mohammed lived his last ten years and was interred. Like Mecca, it is forbidden to unbelievers under pain of death. Positioned along the Pilgrim's Road to Mecca, and being the southern terminus of the Hejaz Railway leading to Damascus, Medina was of great strategic significance. Most of the Turkish garrison was concentrated in the tactically important northwest corner where the train station, aerodrome, and Fort Siler were located. Note the crenellated medieval walls.

▲ Fakhri Din Pasha, the 'Tiger of Medina'. Commander of 12th Corps and later the Hejaz Expeditionary Force, Fakhri Din held Medina in the early days of the Arab Revolt, then stood off the Arab Southern Armies for two-and-a-half years. Reduced to eating dates and transport animals, his officers finally mutinied in January, 1919 and handed him over to the Arabs two months after the Armistice.

Railroad. Only one Arab in five had a rifle, so that the rest fought with the myriad weapons of improvisation.

The revolting levies rapidly discovered that enthusiasm was no match for training and technical arms. The Turkish commander, Fakhri Din Pasha, was a stubborn and grisled veteran of the old school, and he and his soldiers were fresh from punitive massacres in Armenia. From the fortified walls, Fakhri Din's machine guns chattered into the Arab ranks while his artillery blasted swathes into the charging masses. Those Arabs unlucky enough to come to close quarters quickly learned that daggers, sticks, and rifle butts were outclassed by regular troops with fixed bayonets. The Beni Ali men fled, and the Ageyl and Ateibeh went to ground from fear of the big guns to which they were new.

Meanwhile, Sherif Hussein made his opening move 250 miles south at Mecca. Fortunately, much of the Turkish garrison had gone into cooler summer quarters at At Taif, leaving only 1,000 picked guards and Circassian mercenaries in the Holy City. As the first shots reached the Turkish commander's ears he excitedly telephoned Hussein in his official capacity as Amir of Mecca: 'The Bedouin have revolted against the Government,' he exclaimed, 'Find a way out.' Revealing a humourous bent, Hussein replied – 'Of course, we shall –' then ordered the general attack.[2]

On the first day the tribesmen rushed through the city gates, capturing the mosque of the Holy Kaaba, the residential and administrative sections, and penetrated the main bazaar. After three days of street fighting, the garrison barracks were set on fire and the Turks surrendered. Two smaller forts perched on hills outside the city held out for two more weeks.

Hussein had simultaneously coordinated an attack of 4,000 Harb warriors against the port of Jiddah, on 9 June. Initially frustrated by Turkish firepower, the fruit of Anglo-Arab cooperation crystallised in the form of air to ground support from the seaplanes of the *Ben-my-Chree*. Fifteen hundred Turks surrendered, as did the garrison port of Rabegh, to a local revolt 100 miles to the north. By the end of July, Yenbo, another 100 miles north of Rabegh, also surrendered. The Arab Revolt had begun well.

The capture of At Taif, 70 miles southeast of Mecca, was a different proposition. This summer station of the Mecca garrison had been fortified and entrenched and was replete with 3,000 men and ten 75mm German Krupp guns. Abdullah's 5,000 levies sat down to a long investment until Sir Reginald Wingate, as Governor-General of the (British) Sudan, was able to ship a battery of Egyptian artillery with Moslem personnel across the Red Sea. A desultory siege ended on 22 September when the tired Turks threw in the towel.

With the exception of Medina, the southern Hejaz had fallen. From the 5,000 Turkish prisoners of war ethnic 'Arab' elements were coming forward to serve the Sherifian cause. But it was the steady downturn of events at Medina that began to threaten the very life of the Revolt.

Fakhri Din Pasha had skillfully withdrawn his men behind the inner city walls which protected Medina's fabled palaces, fountains and fruited orchards. Inside, he was safe from the few recently acquired Arab mountain guns – for a stray shot might injure the Tomb of Mohammed. As Feisal's tribesmen settled into a lethargic investment of the suburbs Fakhri Din struck one dawn with sudden and brutal force.

The Turks sortied into the Awali suburb where they visited scenes reminiscent of their earlier Armenian slaughter. Males were shot or pushed into the torched buildings while females were raped and carried off. For the Arabs it was a shock. Heretofore they had considered women inviolable and had left immovable property unvandalised. It was the first savage act in the Arabian Campaigns, an act which would inspire an irregular war more dirty and less understandable to the more straight-forward campaigners in Palestine.

The enraged townsmen and tribesmen launched a frenzied counter-attack and were again broken against the bristling bayonets and unyielding stance of Medina's medieval walls. Feisal and Ali met their sheikhs in heart-heavy council and the army broke off to the hills 50 miles to the south in order to block the Pilgrim Road into Mecca.

Moving with uncharacteristic speed, the Turks repaired

the damaged Hejaz Railroad, gathered supplies from loyal elements, and extended their real estate around Medina. Troops had been rushed south so that the Hejaz Expeditionary Force totalled 13,000; half the force was on the road south of Medina, 2,000 were used as a town garrison, and 1,500 guarded the railway. A flight of aeroplanes circled the aerodrome near the train station northwest of Medina.

A mobile column was forming including some armoured cars and camel transport, in order to seize the port of Rabegh, and from thence to march directly on Mecca. Equally astute had been political preparations. Hussein had been formally deposed in Constantinople and the Turkish candidate, Ali Haidar, declared the new Amir of Mecca. This anticipatory figure had already been entrained to Medina with the Turkish 'Holy Carpet' in hand for the triumphal entry in Mecca. The light of the Arab Revolt was burning dim.

The Arab Bureau

By early 1916 a seasoned consortium of Arab experts, known as the Arab Bureau, had collected at the Savoy Hotel in Cairo. The Arab Bureau's chief mission was the collection and analysis of information in the 'Arab' sphere. The Arab Bureau was under the High Commissioner, MacMahon, and supervised by Lieutenant-Colonel C. G. Clayton who wore a triple hat: Sudan Agent, head of General Murray's Military Intelligence, and head of Political Intelligence.

The Bureau's menagerie of experts was legendary: Mark Sykes (of the Sykes-Picot Agreement), Ronald Storrs (Oriental Secretary in Egypt), Commander D. G. Hogarth (former curator of the Oxford Ashmolean Museum), and others, but destined for the halls of history's fame was a 28-year-old junior member, Thomas Edward Lawrence, known to popular history as 'Lawrence of Arabia'.

Lawrence was born fourth of five sons in Tremadoc, Caernarvon County, Wales, in 1888. His parents were Thomas Chapman and Sarah Maden, his father's second wife. Chapman, heir to an Irish baronetcy, ended up losing his estates and changing his name, eventually settling in Oxford. Lawrence spent early years in Scotland, Jersey, and France before attending Oxford High School then Oxford University where he studied the military architecture of the Crusades.

This interest and the required thesis led him to the Middle East in 1909, where he was to spend several years living like the natives and participating on archaeological digs with his tutor and mentor, D. G. Hogarth. Hogarth supplemented his archaeological discoveries with intelligence collection on the side and Lawrence was most certainly involved to some degree, for by 1914 he was an expert on the Turkish order of battle.

Lawrence sat out the first months of the war, however, for Lord Kitchener had asked him to finish writing a book sponsored by the Palestine Exploration Fund which was, in fact, cover for their intelligence activities on neutral Ottoman soil. In any event 'Kitchener's Mob' would have rejected his military service in 1914, because the fair-haired, blue-eyed Lawrence stood two inches below the recruiting standard of

▲ Lawrence of Arabia. Conscious of psychological impression and charisma, Lawrence dressed in pure white silk, often with a head rope of scarlet and gold. At his waist is the curved golden dagger of a Meccan Sherif. To compensate for stature, he often rode larger than average sized camels capable of great endurance and speed. His own endurance became legend even among the hardy Bedouin. Lawrence was widely read in military history, yet with no formal military training might have been judged unlikely to succeed against a deadly environment, a savage foe, and within a harsh, exclusive society. A lover of ideas, he became a mover of men, a dreamer who carried his childhood visions for a foreign people into a practical reality.

five feet five inches. Had they not eventually relaxed such recruiting wisdom Lawrence would have been lost to military history . . . by that criteria, so too Napoleon!

With some assistance from Hogarth and S. F. Newcombe, Lawrence received a War Office appointment to the Geographical Section where he additionally received a direct commission to lieutenant. Because he was fluent in Arabic, with working knowledge of many dialects, and because he knew the Middle East at the village level, Lawrence was able to wangle a transfer to Cairo. From the map department he progressed into enemy order of battle, and then founded a specialist periodical — The Arab Bulletin, in each case winning universal respect for his accurate and authoritative knowledge. At the same time Lawrence continued his inherently relaxed approach to military etiquette so that his inter-departmental workings rubbed conventional noses the wrong way and drove fools and strict respecters of rank to distraction.

His days behind a desk, however, were numbered, as was the life of the revolt if matters were let drift. Ronald Storrs was leaving on a fact-finding mission to see Hussein at Jiddah, and Lawrence was not about to be left behind. Taking personal leave, he induced Storrs to accept him in an unofficial capacity. Few, including Lawrence himself could have guessed that from this journey he would pass from clerk to one of history's greatest irregular warriors, and perhaps the founding father of modern guerrilla war.

The pair sailed via Captain Boyle's Red Sea Squadron to the labyrinthine port of Jiddah in October, 1916. There, in Mecca's old Pilgrim's port they were greeted by Hussein's second son, Abdullah, acting in the portfolio of 'Foreign Minister' for his father, who had assumed the additional self-styled title of 'King of the Hejaz'. Lawrence soon realised his original theory was correct. The Revolt lacked not the enthusiasm or the base of support, but that of a charismatic leader, an armed prophet. He found Abdullah, at 35, too portly, too balanced, and though flushed from his victory at At Taif, more the politician of peace than the driving force.

While Abdullah entertained Storrs with official diatribe, Lawrence obtained Sherifial permission to travel up country in order to better inform Murray's GHQ of local conditions. With Storr's blessing he sailed to Rabegh to meet Ali, Hussein's eldest son. Ali was thin, of average height, and though dignified and pleasant, at 37 he was too tired, too nervous and perhaps too pious to be the leader of armed rebellion.

Zeid, the youngest son, was half Turkish, and having been raised in a Constantinople harem was altogether too shy, flippant, and at 19, too young. More than ever Lawrence longed to contact the third son, Feisal, whose army was poised between the gathering Turkish storm at Medina and the Revolt's last hope – Mecca.

In the best tourist tradition and out of deference for Bedouin opinion – who judge it effeminate to carry provisions for a mere 100 miles overland – Lawrence journeyed to Feisal packed light. The heat and glare turned granules of sand into stabbing pricks of silver light as his camel moved with that swelling roll of tide so fitting for the Bedouin ship of the desert. Exchanged was the bustle of Cairo, the overcrowded office and military regimen, gone for the physical trials and deadly purity of the elements. Not now the bother of conformity, but the nagging menace of a sniper's bullet, a tribe's betrayal, or Turkish torture, while overhead the pestilent pervasiveness of the sun urged an insane desire for water as the broken crust of civilisation crumbled away.

Lawrence met Feisal at the Hamlet of Hamra, a white-robed figure framed against a black doorway:

'I felt at first glance that this was the man I had come to Arabia to seek – the leader who would bring the Arab Revolt to full glory. Feisal looked very tall and pillar-like, very slender, in his long white robes and his brown headcloth bound with a brilliant scarlet and gold cord. His eyelids were dropped; and his black beard and colourless face were like a

▲ Feisal, Lawrence's 'Armed Prophet', commander of the Arab Northern Army, 1917–1918, and King of Mesopotamia in 1920. Feisal in Arabic means 'sword's flashing downstroke'. Training in the Sultan's entourage made him an exceptional diplomat and his military service with the Turks gave him a working knowledge of tactics. Feisal was an impetuous, moody personality, charming and courageous, while at the same time frail in a sense that inspired devotion. 'In appearance he was tall, graceful and vigorous, with the most beautiful gait, and a royal dignity of head and shoulders.' (T. E. Lawrence)

mask against the strange, still watchfulness of his body. His hands were crossed in front of him on his dagger.'[3]

The chemical reaction was immediate, the catalyst to a close, cooperative path to victory.

'And do you like our place here in Wadi Safra?' Feisal asked, amidst the headmen of his army, with meaning more veiled than an obvious answer would satisfy.

'Well,' replied Lawrence, 'but it is far from Damascus.'

Demonstrating comparable diplomatic acumen, Feisal returned: 'Praise be to God there are Turks nearer us than that.'[4]

6

THE GATES OF PALESTINE

BEYOND the watered reserves and palm fronds of El Arish, Chetwode's Desert Column raided southeast against Magdhaba and Rafa, the last Turkish outposts on the Sinai side of the Egyptian–Palestinian border. Moving out the night of 22 December, 1916, Chauvel led his ANZAC Mounted Division and the Imperial Camel Brigade into an envelopment of the 80th Regiment (27th Arab Division), positioned in a circle of redoubts astride the Wadi El Arish near Magdhaba.

Boring produced no water so that, after alerting the Turks, Chauvel found his situation untenable unless he withdrew in defeat or charged to capture Magdhaba's water supply. That afternoon, after directing their three-fold artillery superiority against the redoubts, the light horsemen and cameliers dismounted and went in with the bayonet. The Arab soldiers in Turkish service shot badly so that the casualties of both sides were near 100 and Chauvel made a total haul of 1,300 prisoners and a mountain battery.

The return from Magdhaba was marked with a mysterious series of night manifestations: from the ANZAC commander down through the troopers visions of tall buildings, strange animals, and lighted villages were witnessed in mass. During debriefing, the stories of hundreds of men were corroborated through cross-checking examinations. Officially, as there was no explanation, the incident was recorded as 'lack of sleep', a reference being made to the mysterious 'Angel of Mons' in 1914 when thousands had seen similar manifestations.

Other eastern Sinai revelations were more tangible and irksome. One Scottish patrol was literally attacked and eaten by a pack of wild Bedouin dogs. Omnipresent pests were the scarab beetles, which, after dining near the camel lines, came upon sleeping troopers in bivouac and crawled, foul smelling, into blankets and clothes.

Another 'cutting-out' operation was undertaken against Rafa on 7 January 1917 with two brigades of the mounted ANZACs, the Imperial Camel Brigade, the 5th (Yeomanry) Mounted Brigade and No. 7 Light Car Patrol (of four armoured cars and three tender cars). The column marched under Chetwode's direct supervision for 29 miles. The transit was through pastured country dotted with wild flowers, and also Bedouin country. From the start, the Arab cry of 'Lu-lu-lu!' performed with tongue and wind against the mouth preceded the column's progress, while a chain of signal fires warned the Turks of Chetwode's coming.

Three groups of outerworks guarded the approach to a central redoubt thrust 200 feet over the surrounding terrain. From this hillock seated at El Magruntein was a killing ground of a mile, technically sprawling over the union of the African and Asian continents. The tactical question was whether 5,000 mounted troops with supports could overcome 2,000 entrenched infantry of the 31st Regiment, 3rd (Anatolian) Division, after a night march and with enemy reinforcements at a distance of 12 miles.

In order to lay down adequate suppression, 1,637 field gun shells and 410,000 rifle rounds were expended as the column advanced dismounted with the bayonet. Turkish return fire was again notably poor and while the outer redoubts were pinned the New Zealand Mounted Rifle Brigade carried the central position. The bag this time was costlier – 1,624 Turks and their squad of German advisors for 487 EEF casualties.

Twice, the Turks had left relatively unsupported infantry too far forward; twice, they had lost a full regiment. Ironically, the lesson was similar to that taught previously to the EEF, also the hard way. It is fair to state that von Kressenstein had tried to remove these garrisons but was overruled by Djemal Pasha for the political reason they were the last Sinai toeholds.

Taking Stock

On 11 January 1917, Robertson telegrammed Murray that any offensive in Palestine would have to be postponed until autumn. And while Murray was enjoined to prepare for such an eventuality he was to surrender two of his divisions under the Imperial Reserve concept. The year 1916 in Europe had been bloody and indecisive. Verdun, the Somme, Jutland, the Brusilov offensive . . . Rumania had entered the war and had been overrun by the Central Powers. If Lloyd-George desired a victory in the East, such desire was overturned by pressuring exigencies nearer home.

Turkey's early year exuberance was quickly disillusioned in the Caucasus at Koprukoy, Erzerum, and Trebizond, followed by a Russian offensive destroying the Turkish 3rd Army for the second time, and further defeating the 2nd Army. In Mesopotamia, the 6th Army was crushed under General Maude's two corps advance, undertaken for revenge of the British surrender of 10,000 men at Kut.

Unfortunately for the British Palestine effort, while the War Office set about stripping EEF resources, Germany commenced development of a sweeping plan to bolster the Turkish war capability in 1917. Still, many of Murray's problems had improved or become clearer than at the start of his command in early 1916. His Western Frontier Force had effectively put down the Senussi Revolt threatening Egypt's western border, and the Senussi southern ally, the Sultan of Darfur. The Caliph's call to jihad had also clearly failed, for despite the work of *agents provocateurs* within Egypt, the populace remained pacific.

Having sent his 42nd Division abroad in February, Murray reformed the remaining basis of his command. Garrison battalions of older men and veterans with acquired disabilities provided much of the interior security and guard duties as well as the bulk of the personnel assigned to the Nile Delta areas. The western frontier was held by light, mobile screens and secondary quality troops: the Bikanir Camel Corps, five armoured motor batteries, six light car patrols, seven garrison battalions, and attached artillery. Three infantry brigades and a battalion of the Imperial Camel Brigade anchored the Southern Canal Section. The most important entity was Dobell's Eastern Force. Murray allotted wheeled transport for Dobell's three attached infantry divisions so that they could better maneuver on Palestine's *terra firma*. Three Yeomanry regiments serving without horses were mustered into the 74th Division, and the cavalry was reorganised into two divisions of four brigades. Dobell's own headquarters was shifted across the Sinai from Ismailia to El Arish to be closer to projected operations. By 5 February, the pipehead had reached El Arish and the railhead was beyond.

Eastern Force Order of Battle

Force troops:	Imperial Camel Brigade
	Imperial Service Cavalry Brigade
	52nd (Lowland) Division
	53rd (Welsh) Division
	54th (East Anglian) Division
	74th (Yeomanry) Division
Desert Column	ANZAC Mounted Division
	Imperial Mounted Division
Northern Canal Section:	20th Indian Infantry Brigade
	Two garrison battalions
	Two battalions, West Indies Regiment

The Desert Column was in the vanguard, and by the end of February had taken station five miles east of Rafa at Khan Yunis. Murray was plotting an attack on Shellal but, in early March, the RFC reported von Kressenstein withdrawing to the Gaza to Tel-es-Sheria and Beersheba Line. This was just east of striking range so that a logistical delay ensued.

The RFC reported the arrival of Turkish reinforcements – the 3rd Cavalry Division (lancers) reborn out of their death in the Caucasus, and the 16th Division. RFC intelligence revealed the strength of the Turkish line exceeded anything yet seen. The squadron-sized German 300th Flight Detachment was observing EEF intentions in turn with its new Rumpler aircraft, while its Halberstadt fighters made life uneasy for the RFC. Although only two of the Halberstadts were airborne at a given time, they succeeded in a seven for two kill ratio versus the RFC.

Australian cameliers remarked on the aerial chivalry of one German 'Lieutenant Felmy' in a 'black-tailed Taube' who, having shot down two opponents, risked flying in with messages concerning the flyers. Major Jones of No. 1 (Australian) Squadron then flew over Turkish lines dropping bundled clothes and mail by answer. At fifty feet he was cheered by the Germans and returned their waves.[1]

During early March the RFC explored the modern technique of 'aerial interdiction' in an effort to delay the arrival of Turkish reinforcements into their hardening battle line. Thirty aircraft dropped two and three-quarter tons of bombs over a three-day period. This amount is ludicrous judged by modern standards, but for a three-day exercise of hand-dropping 20 pound bombs it was a notable achievement. As for the result, it would not be the last time in military history that interdiction or strategic bombing would fail to make a decisive difference on its own.

The Turkish force estimated to be in position had about 18,000 combat effectives in March, 1917.

Turkish Order of Battle

Gaza:	79th Regiment (27th Division)
	125th Regiment (16th Division)
	six batteries (one German, two Austrian)
	eight machine-gun companies (two German)
	(3,500 total effectives)
Djenmach:	3rd (Infantry) Division
	seven batteries
	four machine-gun companies
	(5,000 total effectives)
Tel-es-Sheria:	two regiments (16th Division)
	divisional artillery
	22nd Corps Headquarters
	(5,000 total effectives)
Beersheba:	3rd (Cavalry) Division
	(1,500 total effectives)
Ramleh:	two regiments of 53rd Division in reserve

By their own calculations the Turks did not feel unduly secure. Von Kressenstein's memoirs blamed a weaker order of battle return on sickness and Arab desertion into Palestinian villages. In 1915, Alexander Aaronsohn had noted the inefficiency of quartermaster and veterinary procedures dealing with vital transport animals in the Beersheba area: two years later, it seemed such neglect had borne ill fruit as von Kressenstein discovered his transport in deplorable condition.

The First Battle of Gaza

Gaza's very name means 'fortress' and aptly so, for traditionally Gaza has been the 'portcullis' of Palestine. Alexander the Great, Pompey, Saladin, and Napoleon rode within its walls, and the Biblical Samson carried its gates to the nearby hill of Ali Muntar. Now the War Office bade

▶ Top right: *Kameraden.* Five German officers in five separate campaign uniforms stand alternating between six Turkish/Arab personalities (five of whom, if military, are obviously irregulars). Despite the apparent good will, difficulties were widespread between these allies as the transplantation of Teutonic thoroughness and *kultur* did not ride well with the less efficient, but proud and independent Turks and Arabs.

Centre right: Reserves at the Turkish 'Drama' training camp, March, 1917. Note the tents are camouflaged with leafy branches.

Right: A British Yeomanry squadron training near the great Sphinx.

Far right: A patrol of 'A' Squadron, East Riding Yeomanry near Fayyum Oasis during the Senussi Revolt, 1916. The East Ridings were attached to the 22nd Mounted Brigade, ANZAC Mounted Division during the First Battle of Gaza.

General Murray to add his name to the scroll of Gaza's conquerors.

The Turkish lines covered 25 miles from the Mediterranean coastline near Gaza along natural ridges to Tel-es-Sheria, and thence to Beersheba. In the north, Gaza commanded the old coast road and the eastward radiation of roads into all of southern Palestine. In the south, Beersheba guarded the last water supply and acted as anchor against any EEF southern move attempting to circumvent the line through the desert to its south and east. Djemal Pasha's 4th Army had therefore every reason to bolster this front contrary to an EEF breach. As long as it stood the British were relegated to the inhospitable embrace of the desert. Nor could they linkup with their new Arab allies in the Hejaz.

Quite ironically, Murray and Dobell were spoiling for a fight lest the Turks melt away before they could bring the enemy to combat. They conceived a large 'cutting out' strategem. At night, the Desert Column would penetrate east of the town and envelop it before the Turks could react, thus becoming both a rear flank and a bar to any reinforcements coming to Gaza's aid. Meanwhile, Eastern Force infantry, support by the artillery, would plough its way into the town. The critical element was water. The railway had been recently extended to Khan Yunis, but there were no unloading facilities at Rafa Station so that, given the concentration of Eastern Force mouths at Rafa, Gaza had to be captured in one day in order to secure adequate water reserves.

The restriction of water made surprise an even more important consideration. By 25 March, Dobell succeeded in an undetected massing of his five divisions and camel brigade on the western lip of the Wadi Ghazi. The Wadi sliced through the frontier soil in a gash 100 yards long and 45 feet deep, creating a natural 'moat' for the gates of Palestine. Taking up assigned positions, Eastern Force moved across the Wadi in the early morning hours of 26 March, while from the Mediterranean dense sea fog cloaked the intruders with an ethereal shroud.

With visibility restricted to 20 yards the massive penetration and envelopment washed over the unsuspecting Turkish outposts, silent and irresistible. Leading elements scooped up the commander and staff of the Turkish 53rd Division who were motoring on a peaceful morning jaunt to Gaza. As the three-hour fog began to lift at 0800 hours, Turkish headquarters received incredulous spot-sighting reports of enemy cavalry. Soon, the clear sky revealed the extent of the morning's work. By 1100 hours, elements of the ANZAC Mounted Division reached the coast, completing the cordon around Gaza. Arranged over a 15-mile arc in the Turkish rear were 11,000 troopers and 38 guns.

During peacetime, Gaza had hosted 40,000 civilians. On a northeast-southwest axis a series of hills and ridges dotted the town approaches which were themselves covered by large cactus hedges up to 10 feet high and 15 feet deep. The cactus hedges, as formidable as the equivalent depth of barbed wire, were particularly severe along the south-southeast of Gaza, where their intricate patchwork qualified them with the descriptive map reference 'maze'. Two miles

**FIRST GAZA
26–27 MARCH 1917**

inland from the sea set on a low hill, Gaza was dominated by the 300 foot knoll of Ali Muntar.

Against this bastion was aimed 12,000 infantry and 42 guns of the 53rd (Welsh) Division, with 8,000 infantry and 44 guns of the 52nd (Lowland) Division in reserve. The 54th (East Anglian) Division was east of Ali Muntar with 8,000 infantry on the southern apex of the arc across Gaza's rear. The main assault of the 53rd Division had been delayed, however, partly by the fog and partly from lethargic staffwork, unexercised since the evacuation from Gallipoli. At noon, the 53rd struck against Ali Muntar and the southeast ridge, and within an hour had stalled.

Chauvel's mounted ANZACs were ordered into Gaza from the northern approach, his slack to be taken up by a northern extension of the Imperial Mounted Division, part of which would be assumed by the Imperial Camel Brigade farther south. Later that afternoon Chauvel's horsemen had pressed into the northern outskirts while a brigade of the 54th had taken Green Hill, south of the Ali Muntar ridge. This fortuitous support enabled the 53rd to press on and secure much of the Ali Muntar ridge by the shade of dusk.

As some units of the Welsh and ANZACs joined hands in Gaza's outskirts, a staff farce reminiscent of Marston Moor crippled the commanders of both sides. In the twilight of confusion each commander considered himself beaten. Von Kressenstein halted his 12,500 men and 50 gun reinforcements; Major Tiller, Gaza's commandant, blew up his own wireless station, and Dobell recalled his Desert Column, fearful of its exposed situation in the dark without

▶ Top right: The Turkish 3rd Cavalry Division marching out of Beersheba for positions near the Hareira Redoubt, April, 1917. Djemal and von Kressenstein had anticipated Murray's second assault on the Gaza-Beersheba Line.

▶ One of the Turkish (Arab) Regiments near Gaza, April, 1917.

water. Eastern Force troops queried their orders in disbelief.

Further, the break of dawn revealed a miscoordination of night orders between the 53rd and 54th Divisions. Instead of finding themselves in mutually supporting positions, they were bent like a bow back-to-back and exposed to counterattack. The Turkish 'writing on the wall' soon came with triumphal attacks securing both Ali Muntar and Green Hill, and it appeared that 3rd and 16th Divisions were preparing to strike Eastern Force from Ali Muntar to Shellal.

On 27 March Eastern Force phased into general withdrawal with 3,500 casualties and 500 missing, for an exchange of 2,397 Turks and 57 German and Austrian gunners. Though in a tactically strong situation, the Turks had been greatly outnumbered and surprised. The fighting had been stubborn among broken, patchwork ground. The gates of Palestine had held firm.

The Second Battle of Gaza

Frustrated, embarrassed, or possibly in a moment of weakness designed to give his superiors the sort of news for which they were pressing him, Murray issued to Robertson the fateful report of 28 March. In it, Murray tripled the estimate of Turkish losses, ignored his own and mis-

represented the outcome by asserting that the battle had just fallen short of a complete disaster to the enemy.[2]

Such news hit the Imperial General Staff in a euphoric mood over Eastern affairs. Baghdad had fallen to Maude's Mesopotamian advance that March, and the Allies had gone over to the offensive in the Balkans. The first Russian Revolution had removed the Tsar so that at first appearance democratic reforms might allow a more united and vigourous prosecution of Russia's war on behalf of the common Allied effort. The chimeric hope was entertained that Maude's forces might couple with the Russian Caucasian Army to crush the Turkish southeastern flank, while Murray might unite with the Arabs to pierce the Turkish front in Palestine. Turkey might be knocked out of the war.

Murray was ordered to consider Jerusalem his target objective and was promised all necessary supplies and reinforcements pending receipt of his estimated needs. The Prime Minister and the War Cabinet judged the moral effect of a victory in the Holy Land paramount at a time when friend and foe were locked in an endless morale-draining bloodbath in Europe. Murray's EEF could have a major, perhaps decisive influence on the war.

With surprise blown to the winds, however, a resumption of hostilities against the Gaza-Beersheba Line was more likely to resemble a Western Front battle in miniature than

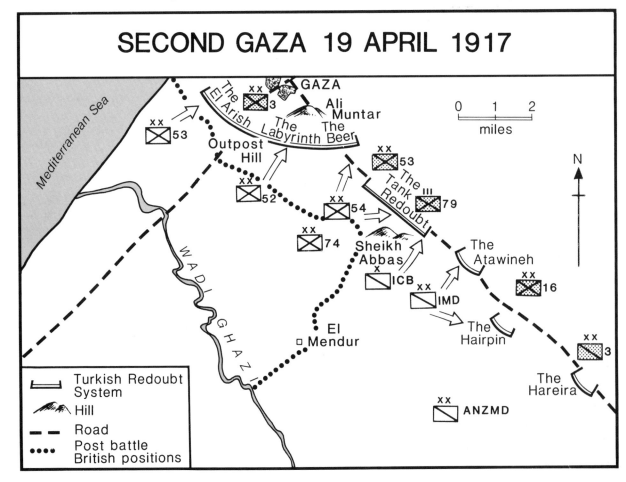

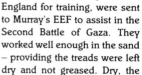
The tank 'Pincher'. Eight Mark 1 heavy tanks, formerly used in England for training, were sent to Murray's EEF to assist in the Second Battle of Gaza. They worked well enough in the sand – providing the treads were left dry and not greased. Dry, the sand passed through, greased, the sand clotted.

the mobile opportunity presented in March. Murray was given eight Mark 1 heavy tanks along with 4,000 gas shells for his 4.5 inch howitzers. For punching power the tanks were grouped with other mobile detachments and placed in the 'Machine Gun Corps' under Dobell's Eastern Force:

'E' Company Mark 1 heavy tanks
Nos. 11 and 12 Light Armoured Car Batteries
17th Motor Machine Gun Battery
Nos. 1 and 3 Armoured Trains

The Turks were also predisposing for round two. Around Gaza trenches were carved into and about the deadly cactus hedges, forming a warren of defences termed 'The Beer', 'El Arish', and descriptively – 'The Labyrinth'. Engineers had sited these redoubts for mutually supporting and enfilade fire, and with direct field of fire along any open-slope approach. Redoubts continued southeast along the Beersheba Road, in strength, but not in a strictly contiguous line.

If tactical works had appreciated, Turkish manpower had not. The two reinforcing regiments in the interim period had merely replaced battle casualties, leaving the Palestine Front with a combat strength of 18,185 men, 86 machine guns, and 68 guns. The 3rd Division garrisoned Gaza, the 53rd Division with the 79th Regiment the centre of the line, while the 16th Division and the 3rd Cavalry Division moored the southeast end of the 12-mile line. From below the Hareira Redoubt only a light screen of troops stood guard for approximately 13 miles into Beersheba, which was itself held by only one regiment.

Despite the attraction of turning this weak flank with his superior mounted arm, Dobell was unable to do so for lack of water. Although the pipeline was pumping 600,000 daily gallons from Qantara to pipehead, only 36,500 gallons were reaching the battle-line soldiers because of needs en route, and natural dehydration. This limitation seems to have impressed Turkish defensive strategy, for the skirmishes in the days preceding 'H' Hour indicated each side had a clear perception of what was coming and where.

Eastern Force battle deployment started on 17 April at the Wadi Ghazi, with a general artillery and naval gun bombardment at dawn on the 19th. It was the largest bombardment and numerically biggest in-theatre battle to date, the EEF having a two-fold advantage in men and guns, but coming up against a tactically strong opponent. As the 53rd attacked up the coastal road, the 52nd struck at southern Gaza, and the 54th and Imperial Camel Brigade assaulted the ridges containing 'The Beer' and formidable 'Tank' Redoubts. With the 74th acting as reserve, the Desert Column's two mounted divisions – the ANZAC and Imperial Mounted – demonstrated counter the southeastern Turkish line.

After a day of battering, lobbing gas shells, and expending the diminishing artillery stock, the Eastern Force was everywhere stymied with superfluous gains. The 53rd still held Samson's Ridge southwest of the 'El Arish' Redoubt, but the 52nd had been ejected from Outpost Hill. The 54th, with infantry, cameliers, and tanks held – then were forced out of – the 'Tank' Redoubt while a withering fire from the height of Ali Muntar inflicted half of the total day's casualties on the 54th alone. Dobell ordered a temporary cessation by nightfall to contemplate further action.

Throughout the night the Turks used their reserve system stationed between redoubts to deliver localised counter attacks. At dawn, as at First Gaza, von Kressenstein desired a full counter offensive, but was again restrained by Djemal Pasha. In the event such a counter attack was not needed, for Dobell had also called off the struggle.

The butcher's bill was 2,013 Turks for 6,444 EEF. Twice Murray's head had butted against an ever-hardening wall denying him the gates of Palestine. Twice the Turks had snatched the laurels of victory, and twice surged in morale. It was a defeat destined to herald sweeping political and administrative reform.

7

THE SERMON CARRIES NORTH

IN October, 1916 Lawrence had gone in search for an Arab leader whom he could recommend to receive British arms and confidence, and he had found Feisal. But before his return to Cairo his mission was to absorb the situation and the essence of the revolt in order to educate Murray's GHQ in the ways of armed rebellion.

Lawrence discovered that the new King of the Hejaz had retained the crust of Turkish civil administration in the liberated areas, but had abolished the Turkish civil code. Islamic fundamentalism, represented by a return to Koranic law, was rife throughout such of the Turkish political house as still remained. The towns, which under Turkish rule had enjoyed the economic fruit of peace, now experienced the diminishing yield of war. It was the Bedouin who provided the warriors and the camels for the Revolt so it was the

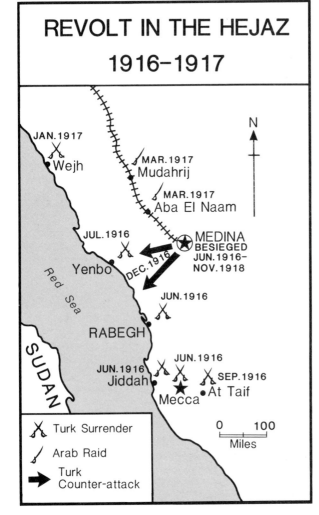

REVOLT IN THE HEJAZ
1916-1917

Bedouin who received Hussein's recompense for service. The Hejaz mutineers were paid £2 sterling in gold for a month's work, and twice that for a camel (in 1916 Arabia these were handsome incentives), while their families were fed by Hussein in patriarchal style.

In fact, the entire rebel army took on the fashion of a feudal assemblage. Hussein, with his immediate family retainers, stood aloof from the actual fighting inside the Holy City while his three eldest sons commanded his field armies. Ali was south-southwest of Medina with 1,800 'trained' Arabs, 6,800 tribesmen, and 11 guns; Abdullah (between diplomacy) was southeast of Medina moving north-east with 8–10,000 and 10 guns, while at Rabegh were 900 Egyptians sent by Wingate and 700 irregulars.[1] Feisal, with his younger brother, Zeid, was based on the port of Yenbo, although Feisal was generally inland with a variable force of 2–8,000.

These warbands were constantly shifting in location, and with the volatile nature of their service, numbers as a strict expression of strength could be misleading. Bedouin definition of a 'fighting man' liberally included anyone 12–60 in age who could pull a trigger. If a family owned a rifle they rotated it among male members after several day increments. Married men divided their time between wife and allegiance, and sometimes a whole clan or sub-tribe would leave the line for an indefinite period.

The basic rebel levy attended his personal sheikh, whose approximate span of command averaged 100 warriors. A Sherif formed the irregular officer spine of the tribal warbands; there were from 8–900 Ashraf (plural for Sherif) so named for their ancient and common blood link with the Prophet. The Ashraf, then, were a rough equivalent of the English knight, in some cases baron, and the fundamental respect afforded them translated into a temporal power of fealty over the Arab masses. In effect, the Ashraf who sided with Hussein became the missionaries of his Arab nationalist sermon.

In early November, Feisal's army numbered 8,000 warriors in the Wadi Yenbo. His men were Ageyl, Billi, Juheina, and Ateiba, four tribes more at ease in the blood feud against each other than in the new spirit of operational teamwork. They were a camp of suspicious, but hardy men and, generously distributed with automatic weapons and set amidst the hill terrain, Lawrence considered their holding of a Turkish thrust from Medina an open bet.

This Turkish threat was real. The ration strength of the Hejaz Expeditionary Force was 15,600 men of the 42nd, 55th, and 160th Regiments (each of 3,200), three companies of engineers, a Medina Garrison Regiment of 1,200, Khairi Bey's Yemen Militia of 3,500, a thousand Camel Corps, six batteries of field guns, three mountain batteries, and four of Maxims.[2]

What the Arabs needed was a backbone of trained regulars commanded by volunteer Arab officers. Fortunately, from desertions and the prisoners of war, notable ethnic Arab officers were coming forward, prior training compliments of the Turkish Sultan. Feisal's *aide de camp* was Maulud el Mukhlis, a former cavalry officer twice demoted for adherence to Arab nationalism. Aziz el Masri, who had commanded Turkish troops against the Italians in 1912, had also joined, fresh from a Turkish death list for his nationalist conspiracies.

El Mazri was assembling regular battalions from Syrian and Mesopotamian prisoners at Rabegh. In Cairo, the Arab Bureau had sanctioned an 'Arab Legion' out of prisoner-volunteers being held in Egypt and India. Lawrence promised to expedite these and British advisors for the Sherifial cause, as well as guns and machine guns. Yenbo was projected as Feisal's exclusive supply base.

Lawrence then sailed with his scroll of knowledge in Captain Boyle's *Suva* to Jiddah, then on Admiral Wemyss' flagship *Euryalus* to Port Sudan, where he entrained to Khartoum to meet Wingate. From briefing the Governor-General of the Sudan, Lawrence travelled north down the Nile by train to Cairo to report to Colonel Clayton.

It was the Arab Bureau's opinion that unless British troops were sent the days of the Revolt were numbered. This assessment provoked the long-enduring political debate over the question of the 'Rabegh Brigade'. Briefly expressed, the French, Robertson, and other proponents desired a dispatch of British troops, and this was opposed by Murray. Murray was delighted to receive the support of such an unlikely on-the-scene ally as Lawrence who forsaw the wider-range complications of commiting European regulars and Christians to the theatre. After some months the agony was laid to rest when Hussein finally refused to accept responsibility for such an action.[3]

Clayton digested Lawrence's impressions on the Arab Revolt then ordered him to return to Yenbo. Incredibly, Lawrence thought his adventure had been a one-off mission and not the prelude to a rendezvous with historical destiny. Believing himself to return to *The Arab Bulletin* which he had founded, Lawrence protested that he was an ideas man, not a man of action. Responsibility, the manipulation of persons, the art of soldiering – these were not his talents. But Lawrence had made his own bed by becoming the indispensable man in Arabia, and Clayton would not be denied Lawrence's lying in that bed. Months would pass before sufficient British advisers and liaison could be put in place. But only days before Lawrence was packed back to Yenbo.

Yenbo

Some good news initially met him after landing in the backwater Arabian port. Feisal's men had driven back the Turkish camel patrols. Feisal's encampment was a day's ride up the Wadi Yenbo, a vast, open waterbed still damp from a late flood. The good news, however, had only been the silver lining in the dark cloud.

Mobile Turkish forces had outmaneuvered the Arab barrier troops in the Wadi Safra, cutting their retreat. A usually effective tactic when dealing with irregulars, this panicked the Harb tribe and the Turks drove over the Dhifran Pass to Bir Said where they surprised and routed a Harb contingent under Zeid. The unruly rebel mob was streaming back on Yenbo and Feisal was trying to plug the breach with 5,000 tribesmen until some defence of Yenbo could be arranged.

Lawrence arrived in camp at night, surrounded by enervating rumours that the Turks would fall on their position at any moment. In that dank early November morn palm-rib fires and hastily prepared morsels of food chased away the grey dawn, and the camels were loaded at the beat of kettle drums. Upon their second drum roll of thunder Feisal's 800-camel bodyguard mounted on each side of the Wadi Yenbo as Feisal rode down the broad streamed avenue on his mare. It was far better to relocate than to allow the Turks a stationary target.

In the following November Lawrence learned of Feisal's basic popularity and charisma at close quarters. When

▼ Essad tribesmen equipped for the Arabian Campaigns.

guards knew Feisal was asleep they would spread their own cloaks over him. His overwork was a worry to his entourage. During recent fighting he had collapsed unconscious with foam-flecked lips from overexertion. Stories from Medina were recounted of how Feisal had ridden about on a white horse in front of Turkish fire in order to better encourage the tribesmen.

The picture of an average day of an Arab 'general' in bivouac also emerged. Before dawn the imam would throatily announce the first of the daily five Islamic calls to prayer, echoed with softer intonation by Feisal's personal imam outside his tent. Feisal's five slaves (a status ranking higher in Arabia than servant) would bring sweetened coffee and after an hour, the private tent flap would be pinned back for conference with the household. Breakfast's staple was dates with occasional biscuits or cereal grains.

After breakfast, bitter coffee and sweet tea would be brought in tandem to Feisal's ordinary bell-shaped tent which quartered his Baluchi prayer carpet, his Kurdish rug,

▼ Feisal's Army entering Yenbo during the dark days of the Arab Revolt, December, 1916. Feisal is riding his Arab charger in the front rank, just right of centre, in the rear of the foreground infantry. A white-robed Lawrence is mounted on a camel, two ranks behind Feisal, and in front of the Ageyl banner. The absence of baggage encumbering European or Turkish expeditions gave Arab warbands phenomenal long-range initiative. Each man carried 45 pounds of flour from which he made unleavened bread, baked in ashes. During a six-week adventure an Arab camelier could cover 2,000 miles with a mouthful of water per day and long drinks at wells spaced two days apart.

his camp bed, and a liberal provision of his ever-present cigarettes. At 0800 hours his Sherifial ceremonial dagger would be strapped on and he took business matters into the reception tent. Everyone squatted Arab fashion or lay in the sand – semi-circle out from Feisal until noon when the household and special guests reassembled in the living tent. Luncheons provided as much variety as possible, normally a selection of beans, rice, lentils, spinach, and sweet cakes. Food was taken with the fingers while squatting, and fingers were afterward rinsed with water. Lunch would be trailed by two rounds of coffee and two rounds of syrup-thick green tea.

If the master rested or conducted private matters it would succeed this ritual until 1400 hours when he would return to the public reception tent. Sometimes there was time for a walk before the early evening meal which unremarkably resembled lunch. Then talk wound down and slaves continued intervals of tea as Feisal relaxed – frequently with poetry, and sometimes with chess.

Lawrence learned much as a student of Feisal, much of the personal nature of irregular command, and of the extreme patience necessary in tribal exigencies with all its interrelationships of man, family, and tribe. It was during these weeks that Lawrence, at Feisal's request, adopted native dress, specifically Feisal's own white silk garments. Thereafter, Lawrence would build a psychological and charismatic image around the wearing of pure white silk, gold and crimson headrope, and golden Sherifial dagger.

Lawrence chose for himself not the role of a hovering martinet of transplanted British culture, complete with a

Left: The vanguard of the 1,200 strong Ageyl Camel Corps, recruited from the Nejd towns by ibn Dakhil ostensibly for Turkish service. When the Arab Revolt broke out the entire band went over to Hussein. Most were 16–25 years of age and had joined for a period of several years so that as a body they were more reliable than the average Arab levy. Depicted in the front rank are the three gilt-topped spears carrying their three crimson banners. Of fairer skin, higher education and a less fiery temperament than the standard Arab, they could fight with brains as well as courage. Their clothes were a gaily coloured rainbow as were their fanciful saddle ribbons. On the march they rode in a centre body with wings, accompanied by mobile tom-toms and marching song.

Above right: Ateiba troops at Yenbo. 'They were a tough-looking crowd, dark coloured, some negroid. They were physically thin, but exquisitely made, moving with an oiled activity altogether delightful to watch. It did not seem possible that men could be hardier or harder. They would ride immense distances day after day, run through sand and over rocks bare-foot in the heat for hours without pain, and climb their hills like goats. Their clothing was mainly a loose shirt with sometimes short cotton drawers, and a head-shawl usually of red cloth which acted as towel or handkerchief or sack as required. They were corrugated with bandoliers and fired joy-shots when they could.' (T. E. Lawrence, The Seven Pillars of Wisdom.)

soldier's textbook on 'civilised' warfare, but rather the role of becoming like the people he would advise. Sleeping, eating, riding in native fashion, walking barefoot when they did, drinking only when his hosts drank . . . and, above all, learning their soul, to the extent that Arab thought as well as dialect, honed his very reaction and instinct. It was a tough assignment, even impossible, except that he did it. And in the completion he may be regarded as history's greatest role-player.

Lawrence took leave of Feisal at Nakhl Mubarek to help organise the defence of Yenbo with elements of the Royal Navy's Red Sea Squadron under Captain Boyle. Scarcely had he gone when the Turks outflanked Feisal with three battalions of infantry and several companies of mule and camel troopers. In an attempt to regain the initiative, Feisal held his centre and right, throwing out the Juheina tribe on his left.

His two antiquated Egyptian 15 pounders grunted at the Turks with mouldy green Boer War vintage fuses, no sights, no range tables, no high explosive shells. Yet their din was voluminous and the tribesmen judged a gun's effectiveness by it: 'By God' said one Arab, 'those are the real guns: the Importance of their noise!'[4] Rasim, the colourful Turkish-trained Syrian battery commander, blasted his shells off quickly in sporting merriment, giving the tribesmen such a boost in morale that they surged forward.

Suddenly, however, the Juheina vacated the field as if in rout. Feisal had no choice but to retire on Yenbo with only 2,000 men still clinging to the colours. Strangely, the Turkish pursuit was slowed as if by an unseen hand. As the Juheina rode into Yenbo the next morning they chided Feisal for his 'flight'! During the battle they had retreated only to drink coffee, then had faced about and fought the Turks unaided all night! Such an anecdote is illustrative of the problems which would have driven a more doctrinaire textbook advisor to madness.

The skirmishing interlude had not been wasted. In Yenbo, bastions had been constructed from the crumbling medieval town walls along with rifle-proof ramparts and barbed wire. Machine gun nests covered the angles of fire. Overhead a naval signals team perched in the slender minaret of Yenbo's mosque to alert Boyle's five Royal Navy vessels assembled offshore. Monitor M31 lay in the shallow southeast portion of the harbour while the ships of heavier draught were moored at the deeper northern end. Naval searchlights played across the dead ground leading to the port of Yenbo. That mid-December night the Hejaz Expeditionary Force gazed in awe at the interplay of searchlights over the repaired walls and imagined the impact of naval artillery. Indecisively, the Turks stepped back and the Arab Revolt was reborn.

Wejh

Often the best defence can be a good offensive. At Colonel Wilson's suggestion, Feisal and Lawrence conceived a brilliant plan on New Year's Day, 1917. From Yenbo to Wejh was 180 miles. If the port of Wejh could be taken the Arab Revolt would be extended into the northern Hejaz. Wejh was 150 miles west of the Hejaz Railway, an easy raiding run for the Bedouin. Also Wejh was northwest of Medina so there were almost unlimited possibilities of interdicting the rail, which was Medina's virtual lifeline to Turkish-occupied Palestine–Syria.

The ploy was a gamble. Feisal's brother Ali would have to cooperate by moving 60 miles north of Medina, thus interposing his forces between Feisal and the Turks. The plan carried the risk that a vigorous Turkish thrust might drive on the Arab supply base at Yenbo while Feisal's column was in progress north. By pound of prevention, Boyle's Indian troop ship *Hardinge* took on supplies and water at Yenbo and became a floating logistical base following the Arab exodus up the coast. Feisal's following had swollen to over 10,000 tribesmen. As a testimonial to Boyle's support and to the paucity of Bedouin need on the march, Feisal's 5,100 camelry and 5,300 infantry, four Krupp guns and 10 machine guns required only 380 transport camels. Providing such an assemblage could manage to shift to Wejh, the outcome of its struggle with the 1,200-man Turkish garrison was almost guaranteed.

Having secured Ali's coordination, the expedition began on 3 January 1917. Boyle had arranged a 23 January flotilla of five ships, with 50 guns and a seaplane carrier, to lie offshore Wejh and unload, by amphibious assault, several hundred Harb and Juheina footmen north of the port into its Achilles heel. This was no ordinary advance, but a show of force for the Sherifial cause consisting of multi-columns of multi-tribes, specifically designed to foster the image of the national movement.

At Bir el Waheida the columns were drawn up for the final convergence on the tiny Wejh garrison. First came the great camel body of 1,200 Ageyl under Ibn Dakhil, sheikh of the Russ, who had originally raised such men for Turkish service against the Canal, and then had defected them *en masse* to Hussein. Three large gilt-spiked crimson banners rippled in their van and set off their brilliantly diverse dress and ornate camel blankets and saddles which were bedecked with fluttering ribbons.

Then marched Abd el Kerim's 700 Gufa camelry with an equal number of infantry in train. They were in white with large head shawls of red and black striped cotton, and they waved green palm branches instead of banners. Beside them rode Sherif Mohammed Ali abu Sharrain's 300 Ashraf

camelry of Aiaishi-Juheina blood – all of them Sherif paladins, but none of inscribed pedigree in Mecca. Each wore brick red henna-dyed robes under black cloaks, and each a sword, with a loinclothed slave to carry his rifle and dagger, to tend his camel, and to cook his food.

Next, under their crimson banner, came the 1,000 Rifaa under the last of the Arabian sea pirates, Owdi ibn Zuwied. As if in material profession that brigandage could still pay, Owdi sported a German officer's coat relieved from the von Stotzingen Mission. Behind him, came the Krupps ported by Egyptian pack mules under the personable Damascene, Rasim.

One of the Arab Bureau's first advisory augmentees was Lieutenant-Colonel S. F. Newcombe, Royal Engineers, and new head of the British Military Mission in Arabia. As one of the pre-war's brightest engineers, Newcombe had built the Nile to Red Sea railway across the Sudan. For the next seven months he proved equally adept in antithesis – that of demolishing the Hejaz Railway. As Lawrence wrote: 'Newcombe had constant difficulties owing to excess of zeal, and his habit of doing four times more than any other Englishman would do: ten times what the Arabs thought needful or wise'.[5]

'Skinface' Newcombe was one of the desert's own legends, worthy of biographical acclaim and the stuff of novels. But he exhibited an even finer trait than quality of engineering and the inspiration of high adventure . . . though Lawrence's superior, he did not muddy the water with Lawrence's contacts nor did he cramp Lawrence's style. More than this cooperative teamwork, Newcombe brought a privacy-giving tent, a luxury Lawrence had not enjoyed for weeks.

The Arabs were running behind schedule, so Newcombe rode ahead to Hobban to inform Boyle to postpone the attack for two days, and to coordinate the critical drop-off water at Hobban on 24 January. Boyle and Newcombe were concerned lest the Turkish garrison try to slip away before the battle.

Newcombe had done his work well, and Boyle even better . . . As Feisal's column approached Wejh from the desert the crimson Ageyl banners were unfurled and the colourfully caparisoned tribesmen disrobed in their old fighting tradition in order to ensure 'clean' wounds. Then, with a six-mile-per-hour dead silent advance on camel back, they crested the ridge overlooking Wejh to discover Boyle's ships and the amphibious assault party had already gone in and Arab footmen were in possession of Wejh. The sermon of nationalism had reached the northern Hejaz.

Pillars of Wisdom

The advance on Wejh had been a political and military masterpiece. In one stroke the Arabs had regained the initiative, their base of power had been extended, and the Turkish threat to Yenbo and Mecca receded, never to seriously rise again. In fact, Wejh caused a northward lengthening of the Hejaz Expeditionary Force as well as a reinforcement from 7th Division in Syria. The '1st Composite Force' was created at Maan with 3,000 Turks, a sum

▲ A review at Wejh, January, 1917. Wejh was Feisal's Headquarters from January till August, 1917, when his army was
transported by sea to Aqaba. The encampment as Wejh was
spaced widely, a mile from the coral reefs and foothills along
the Red Sea. The tents are British supplied, the more traditional
Bedouin tents usually being black.

▶ Lieutenant-Colonel S. F. Newcombe in native dress but
foregoing sandals or bare feet for British boots. Newcombe was
Lawrence's occasional tent mate, technical boss, and head of
the British Military Mission to Arabia. Like other Arab Bureau
agents he played the *beau sabreur*, accomplishing his camel
raids at such a trot as to wear out man and camel. The Arabs
claimed Newcombe was like 'fire' and that he slept with his
head on the Hejaz Railway. After his suicidal mission up the
Hebron Road he was imprisoned in Constantinople, but was
aided to escape by the pretty Syrian lady he later married.

which would more than double by December, 1917. South
of Maan at Tebuk and 300 miles north of Medina was
located the '2nd Composite Force' of 5,000 men. General
Murray was gradually appreciating that this 'sideshow of
amateurs' was containing as many Turks as his own regular
EEF.

This general ignorance of, and even predjudice against
the value of the Arab Revolt permeated nearly all EEF levels
and would largely remain so until the advent of General
Allenby – and equally important – until the Arabs fought far
enough north as to virtually become the EEF's right flank.
No one was more a proponent of this strategy than
Lawrence, who counseled Feisal that the Revolt's freedom
would be *taken* not granted.

In his burden of serving two masters, Lawrence was
increasingly ashamed of his liaison role. How to be with

honour to both and traitor to neither, that was the question. This acutely developed higher sense was the root of his refusal to accept many of the battle honours tendered him for meritorious and courageous service. The Arabs accepted, through his significant reputation and assurances, proof of Britain's rhetorical, even written promises. But although he could not know the secret clauses of the Sykes-Ficot Agreement, enough common sense and misty rumour dictated that certain Allied clauses would be inimical to Arab aspirations in a post-war settlement.

'In revenge I vowed to make the Arab Revolt the engine of its own success, as well as handmaid to our Egyptian Campaign: and vowed to lead it so madly in the final victory that expediency should counsel to the Powers a fair settlement of the Arabs' moral claims.'[6]

During the weeks at Wejh, Lawrence reconsidered the position of the Arab War. As a conventional question of strategy Medina was a prize. Ali's spies reported the civil populace awaiting only a close-investment of the environs as a signal for their own cooperative rising. Murray was anxious lest Fakhri Pasha evacuate the Medina garrison in favour of reinforcing the Palestine Front. This was the very course the German High Command was pressuring the Turks to take. The ideal scenario was for Medina to fall in a bag with its garrison and the salient thorn in the Arab side would be thus removed. On 26 February 1917, Ali's army was reported as:

'1,500 trained Arab troops under Syrian Arab officers; 1,500 Beni Assam; 1,500 Beni Saad; 800 Baladia; 400

▲ Turkish heavy Maxim machine guns in action and officer observing effects. Surprisingly, with open terrain, cavalry could and did succeed in charging home against modern machine guns. The natural tendency was for gunners to fire high at the horsemen thundering towards them at 45 feet per second.

Meccans; 250 Ateibah Camel Corps; 200 Bisha; two 5-inch (breech loading) howitzers; two 15 pounders (quick-firing field guns); three 2.95 (Egyptian Army) mountain guns; one or two Turkish mountain guns; three four-gun batteries of Maxim guns.'[7]

Medina had been developed with extensive Turkish outerworks. The north and northwest were the best defended approaches, where was the aerodrome, train station, and Fort Siler in the hills over looking the city. Even with the cooperation of Abdullah's army in the Wadi Safra the capture of Medina was bound to be a hotly contested issue.

Lawrence's strategy for Medina was in the radical vein. His thesis was that Medina was a thorn in the *Turkish* side and could be made increasingly so by stepping up pressure against the garrison and its lifeline, the Hejaz Rail; pressure which would result in a maximum Turkish commitment of life and material resource, but not enough pressure to cause its fall. Lawrence believed not even German persuasion could make the Turks quit Medina. After losing Mecca, the further loss of a Holy City would damage Turkish confidence as an empire and injure its prestige within the Moslem World. As long as Medina and the Hejaz Railway – slender ribbon though it was – remained in Turkish hands, the

illusion would be that they 'controlled' more territory than was reality, and it would serve to reinforce them in their folly. Medina and the railway would be an economic sieve while in the military sense the railway's unprotectable length would create an 'absurd position — all flanks and no front.'

Whereas the necessary dispersal of Turkish strength along the rail would prove his weakness, dispersal was the historical strength of the irregular Bedouin. Arab effectiveness naturally lay in *depth* not *front*, for he could neither attack nor defend fixed points, nor fight regular pitched battles except at his own choosing. The advantages of terrain knowledge, support of most local inhabitants, his natural toughness in his native elements, and his traditional mobility would be enhanced while the war-fighting capabilities of the Turks would be correspondingly decreased. Further, intelligent strategic application could act as a regulator valve; the pressure of raids could be lessened if the Turk showed panic or evacuation, or amplified if he demonstrated complacency or strength. In this way might his entire Arabian effort be bankrupted.

Aqaba

Lawrence's appraisal of tactical matters, enemy intentions, and the material-economic factors of the equation distinguish him as a founder of modern guerrilla war. Not surprisingly, perhaps, it would take his superiors some weeks to come to the same appreciations. Turkish secret messages had been decoded and it was apparent that, in a

▲ Lieutenant-Colonel Newcombe (second from left) and Captain H. S. Hornby (far right) led demolition parties out of Wejh and Aqaba against the Hejaz Railway. Hornby, of the Royal Engineers, had seen adventure in West Africa and was regarded as a reckless lunatic in his exploits. The Arab legend was that Hornby chewed the rails with his teeth when gun-cotton failed. He and Newcombe remained in the wilderness for weeks with small parties of Bedouin. In 1918 part of an explosive discharged in Hornby's face, leaving him partially blind and deaf, and chaffing behind an administration desk in Aqaba.

temporary fit of pique, Enver had bowed to his German mentors and ordered the evacuation of Medina. His communication revealed his understanding that now, so late in the Revolt, it would not be easy — for he advised the garrison to load supplies on trains and, enclosing them with moving columns, march north in enormous protective squares. Enver could not know Fakhri Pasha would defy his evacuation order, nor the British know that Enver would change minds again; the threat of a 25,000 ration strength of Turks descending on Beersheba, doubling the odds against the EEF, was too much for Murray to bear.

The red flag waved, all sources moved to strangle Medina before the event. Fakhri Pasha had assigned garrisons at all water stations between Medina and Tebuk and smaller posts in connection with these along a 300 mile course. Newcombe raided northeast of Wejh and Captain Garland southeast. After fragmenting the line with explosives they converged their warbands with the intention of inviting Feisal's army to Medain Salih to actually occupy the line.

▲ Auda abu Tayi, the Bedouin 'Robin Hood' (standing, left). Chief of the abu Tayi of the eastern Howeitat, Auda was probably Arabia's greatest warrior with 75 kills and an undisclosed greater number of Turks (which honour did not permit him to count). Ostentatiously, Auda had declared personal war by letter on the Sultan and the Young Turk leadership. At age 60 he had had 28 wives and had been wounded 13 times during his 100 victorious raids. Despite having taken kings' ransoms in booty, Auda was perpetually poor because of his renowned gifts and hospitality. Hard-headed, hot-headed, a tale-teller of life which spun around him as a saga, Auda was yet simple and loved by his friends – to whom he was often most embarrassing and trying.

Lawrence travelled southeast to Abdullah's headquarters at Wadi Ais near Medina to secure his cooperation with the forces of Ali and Feisal. The journey was a disappointment. Abdullah was too slothful, too indifferent in martial pursuit, and a touch jealous of Feisal's more laudable success. On the way to Wadi Ais Lawrence had tried his hand with automatic mines which were triggered by a train's passing. He left satisfied that enough raids were in progress, even if doubtful of Arab chances to compel the stubborn Fakhri Pasha to surrender.

The port of Aqaba now seemed the greater reward for effort. The Arab Revolt had accrued enough friends in high places, who had watched its growth with amazed interest, for the EEF to countenance a brigade landing in amphibious assault against the tiny disused port of Biblical Solomon. Aqaba would be the linking base between the EEF and the Arabs, and its supply a convenient shipment from Suez. Lawrence knew first-hand, however, that Aqaba was as naturally strong on the seaward side as it was potentially vulnerable on the landward side. Embroiled with the battles of Gaza, Murray was content to let the amphibious issue subside while the Arabs busied themselves against Medina. It was up to Lawrence, without authorisation and in apology to Clayton, to capture Aqaba in Nelsonesque fashion.

The house at Wejh had meanwhile been put in order. Colonel Joyce was acting as commandant over the transferred Yenbo troops and stores, the two Rolls Royce armoured cars, and the flight of aircraft from Rabegh. Politically Feisal's achievements were prodigious. Daily, an honour roll of sheikhs and Ashraf came in to submit to the new cause, swearing on the Koran between Feisal's hands: 'to wait while he waited, march when he marched, to yield obedience to no Turk, to deal kindly with all who spoke Arabic, and to put independence above life, family, and goods.'[8]

Traditional blood feud was healed or put in abeyance for the common cause of nationalism. Feisal's informed tact, splendid memory for personal intricacies, and just decisions allowed him to sit as Supreme Court and Court of Appeal for Western Arabia.

Two great figures came forward. Nuri es Shalaan, the Amir of the Rualla, was one of the four great princes with his power base in southern Syria. At 70 years of age, Nuri had ruled his tribe for 30 years with an iron hand, and through sheer force of character. His word was law, his opposition brief. Nuri agreed to appear friendly with the Turks while biding his time till Feisal was in position to threaten Damascus. In the meantime, Lawrence received his blessing to cross the vile waste of the Sirhan in a wide turning movement against Aqaba.

Equally important to this ambitious project was the support of Auda abu Tayi, the Bedouin 'Robin Hood' of the Eastern Howeitat. It was a small tribe but a respected one whose support was critical to a landward approach on Aqaba. And Auda abu Tayi was a virtual legend throughout Arabia . . . and recognised as probably its greatest warrior.

The sweeping flank Lawrence envisioned was a 600-mile track so bleak and torturous as to preclude artillery or machine guns. The movement was a turning point. Heretofore, Feisal had always been seen as the public leader. It would also mark a turning chapter in Lawrence's personality: the meek man of ideas was – despite himself, or in spite of himself – metamorphising into the man of action in pursuit of the dream for which he would burn so brightly – too brightly – and from which he would later climb down in body and spirit, fulfilled, yet scarred.

On 9 May 1917, Lawrence and Auda set off north with 35 Ageyl and a small warband of Howeitat who cheerfully chanted their tribal three-note medley of 'ho, ho, ho,' up and down, back and forth, in tribute to the new adventure. Across the desert, through the snake-infested Sirhan district, the journey absorbed much of May in the trial of elements. At each well the Arabs drank to the point of disgorgement then went dry with usually a day between waterings.

During the first two weeks of June Lawrence endured a solo 400-mile trek, from Nebk through Syria, to secure a barometer reading of local conditions pursuant to the planned phase after Aqaba. He penetrated as far as Baalbek, accomplishing a bridge demolition, and visited Nuri es Shalaan in his own domain.

Auda's presence and the whisper of battle had meanwhile attracted 500 loyal Arabs as well as Turkish attention. Presence, but not Arab intention the Turks had divined, for wells were found demolished in effort to drive the war band from the district.

Bedouin had weakened from exhaustion. Tempers flared and Lawrence taunted Auda abu Tayi at the seeming check which would mean mate. Angry, Arabia's legendary warrior stormed off with 50 horsemen to gallop the Turkish rear. Lawrence and Sherif Nasir hastily drew their 400 camel warriors along the heights, awaiting the moment of Auda's charge. It came and paced on through the first volley, some horses tumbling at the impact of metal. The Turkish line seemed uncertain of its strength, and the camelry launched down the slopes in Auda's support, gaining a momentum uncontrollable and terrific. Bullets failed to check the 30 mile-per-hour impetus of charging camels as they staved in the quavering Turkish infantry. Lawrence was in first, revolver barking, when his fifth shot accidently killed his

▲ The triumphal rush into Aqaba, 6 July 1917. One of the gilt-spiked crimson Ageyl banners ripples in the sandstorm.

Aqaba would fall if the critical pass of Nagb el Shtar toppled with its garrison at Aba el Lissan. If the 1st Composite Force at Maan received wind sufficient to sally against the Arabs before the fact, the plan would be undone. Pains had already been taken to keep the Maan garrison in ignorance about Aqaba. Rail raids to the north diverted suspicions to Maan's railway link to Dera. Newcombe had leaked 'secret' papers to Turkish authorities while Lawrence's agents at work with Nuri es Shalaan 'warned' of impending raids. To lend concrete credence Lawrence and a company-sized party struck north of Amman where they left misleading information purporting their base to be at Azrak Oasis. The Turks in southern Syria were discovered to be more than usually alert.

On the road to Aqaba, Aba el Lissan consisted of a blockhouse and positions sited to restrict unwanted passage. The Turkish garrison battalion, however, had fortunately taken bivouac in June amidst the more comfortable natural springs laced with shade-giving palms. They presented just the sort of vulnerable target the desert-hardened Arabs sought as they infiltrated the higher ground commanding the oasis.

At first, Arab sniping made little impression on the Turks who returned an ineffective mountain gun fire. The day was the hottest in Arabia that Lawrence could recall. Even the

own camel and sent him into a head-over spin. Above him the camelry plunged in ringing stampede, exacting a terrible price among the Turks out of revenge for one of their recently sacked Arab villages. Of 460 Turks only 160 were left standing. Auda had lost his horse and proudly sported six bullet holes in his robes. The Arabs had only two dead.

The rout at Aba el Lissan, combined with two small, rapid raids by Lawrence, completed the temporary panic of the Turkish Maan garrison. Maan would be in no temperament for a riposte as the main Arab force drove in the post of Kethira on 4 July and negotiated the narrow defile of the Wadi Itm towards Aqaba.

Aqaba lay below with a mere garrison of 300, shaken by unfortunate news and hungry from meagre supply. Flushed with success, the Arab levy had swollen double. The Arab leaders demanded immediate surrender or they disclaimed responsibility for a Turkish massacre. The Turks considered their unattractive options and agreed to surrender at dawn. The night of 5 July an enthusiastic human tide again doubled the Arab mass, to 2,000. And the next morning the Arab Revolt rushed in victory through a howling sandstorm and splashed their animal's fetlocks in the Red Sea.

Above: New faces for the front. Note the empty beer bottles (front and right) and the dismounted soldier's indiscretion. Below: Dugouts of the 1/4th Northamptonshires at Gaza, 1917. Right: An Australian battalion of the Imperial Camel Corps outside Beersheba, 1 November 1917.

PART 3
THE ADVANCE
July to December 1917

8

COMES A CRUSADER

'I have too happy a life at home to make a really good soldier. I catch myself often half hoping that the war may be over by the time we arrive. — Allenby to his wife, 6 November 1899

THE débâcle at Gaza produced inevitable changes, and first in the structure of command. Dobell was recalled to England, with General Sir Philip Chetwode assuming command of Eastern Force. General Sir Henry G. Chauvel replaced Chetwode in command of the Desert Column, and Brigadier E. W. C. Chaytor succeeded Chauvel in charge of the ANZAC Mounted Division.

Murray and Chetwode concurred in the consolidation of positions gained north and east of the Wadi Ghazi, and in preparations for a hot summer of desultory trench raids perched on the edge of the desert. A major problem was the water and supply of Eastern Force so far from Egypt. Half the train traffic was absorbed in merely keeping the track active with only half servicing the needs of the troops. Murray had submitted a plan to the War Office for doubling the track, but completion would take eight months even after authorisation. A lucky strike at Khan Yunis was yielding 100,000 daily gallons of water, also boring parties discovered potable reserves at Shellal and wells at Deir el Balah suitable for animals. Biblical research even uncovered ancient water cisterns at Um Jerrar, mentioned in the Book of Genesis!

In early May, the Palestine Line of Communications Defences came into being under Brigadier Watson with administrative responsibility stretching from the northern Suez Canal across the Sinai to Khan Yunis. Guarding the rail and pipeline were the Bikanir Camel Corps, Imperial Service Cavalry Brigade, the French and Italian allied contingents, and smaller detachments of Indians, West Indians, Imperial Camel Corps, and Yeomanry.

From May through June, a series of reinforcements coincident with order of battle changes took place. The 7th and 8th Yeomanry Brigades were transferred from the Macedonian Front, giving the EEF a total of five Yeomanry, four Australian, and one New Zealand mounted brigade. These Murray organised into three divisions of three brigades each, with one brigade under GHQ. The Yeomanry Mounted Division came into being, and the Imperial Mounted Division designation was changed into the Australian Mounted.

Artillery allocations were increased. Four-gun batteries of 13 or 18 pounder guns were attached to the mounted arm — an artillery brigade to each division. Seven or eight six-gun batteries of 18 pounders were attached to an infantry division.

Transferred from Salonika was the 60th (London) Division of second-line territorials. A 75th Division was formed of British territorials and Indian battalions, both the 75th and the 74th (dismounted Yeomanry) being below war standard in men, training, and material. The French loaned two battalions of Algerian and one of territorials, while the Italians dispatched a battalion of Bersaglieri.

Murray presided over the preliminary changes but was not to survive in command of their fruition. On 11 June 1917, the War Office informed him of his recall to England and of the subsitution of General Sir Edmund Allenby.

If Murray's operations and reporting judgment were unhappy, his contributions in the administrative and logistical field were enormous, and had laid valuable, even critical groundwork for his successor. The Suez Canal was freed from threat and the Sinai conquered. Egypt was pacific, and the Arab Revolt in virulent swing.

The theatre only awaited the advent of a modern Crusader, of a modern Richard the Lionheart.

General Sir Edmund H. H. Allenby

Edmund Allenby was born in 1861 to a family of North Country stock residing variously in Lincolnshire and Felixstowe. By twist of fate, this son of lesser landed gentry — who was destined to become a great cavalry leader — possessed an Eighteenth-century blood link to the great cavalry leader and Lord Protector of England — Oliver Cromwell.

After twice failing exams into the Indian Civil Service, Allenby entered the Royal Military Academy at Sandhurst in 1881 and graduated with honours the same year, ranked twelfth in his class. At age 21 he was posted as a subaltern in the 6th Inniskilling Dragoons to South Africa where he would remain for six of the ensuing eight years. Here, he became noted as a swordsman and a strong rider in the rough sense — lacking, some noted, a certain country club finesse. But Allenby was not after form, and was probably too large a man for effete grace; instead, patrol, reconnaissance, bivouac, and field matters practised across Zululand, Bechuanaland, and South Africa were his handmaidens.

In 1881 he was promoted Captain and Mess President along with the nickname of 'Apple-pie' by play on name. In the next years peers pronounced him 'easy going' and considered him more widely read than sport serious. At the same time, his responsible orderliness earned him promotion to Adjutant the next year, followed by a six-year posting to England.

At age 34, he married Mabel Chapman after a whirlwind courtship during a Scottish hunting trip. After a second try, Allenby became the first cavalry officer to qualify to attend the Staff College. In 1897, during Queen Victoria's Diamond Jubilee, he graduated alongside Captain Douglas Haig. It had been the start of an uneasy relationship that would continue with repercussions into World War One. In the words of

Viscount Wavell: '. . . Allenby was the more broad-minded and the more human; Haig, by virtue of concentration, the more technically efficient.'[1]

It was during the Boer War that Allenby demonstrated his remarkable qualities as a field commander. Bold in action with no fear of danger or responsibility, he took risks, but no unnecessary risks with his men. Avoiding Boer tactical traps by use of common sense became his knack as did skill in independent operations. These attributes caused him to be selected as a column commander along with such future notables as Haig, Gough, Byng, Smith-Dorrien, Plumer, and Rawlinson. Yet he was one of the few to emerge with reputation intact, for Allenby never suffered a personal reverse, lost a patrol or convoy, or received unnecessary casualties.

Service against the Boers showed him how generals exhausted the horses of their troopers by a poor appreciation of resource and objective so that they were expended on hare-brained chases and transferred from uncompleted tasks. Detached units were not properly supported. He learned that cavalry pursuit of flanking moves depended on the prior state of horses and remounts, and after Bloemfontein he bitterly noted the wage of allowing a beaten enemy breathing space to recover. In these mobile actions, Allenby early developed the policy of giving trusted subordinate officers the widest autonomy in achieving their given missions.

Beyond tactics, Allenby absorbed the strategic lessons of using cavalry to block the withdrawal of a larger force, as with Lieutenant-General French's maneuver against Cronje's troops at Koodoosrand Drift. Or, the value of dash correctly applied even against a ring of fire, as French's cavalry gamble before Kimberly. And especially of the aesthetic simplicity of Lord Roberts' grand strategy of feinting one flank then crushing with the other – completed only by the subtle intricacies of deception, concentration, and mobility. Palestine would witness this faithful execution in Allenby's campaigns of 1917 and 1918.

When peace came in 1902, Allenby received a brevet promotion to Colonel, a Companionship of the Bath, and he became commander of the 5th Lancers. From 1902–1905 the 5th was stationed in England, and from there Allenby moved on as Brigadier-General in charge of the 4th Cavalry Brigade at Colchester. Promotions in England continued; Major-General in 1909 at age 48, then Inspector-General of Cavalry in 1910 with headquarters in London with the Horse Guards.

The Boer War and the following Russo–Japanese War provoked two divergent schools of thought concerning the role of cavalry on the contemporary battlefield. On one side were the diehards of the *arme blanche*, the age-old cavalry spirit of shock action, and on the other side the proponents of mounted infantry. As Inspector-General, Allenby used his considerable power to steer a middle course which emphasised the techniques of firepower and the introduction of the machine gun, while preserving the option of shock.

As early as 1911, he had predicted the course of European conflict accurately enough to have exercised a staff scenario wherein the Hibernian (British) Cavalry

Lieutenant-General E. H. H. Allenby as he appeared in *Sport and General*.

Division was pitted contra Blue Force (Germany). More prophetically, he had pressed the unpopular role of cavalry in retreat, and had studied French cavalry on maneuvers as well as the lie of the land in northern France. Fortunately, Allenby had been selected to lead the British Cavalry Division in event of war.

Despite his technical competence and wide experience, Allenby's personable nature often seen in his early career began to wear off under the increase of responsibility. He was not a popular Inspector with the Cavalry. His inspections were brusque, and his presentation critiques rough. Physical size combined with these non-endearing mannerisms and with increasingly manifest explosions of temper to earn him the accolade of 'The Bull'.

The Bull

The First World War came, and by 20 August 1914, the Cavalry Division had concentrated near Maubeuge. Allenby's division was of four brigades numbered one to four, with supporting artillery of (32) 13 pounders, a squadron of engineers, and one of signals. A fifth brigade acted independently under Sir Philip Chetwode of later Palestine fame.

British cavalry was judged splendid, but its gremlin was the absence of pre-war practice as a working whole. As a division it was an unfamiliar entity so that higher staff and supporting arms had difficulty in the translation between peacetime and wartime footing. This was not aided by the cavalry's shackled mission to aid the notably unrealistic

French Plan 17. Thus, while the main French effort failed, and a weakness on the German left was bolstered by natural obstacles, the colossus of the German right smashed its path as a consuming juggernaut across neutral Belgium and into the vulnerable plains of the Allied left.

Allenby, in fact, had been one of the first to recognise the unfolding danger. Within four days the Cavalry Division was in retreat from Mons to the Marne; throughout the retreat he maintained the steadiness of its brigades, exemplified personal courage, and showed judgment under crisis at Le Cateau. In September, however, opportunity was missed on the Aisne to exploit the slowed and erratic momentum of the German right. At this time the cavalry was expanded into two divisions with Allenby commanding the 1st Division. A month later, a full Cavalry Corps was born with Allenby in overall control.

During the 'race to the sea' the cavalry drove off a German cavalry corps southwest of Ypres, then acted dismounted as infantry in the trenches at First Ypres, suffering heavily for the clash with a three-fold foe. A third cavalry division arrived under Allenby's care and acted in the role of a mobile reserve for the trenchlines.

The opening months of war revealed the Germans usually out-matched in sabre-to-sabre work, but advantaged in the superior range of their horse artillery, and by the dual employment of *jägers* (light infantry with machine guns) which worked with their cavalry. The British division of four brigades of three regiments each was found to be more cumbersome than the German division of three brigades of two regiments each.

◀

British cavalry in helmet, great-coat, full kit, with rifles and slung lances. During the April, 1917 battles of Arras a five-mile wide breach opened in the German lines. Cramped and muddy conditions and the fact the nearest cavalry was seven miles away from the 'G' in Gap caused the desired exploitation to fail. Allenby and staff were determined not to let such failures on the Western Front impair the success of their cavalry in Palestine.

Prime Minister David Lloyd-George.

Lessons noted, and with a career familiarisation of cavalry behind him, the Army decided to promote Allenby to command 5th Corps which he would head throughout most of 1915, and through Second Ypres. In 5th Corps, Allenby associated with several of his future officers in Palestine; Bulfin — later of 21st Corps, Bols, later his chief of staff, and Longley — later of 10th Division. It was a costly year, and Ypres a battle of attrition. Allenby's stubborn purpose of mission and his loyalty to superior orders maintained his nickname as the 'Bull' as he persevered through the same terrible casualties of attack and counterattack that were sustained along the entire front.

In October, General French appointed Allenby in command of 3rd Army shortly before being replaced himself by Allenby's former uncomfortable Staff College associate, Sir Douglas Haig. Third Army at first consisted of 7th and 10th Corps, and eventually of the 13th and 14th Corps in addition. During the 1916 Battle of the Somme, 3rd Army's task was to divert the bulk of the German counterattack onto itself and to strike Gommecourt, a particularly formidable strongpoint of the enemy line. In the 90-mile British sector of the Western Front two British armies lay to 3rd Army's north, and one to the south. As in all sectors of the Somme Offensive, 3rd Army's lot was costly failure.

Even at an army command level Allenby was up front as much as possible to learn of conditions and events first-hand. Neuritis of the arm did not make his increasingly strained relations with Haig any better during the early

months of 1917. At this time thoughts of Murray's operations in the Sinai and the Arab Revolt were only passing newspaper words. But as Murray's final effort in the Middle East was playing out in the battles at Gaza, Allenby's final Western Front action was playing out at Arras in April, 1917.

The planning had taken six months and near the end of it the Germans threw a clever wrench in the works by shortening their line. But Arras was too big to halt. The overall Allied commander, Joffre, had been replaced by the polished Nivelle, whose promises and high sung optimism seemed to offer a solution to the stagnant attrition. David Lloyd-George coerced Haig to fall in with a British plan supportive of the French offensive on the Aisne. The majority of the 'holding' action fell on Allenby's 3rd Army from Arras to the Somme. The official order made Allenby responsible for taking 'the German defensive line, which ran from Arras towards St. Quentin, by turning it and attacking it in flank and rear, continuing to operate in the direction of Cambrai.'[2] First Army would cooperate to take the Vimy Ridge to the north.

Arras had been a picturesque enough town. It was the site of one of Marlborough's most classic maneuvers, and of the famous scene of siege in Rostand's *Cyrano de Bergerac*. In spring of 1917 it was a quagmire. The town's position made it the terminus where through the main assault, supply and reinforcement must pass during the offensive. The immense congestion was only in part alleviated by the natural underground tunnels.

Allenby had already been at loggerheads with Haig and the General Staff over the tender subject of bombardment. Experimentation had shown Allenby that a furious but short bombardment would not only exact that psychological edge but would still confer the advantage of surprise to the follow-up infantry assault. In some of his ideas Allenby was predating the advent of the dread German *stosstruppen* tactics. The General Staff, however, had foregone surprise for the sledgehammer effect of massive bombardment. One gun had been allotted to every 36 feet of frontage.

Despite the four day bombardment (cut short one day as a compromise to Allenby) the Germans *were* taken by surprise on Easter Monday, 9 April 1917, as five miles of front opened up before 17th Corps and 4th Division marched through unimpeded for seven hours. Unfortunately, the British were also surprised by their greatest Western Front success to date. Much hope had been placed on the cavalry finding the 'G' in Gap and 40 tanks from Heavy Branch, Machine Gun Corps had been allocated for extra push. Nevertheless, the nearest cavalry was seven miles from the breakthrough. By the time command and control reacted and the cavalry and artillery fought their way through the clogged potholes, the opportunity had passed.

In three days, 3rd Army paid a price of 8,238 casualties for a haul of 7,000 prisoners, 112 enemy guns, and 21,000 German casualties. Further British and Canadian efforts in April ended in the usual toll of death while Nivelle's will-of-the-wisp promises led the French Army toward the ugly swamp of mutiny.

Seeking a way around the disenchanting impasse, Lloyd-George remembered his Eastern school of thought. General

Smuts – recently returned from capaigning in East Africa – was invited to replace Murray in Egypt and to revitalise fortunes in the East. Smuts declined, and the Chief of the Imperial General Staff recommended Allenby to the Prime Minister.

Allenby's appointment covered manifold purposes. Allenby was a robust general of determined drive. He was a cavalry general and the EEF held a very high proportion of mounted troops. The Boer War and Allenby's expert handling of cavalry in 1914 were recalled. Palestine was a mobile fight ready for one of independent initiative; in these Allenby excelled. And his passing would not be mourned by Haig.

Lloyd-George and Robertson gave Allenby successive briefings concerning his new assignment. At first, 'The Bull' was resentful at being relegated to a 'sideshow' now that the planning for a new Flanders offensive was underway. Having witnessed the 'G' in Gap open wide then close before he could thrust through his cavalry, he was still in mind refighting the lost opportunity at Arras. But the Prime Minister made it apparent this was no ordinary sideshow, nor indeed, a sideshow at all, but the most important theatre after France. The British people needed a perk in morale and Palestine and Jerusalem held a special place in the morale and psychology of a Christian people bogged down in a dragging war. In Palestine, great victories might be won by the right man. Lloyd-George wanted Jerusalem 'as a Christmas present for the British nation' and he presented Allenby a mandate for victory.

A

B

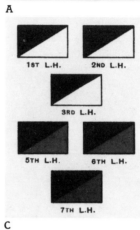

C

Divisional and Corps signs.
A: 21st Corps: Green with white numerals and letters.
Desert Mounted Corps: Black and white.
B: ANZAC Mounted Division: Patches illustrated are of the 1st, 2nd and 3rd Light Horse of the 1st Australian Light Horse Brigade, and 5th, 6th and 7th Light Horse of the 2nd Australian Light Horse Brigade.
C: 1st L.H.: blue/white; 2nd L.H.: green/white; 3rd L.H.: black/white; 5th L.H.: blue/red; 6th L.H.: green/red; and the 7th L.H.: black/red.

Left: The 120th Anti-Aircraft Section with gun mounted on lorry at Tel el Ajul.

9

REVITALISATION

ALLENBY assumed official command of the EEF at midnight 28/29 June 1917. If the troops were demoralised by the recent Gaza reverse, they were nonetheless splendid fighting material. Already seasoned veterans, the EEF had not experienced the terrible drain of casualties which had so debilitated teamwork and effectiveness on the Western Front.

A lesser mortal might have foregone the heat of the field in dalliance with staff reports and opinions. Allenby immediately went to the front where he inspected Eastern Force over a five day tour. It was symptomatic that he announced GHQ would be relocated from Cairo (300 miles distant) to Um el Kelab near Rafa and the Palestine border. Allenby's great size and determination brought credence to the rumour that the War Cabinet was at last behind the EEF. Morale improved. According to the *Australian Official History*:

'He went through the hot, dusty camps of his army like a strong, fresh, reviving wind. He would dash up in his car to a Light Horse regiment, shake hands with a few officers, inspect hurriedly, but with a sure eye to good and bad points, the horses of, perhaps, a single squadron, and be gone in a few minutes, leaving a great trail of dust behind him. His tall and massive, but restlessly active figure, his keen eyes and prominent hooked nose, his terse and forcible speech, and his imperious bearing, radiated an impression of tremendous resolution, quick decision and steely discipline. Troops who caught only one fleeting glimpse of him felt that here at last was a man with the natural qualities of a great driving commander who, given a great task and supplied, as Allenby was, with a great scheme for its accomplishment, would relentlessly force it through to its conclusion. At last they had a commander who would live among them and lead them. Within a week of his arrival Allenby had stamped his personality on the mind of every trooper of the horse and every infantryman of the line.'[1]

The ration strength of the EEF had tipped 200,000 with an additional 60,000 labourers to be fed. 'The Bull' had submitted requests for two infantry divisions with full artillery complements and three squadrons of aircraft with an extra flight to replace 'X' Flight operating in the Hejaz. Murray had previously scratch-built the 75th Division, while the 10th (Irish) Division was transferred from Salonika. In August, the 'Eastern Force' concept was disbanded in favour of the three corps system order of battle.[2]

Desert Mounted Corps (Chauvel)
ANZAC Mounted Division
Australian Mounted Division
Yeomanry Mounted Division
Imperial Camel Corps Brigade

20th Corps (Chetwode)
10th (Irish) Division
53rd (Welsh) Division
60th (London) Division
74th (Yeomanry) Division
Four Brigades Heavy Artillery

21st Corps (Bulfin)
52nd (Lowland) Division
54th (East Anglian) Division
75th Division
Three Brigades Heavy Artillery

Nominally retained under GHQ were the 10th Division, the 7th Mounted Brigade, and a 'Composite Force' of French, Italians, Imperial Service Indian cavalry and infantry, and the West Indians. Excluding the 10th Division, the EEF counted a rifle strength of 95,737.

Chetwode, in conjunction with Brigadier Guy Dawnay, had formulated a complete strategic appreciation of the Turkish Gaza-Beersheba Line. This plan, accepted by Allenby almost in entirety, considered a direct assault on Gaza could only accrue another expensive siege. The centre of the line was still strong, but the weak point of the 30-mile long defences was at the southern end at Beersheba. Here the defences were less prepared and if the higher ground north-west of the town could be taken, it would dominate Beersheba. When Beersheba fell, the mounted arm could expand east and northeast, blocking enemy reinforcements through the hills from Jerusalem and laying open the entire Turkish rear with a cutting-off drive to the sea. The infantry could hit the centre line hard near Tel-es-Sheria, and participate in rolling up the Turkish line in toto. The plan artfully ignored Turkish strengths while fully exploiting their weaknesses.

There were three critical hingepins to the grand strategy. The first was water. Beersheba sheltered wells vital to capture on the first day. The waterpipe had been extended to Shellal where had been constructed a rock basin reservoir to store a half million gallons. Smaller pipes were laid from forward area springs and wells to reach the front lines. Man and beast would require a daily 400,000 gallons in 20th Corps and the Desert Mounted Corps alone.

Transport was the second problem. A 7,000-camel convoy was arranged to fill 2,000 fanatis containers of 25,000 gallons per hour, and the railway was doubled to Allenby's headquarters. The troops designated against Beersheba could not use wheeled transport for the sandy nature of the ground; therefore, 21st Corps, opposite Gaza, surrendered its horses, mules, and camels to the southern corps. The men were trained to march on decreasing amounts of water in order to acclimatise them for the operations. (The United States Marine Corps of the 1980s recognises this technique as actually hindering operations on the day by weakening the man beforehand).

Secrecy of concentration and intent was the third problem. Raids toward Beersheba had been a fortnightly event in order to deceive the Turks of the timing of the main attack. To give the cavalry practice over the chosen ground, a tandem system of one division working opposite Beersheba while two rested near the Mediterranean was instituted. This helped keep alive the illusion that Gaza would again be the primary target. Assisting in this were the systematic infantry trench raids counter the Gaza environs.

The EEF 'leaked' cipher messages to intercepting Turkish ears. The carefully orchestrated message traffic emphasised the importance of Gaza and the desirability of an amphibious landing behind the town. A week's preliminary bombardment of Gaza was planned in conjunction with the Royal Navy to firm up any remaining doubts. During these days, of course, the main EEF attack troops would be deployed on the Beersheba flank.

Reminiscent of the 'Man Who Never Was', an elaborate deception known as the 'Haversack Ruse' was perpetrated by an officer of the Intelligence Branch named Meinertzhagen. With a small patrol, Meinertzhagen allowed the Turks to spot and fire on him. As the Turks pursued, he feigned wounded and dropped a haversack, prestained with blood and carrying odd £20 sterling notes, personal letters, and a cipher 'code' in simple dummy messages. The messages recorded the 'impossibilities' of any move against Beersheba, yet 'objected' to the imminent offensive on Gaza.

The 'Haversack Ruse' was given validity by mock Desert Mounted Corps orders demanding retrieval of the 'lost' haversack. These 'orders' were left cleverly crumpled among sandwich wrappers in the van of a local Turkish advance where they would be sure to be found. The Turks thought they were on to something big, for amusingly enough, the commander of 20th Corps congratulated his sergeant for finding such valuable intelligence and warned

his officers about carrying such similarly compromising material!

Deception was the hardest problem of the three, however, for the Turks had friendly Arab spies located behind EEF lines. These deceptions would have been virtually impossible without an upgrade in the technical status of the RFC. German aerial strategy had been to apportion some of its most advanced aircraft to each of its operational theatres in the belief quantity did not offset quality. EEF flyers who had engaged superior enemy machines had agreed with this theory all along, so that during summer and early autumn the RFC was pleased with the arrival of Bristol Fighters. As the Bristols were equal to any of the German 300th Flight Detachment aeroplanes, the EEF with its greater numbers was almost immediately able to regain mastery of the skies. This prevented the sort of enemy aerial reconnaissance which had proved so useful to the defence before Second Gaza.

A new RFC command designation had, in fact, been formed; the 'Palestine Brigade', consisting of 'X' aircraft park at Cairo, and all air assets east of Suez. The Brigade was commanded by Brigadier W. G. H. Salmond (head of RFC Middle-East), and was concentrated near Allenby's GHQ at Deir el Balah.

5th Wing

No. 14 Squadron	(16) BE 2e aircraft
No. 113 Squadron	(8) BE 2e aircraft
	(5) RE 8 aircraft

40th Wing

No. 111 Squadron	(6) Bristol Fighters
	(5) Vickers Bullets
	(3) DH 2
	(2) Bristol Monoplanes
	(1) Bristol Scout
No. 67 Squadron	(7) BE 2c and e
	(5) RE 8
	(5) BE 12a
	(1) Martinsyde

No. 21 Balloon Company (49 and 50 sections)

The Gaza-Beersheba Line

The Turks had also been under preparation. A second defensive position was sited north of Gaza, strongpoints developed in the line centre at Tel es Sheria, and concrete shelters around Beersheba. 'The Turkish position comprised several trench lines with switches and communication trenches, and in the dunes consisted of sandbag breastworks, without dug outs.'[3] Unfortunately, lack of material prevented the extensive and formidable placement of barbed wire.

By May, the 7th and 54th Divisions had been transferred from Constantinople, in August the 26th Division arrived, and a month later the 24th. Despite the impressive ring of these reinforcements, a Turkish division was a very different thing from a British division. The 24th had only 500 combat troops. Comparative low strengths lead to a denial of most

◀ Turkish telephone listening post in 1917.

▲ German-manufactured Gotha WD 13 with Turkish Air Force markings of black on white. The wheels to this seaplane belong to the beaching trolley.

leave or relief in order to keep a maximum count in the front line.

Further, the greater stocks of EEF shells allowed the EEF to pound the Turkish trenches which resulted in a monthly affliction of 500 casualties. Further, one-quarter, or 10,000, of the whole army personnel was sick in hospital at any given time. Desertion took its deadly toll. By the middle of 1917 the reported cases reached 300,000, a legacy the Germans attributed to the deteriorating efficiency of Turkish headquarters staffs. A piecemeal strategy of insufficient training, little emphasis on welding unit cohesiveness, and the regionalism and illiteracy of the average Turkish recruit merged with poor leadership to encourage an aura of inexperience, indifference, and even fear.

'When sent to the railroad station, the men for the most part did not know each other or their superiors. They only knew that they were being sent to some bad place. Hence they ran away whenever they could, and risked being shot while running. They jumped form the cars in motion, from the marching column in covered terrain, or from the bivouac, or from their billets.'[4]

In the spring of 1917, Germany and Turkey colluded on a daring plan known to the Germans as 'Army Group F', and to the Turks and to subsequent history as Yilderim, or 'Lightning'.

Yilderim

Yilderim had been previously coined twice in Turkish history. The first time to describe how Sultan Bayazid destroyed the Crusaders at Nicoplis in 1396, and the second time with reference to Napoleon's Egyptian Campaign. By implication, the new Yilderim was intended to fall like a 'thunderbolt' out of the desert with the best troops Germany and Turkey could spare.

The Turks withdrew four divisions from service with their allies Austria–Hungary and Bulgaria, and two from the Roumanian Front. The Germans contributed a body of 6,500 men hand-picked to withstand the rigours of a tropical climate. As Turkish Lieutenant-Colonel Hussein Husni noted in his book, Yilderim, the German blackboard briefings and the training at Neuhammer, deep in the Silesian forests, recalled the romance of a Jules Verne novel.

The German Asien Korps (generally known by the Turks as Pasha II) was established by the Prussian War Ministry on 2 July 1917, and it absorbed the technical arms of 'Pasha I').

Asien Korps

Colonel von Frankenberg-Proschlitz, commander 701st, 702nd, 703rd infantry battalions (three companies each, with six Maxims and 18 Bergmann light machine guns)
Three machine gun companies of six guns each
Three platoons of cavalry with two machine guns each
One artillery battalion of two light howitzer batteries and one field gun battery
One light mortar company
One anti-aircraft battery
Two mountain howitzer platoons
One pioneer section with platoon of flamethrowers

◀

German marching band and infantry parading on Good Friday in Jerusalem, 1916–1917. Because the tropical helmets resembled the helmets of the British, Turks and Arab sympathisers sometimes mistakenly fired on such German formations. In 1918, Liman von Sanders forbade their wear.

Machine-gun detachment 'Hentig'
Auto echelon and ammunition columns
Three heavy and five light wireless stations
Two fields hospitals and one sanitation company
Four aviation sections
One army and one division of telephone equipments

Several months later, the *Asien Korps* would be supplemented by the 146th (Masurian) Regiment of (three battalions, each with six machine guns), the 11th (Reserve) *Jager* Battalion (with six machine guns), a mountain artillery detachment of 12 (105 milimetre) howitzers, and four machine gun companies. In 1918 the *Korps* would be commanded by Colonel von Oppen and Lieutenant-Colonel Freiherr von Hammerstein-Gesmold. The in-theatre impact of the *Asien Korps* was fully that of a Western Front Division, considering its impact on Turkish morale, and the technical arms. Its 400 lorries were divided into 24 German, six Turkish, and three Austrian transport columns. The *Korps* could operate as a whole, or in battalion detachments, each with its own cavalry, artillery, and machine gun support.

The Germans supplied 'Army Group F' or *Yilderim* with a special fund of £5,000,000 sterling. Considering the value of the 1917 pound and adjusting for the ravages of modern inflation, the sum was roughly equivalent to President Reagan's 1986 projected loan to the 'Contras'. They also gave it perhaps their most distinguished soldier as commander – General (Marshal in the Turkish Army) Erich von Falkenhayn.

From September, 1914 to August, 1916 von Falkenhayn had headed the General Staff serving directly under the Kaiser. His swansong had been the planned destruction of the French national will at Verdun. Hindenburg and Ludendorff then collaborated in a political coup to cast him from the favourable eyes of Kaiser Wilhelm, and von Falkenhayn was sent to the Rumanian Front. Here, in Napoleonesque fashion he coordinated two armies over mountainous terrain and in the face of superior numbers effectively kicked Rumania from the war.

Von Falkenhayn's next mission was the restoration of Turkey. He had arrived in early May, 1917 at Constantinople, toured the Mesopotamian front, and met Djemal Pasha in Syria. At inception, *Yilderim* aimed at the recapture of Baghdad, but its implementation would devolve against the Palestine Front.

Yilderim Order of Battle
Commander in Chief – Marshal Erich von Falkenhayn
Chief of Staff – Colonel von Dommes
7TH ARMY (General Fevzi Pasha)
3rd Corps (Colonel Ismet Bey)
3rd Cavalry Division
24th, 27th Divisions
48th Regiment
8TH ARMY (General Freiherr Kress von Kressenstein)
20th Corps (Colonel Ali Fuad Bey)
16th Division (less 48th Regiment)
26th, 54th Divisions
13th Corps (Colonel Refet Bey)
3rd, 7th, 53rd Divisions
GHQ TROOPS
Asien Korps
Yilderim Flying Command
1st Pursuit Detachment
302nd, 303rd, 304th Reconnaissance Detachments

A special June conference had met in Aleppo to brainstorm the *Yilderim* question. In attendance were Enver, Djemal Pasha, Brousart von Schellendorff (Chief of the General Staff and Under Secretary to the Minister of War), Izzet Pasha (commanding the Caucasian Front), Halil Pasha (commanding 6th Army), and Mustapha Kemal (later Turkey's first President, currently commanding 2nd Army). Understandably, Djemal, as commander of 4th Army in Palestine and Syria, warned – as did Kress von Kressentein – of the building EEF commitment opposite 4th Army. As an advance against his army would also threaten Turkish Mesopotamian forces, Djemal argued his was the strategic need for the reception of *Yilderim*. The emotionalism for

Baghdad, however, was too strong a magnet. Djemal and proponents then argued for at least a concentration of *Yilderim* at Aleppo where the railway forked in service to both fronts and where it could act as a general reserve in event of a Russian push through Persia.

The result of the Aleppo conference was a strategic quarrel and political confusion throughout the summer. Mustapha Kemal, who was becoming recognised as Turkey's best general, refused to serve in *Yilderim* which he rightly thought a German tool. Djemal badly wanted reinforcements for 4th Army, but not at the price of von Falkenhayn's superimposition over his own political and military satrapy in Palestine and Syria.

Von Falkenhayn, meanwhile, was making his own reappraisal. Allenby's EEF preparations left little doubt as to his offensive intent. In early September, von Falkenhayn visited the Palestine front, personally going forward of the front lines near Kharm to observe first-hand. His proposal to Enver was the transfer of *Yilderim*'s 7th Army to Beersheba where he would strike the EEF right flank and take the wind out of its offensive sails. In order to please his German mentors and politically to neutralise Djemal, Enver agreed. However, Machiavelli would not have approved of Enver's

solution. While *Yilderim* was given operational sway in Palestine and Mesopotamia, the damaged Djemal was left not only as commander of Turkish forces in Arabia, but in Syria, which was the rear communications of *Yilderim*. Friction between the emasculated Djemal and *Yilderim*'s headstrong German staff was inevitable. Von Kressenstein, under no illusion as to Djemal's military talent, nevertheless praised his energy and influence in the civil and administrative arena. He viewed this change with apprehension.

General Liman von Sanders was also incredulous at this turn of events. During *Yilderim*'s conception, the German Military Mission was not even consulted. Von Sanders and von Kressenstein had previously worked through Turkish staffs and had allowed for national characteristics, local conditions, and the Turkish proverb 'all haste is the devil's'. German assistance was now not on the cooperative, but on the *directive* basis. *Yilderim* had been organised along the lines of a German army group, and of the 74 senior officers, 65 slots were filled by Germans, the remainder by Turks in liaison roles, of which the most senior rank was *major*. Turkey was paying the historically inevitable price between patron and beneficiary when increasing deterioration demands increasing assistance.

Field Marshal Erich von Falkenhayn (centre, tallest figure in cape and Turkish fez) with German officer of *Yilderim* on inspection in Palestine. Two Turkish officers are at right; the officer at attention with short sword appears to be reporting on local conditions.

◀

Below: British trenchworks of the 75th Division near Gaza, 7 November 1917.

Sand

There's sand in the desert in bountiful store,
There's sand and then sand, and still a lot more:
There's sand in the axles and sand in the breeze,
There's sand in the marmalade, sand in the cheese:
There's sand in your mouth, in your hair, in your eyes,
There's sand in your blankets, and sand in supplies,
There's sand in your watch and sand in your shoes.
There's sand in the coffee and sand in the stews,
There's sand in your pockets, and if there's a home
In the sky for poor mortals whose summons has come,
Let us hope the bright landscape in that happy land
May lack that disgusting ingredient, sand.

Palestine News, 1918.

Below right: Turkish infantry in a shallow trench await the British onslaught.

The following letter was captured in a trench at Rafa on the Palestine border. Stamped by Turkish officialdom 'Passed by Censor' it was translated as an example of the ordinary Turkish soldier. (From page 105, *Diary of a Yeomanry Mounted Officer*.)

My life-giving and revered Father, Abdullah Agha,

I am awfully worried at not having received any letters from you for more than a year to tell me whether you are quite well. I think that it is hardly fair of you to let your son worry like this, when he has joined the army to serve his Fatherland and fellow-countrymen. I can only attribute this to the fact that you must be very busy in your office. By the grace of God, my health is quite good. May it please Providence to grant my mother, yourself, and all my relations the best of health. Under the auspices of our Government and nation I am quite well, and you need not worry about me at all. I beg to kiss both my little gracious mother's hands, and am always in need of her dear prayers. Trusting you are quite well, my dearest father, I kiss your two holy hands, and anxiously await the answer to my letter.

(Signed) Corporal —,
Regiment No. 8,
2nd Battalion,
No. 3 Company.

BREAKING THE GAZA–BEERSHEBA LINE

EARLY October found Robertson and the War Cabinet urging Allenby to move ahead with his offensive plans. In late July, Allenby had lost his only son, Michael, who had been killed serving as a horse artillery lieutenant in France. As consolation, Lady Allenby had arrived in Egypt in early October to assist in Red Cross work. This personal tragedy did not appear to debilitate his work. As the days waxed his appearance became so frequent and sudden throughout the lines that crafty staff officers 'employed' one signal officer to monitor Allenby's sorties and give a signal warning with the abbreviated letters 'BL' or 'Bull Loose'![1]

On 22 October General Allenby issued his orders. Bulfin's 21st Corps was to direct a holding action against Gaza while Chauvel's Desert Mounted Corps and Chetwode's 20th Corps delivered the master stroke to the Turkish left at Beersheba. Holding the more than 15-mile long gap between the concentrated Corps would be the thinly-spread Yeomanry Mounted Division.

Over the next week the critical EEF concentration was carried out. Fortunately, there were few cavalry brushes so that the RFC was able to use its aerial mastery to prevent enemy discovery of the southeasten deployments. Troops lay low by day and secretly deployed by night. Daily alarm systems warned of any overflying enemy aeroplanes. Only once did a German observer manage to snap photographs

which would have lead to a radical reassessment of EEF strategy, and during egress his plane was shot down by a Bristol Fighter. Completed by 30 October, the concentration had been no mean feat, for the transport of the Desert Mounted Corps alone had been a compromising six-miles long. Irresistible force was now in position.

Comparative Strengths

	Turkish in line	EEF in line	EEF total available
Cavalry	1,400	12,000	15,000
Infantry	33,000	60,000	80,000

The EEF thus possessed twice the infantry, nine times the cavalry, and three guns for every two Turkish guns, generally throughout the battle line. The concentration, however, had made the threat against Beersheba far worse. Turkish 3rd Corps, defending the Beersheba environs, positioned 4,000 infantry, 1,000 cavalry, 60 machine guns, and 28 guns, while in men alone the Desert Mounted Corps and 20th Corps had 40,000, or a total ratio advantage of eight to one.

The name Beersheba was a modern corruption of the Arabic *Bir es Sabe*, meaning 'Seven Wells'. Belying its Biblical importance, Beersheba was a poor native town of 800 settled Bedouin before the war. Its position as an operational base against the Suez Canal and the coming of the rail transformed it into 'a military settlement built on

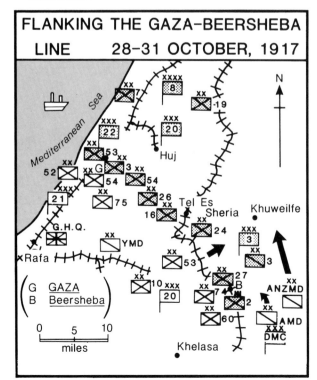

▲ A dismounted Turkish Maxim machine-gun detachment with rangefinder (foreground) awaiting the attack on Beersheba, 31 October 1917.

FLANKING THE GAZA-BEERSHEBA LINE   28-31 OCTOBER, 1917

G   GAZA
B   Beersheba

0   5   10
miles

German lines'.[2] Beersheba was a locally significant junction of road and track. Northeast ran the winding road to Hebron, Bethlehem, and Jerusalem, northwest, the open plain road to Gaza, and south to Aqaba, the new logistical base of the Arab Revolt. But it was the wells that were most critical to the gameplan and they would have to be captured undamaged at the first rush.

Von Kressenstein was still in command of the Palestine Front for, although the *Yilderim* structure was in charge on paper, von Falkenhayn and his entrained units were still in transit. Despite contrary reports from native spies, von Kressenstein remained convinced that Allenby was bent on a third try for Gaza. For five days during the secret concentration the EEF had rained a vicious broadside into Gaza, 'confirming' the illustrious 'Haversack Ruse'.

At 0555 hours in the breathless dawn of a hot day, 20th Corps artillery opened against Hill 1070, a Turkish-held prominence west of Beersheba. Twenty miles to 20th Corps' left the horizon flickered and rumbled with the storm of shot and shell at Gaza. Within an hour a pall of dust obscured observation of Hill 1070 so that the guns halted, then recommenced at 0745 hours under a clear sky. Shortly after, the 60th Division scrambled forward and the artillery was shifted into 'wire-cutting' range.

At noon, elements of the 60th and 74th Divisions fought their way into the sparse clumps of barbed wire, hitting the Turkish positions over a three-mile line. The Turks soon surrendered six guns, and 419 personnel, but some trenches had fought to the last man. Corporal John Collins of the Welsh Fusiliers bayonetted 15 Turks, then advanced with a Lewis gun section in pursuit, winning the Victoria Cross. By early afternoon, serious resistance was over with an EEF casualty bill of 1,151.

Chauvel's Desert Mounted Corps had moved out the evening of 30 October so that by Halloween's dawn the formations had covered from 17–30 miles in rear flank of Turkish 3rd Corps. Each trooper carried two days rations plus one day's forage for his horse and two days emergency grain in a sandbag. All told, each horse was carrying about 280 pounds. The ANZAC Mounted Division held the van, followed by the Australian Mounted Division, then the 7th Mounted Brigade, which was holding the line south of Beersheba between the Australians and 20th Corps. Beyond the ANZACs, on the extended far right was a company of British camelry with Bedouin scouts under Colonel S. F. Newcombe, recently transferred from the Military Mission is Arabia. Newcombe's fantastic mission was to block the Hebron Road into Beersheba, and if possible, raise the tribes in rebellion.

Mid-morning of 31 October found the Desert Mounted Corps in place, to the total surprise of the Turks. Beset by infantry to the west, 3rd Corps commander Ismet Bey now found enemy cavalry to the east. Urgently, he requested assistance from von Kressenstein, under apparent siege himself in Gaza. Still mis-reading the situation, von Kressenstein refused.

Blocking the soft approach into Beersheba was the flat-topped mound of *Tel es Sabe*, a 20-acre obstruction harbouring a battalion and machine gun company. As the Somerset and Inverness batteries offered covering fire, the New Zealand Mounted Rifle Brigade closed on the mound with leap-frog rushes from cover to cover. Overhead, Turkish aeroplanes bombed targets of opportunity on the plain. That mid-afternoon, the Auckland Regiment made the final rush and secured the height.

Day was wearing down and Allenby ordered Chauvel to take Beersheba before dark. In the hour before dusk Brigadier W. Grant's 4th Light Horse Brigade charged on a front of two regiments, each regiment drawn up in three long squadron lines, 300 yards between each squadron, with nearly five feet between individual troopers. It was a stark test of the *arme blanche* against rifles, machine guns, and shallow trenches. As Grant's troopers became visible in the intervening plain, the Turks opened fire. Speed and loose formation were the essence to minimise casualties. Cannons volleyed, then machine guns chattered on the Light Horse left. Allied guns pinpointed then stabbed at the Turkish machine guns. Then the sustained rattle of riflery from the shallow trenches thinned the leading lines. Grant's full gallop continued, unrelenting. As the mounted arm closed, the Turkish musketry became erratic, then almost hushed as the Light Horse galloped over the first two trench lines. Some troops dismounted to fight in bayonet *mêlée* – which they carried in preference to the sword – while other troops rode straight into the town where they prevented the planned Turkish demolition of the Beersheba wells.

For less than 200 casualties the Light Horse bagged 1,500 Turks with nine guns. It was the end of the 27th (Arab) Division. Ismet Bey and part of the 3rd Corps staff barely managed to shoot their way free of the trap. These impressive results were achieved not only from loose formation and rapid movement, but from the psychologically enervating effect on infantry caused by a mounted charge. Habitually, rifles and machine guns fire high at rapidly incoming targets and the less steady the soldiers the more is forgotten in sight correction. The same can apply to artillery who, in the excitement fail to shorten sight ranges and so sail their shells harmlessly overhead. Far more casualties were caused by the aircraft which found any clump of horses a particularly rewarding target. This was not an isolated instance, nor was Palestine an only case. These same lessons were proved consistently during the contemporary Russian Civil War of 1918–1920 when White Russian and Cossack cavalry demonstrated the same prodigies as British Yeomanry and Light Horse. Grant's charge became a landmark for the duration of the campaigns. Thereafter, the value of the frontal charge in specific situations was recognised and a competition for *élan* sprung up among the EEF mounted arm.

Rolling up the Line

Two days were now needed to reorganise and to prepare the storming of the Turkish centre at *Tel es Sheria*. Once again Allenby distracted enemy attention to the orchestral rehearsal while off-stage the maestro composed the virtuoso performance. Bulfin's 21st Corps stepped up pressure on Gaza during the first two days of November and were now joined in the bombardment by elements of the British and French Mediterranean Fleets. The task force included three seaplane carriers which acted in a counter air profile. Bulfin held a compliment of 218 guns (half of 18 pounders), which included 68 medium-heavy pieces for counter battery suppression. Gas shells had already been in use although, according to the Turkish reports, they exploded with only a harmless yellow smoke.[3] It was the heaviest cannonade yet seen outside the European theatre.

A convincing holding attack involves more than mere demonstration. A night assault had been selected to minimise casualties in crossing the 5,000 yard frontage of heavy sand which rose in places as 150 foot high dunes. Occupational objectives were Sheikh Hasan, which overlooked Gaza's modest harbour, and Umbrella Hill at the southeast point of the attack.

The 75th Division had already engaged in activities near Umbrella Hill, and the hill itself fell to the 7th Scottish Rifles of the 52nd Division before midnight on Halloween. A four-hour pause tricked the Turks into believing it had been a separate or disjointed phase: in fact, it had only been the prelude to the main holding attack at 0300 hours. Under cover of darkness, and assisted by six tanks of the Palestine Tank Detachment, the 52nd and 54th went in, losing the first wave of a leading battalion to cleverly concealed landmines before taking Sheikh Hasan. As dawn's rays sparkled over the turquoise Mediterranean blue, Bulfin discovered his men had held against Turkish night counter attacks. One thousand Turkish dead were found with 550 prisoners taken. The EEF left flank had lost 2,700 casualties.

Allenby now pressed for a 4 November reopening against the Sheria centre. A delay dangerous to Allenby's plan, however, had intervened. The Beersheba wells had yielded less than calculated while the dry *khamsin* winds had resumed to parch the throats of man and animal. There seemed no alternative to awaiting further solution of the water predicament. After touring his three corps by staff car Allenby reluctantly postponed operations till 6 November.

This serious delay was fortuitously eased by Turkish confusion and paranoia on the one hand, and by a chivalrous mission on the other. By 2 November the ANZAC Mounted Division had ridden so far behind Turkish lines that the Turks were afraid of a raid up the Hebron Road to Jerusalem. Colonel Newcombe's 70-strong camel party had already reached Hebron itself, gallantly rupturing communications.

Newcombe never came close to causing the Arab tribes to revolt, but in the shadowy scenario of a communications blackout the Turks could not be so sure. Doubt made his warband and the ANZACs into a momentous flanking menace. As the staff of the EEF plotted the move on Sheria, the Turks, at first having ignored the threat to their left, then overreacted. The 3rd Cavalry Division, the 19th (Anatolian) Division and remaining elements of the 24th and 27th were rushed to Khuweilfe, ten miles north of Beersheba, to intercept the imaginary menace.

Static fighting ensued from 3–6 November with Allenby's 53rd Division and elements of the Desert Mounted Corps. Not surprisingly, such superior forces hit Newcombe's cameliers that 20 were killed and the rest captured. Colonel Newcombe became the most senior EEF officer taken thus far by Turkish arms.

In the centre of the Turkish line the Sheria emplacements extended over four miles of well-sited trenches overlooking a frontal plain. Wire entanglements covered some lines, but elsewhere lay bare approaches. By the night of 5/6 November 20th Corps and the Desert Mounted Corps were ready for a resumption of hostilities. From left to right the 10th, 60th, and 74th Divisions would attack the Sheria positions while the Yeomanry Mounted Division, the Imperial Camel Brigade and the 53rd Division wrestled with the Turks at Khuweilfe. Interposed in the 15-mile gap between 20th and 21st Corps was the Australian Mounted Division.

Once again it was a case of maximum concentration at the desired point. The leverage gained after Beersheba allowed 20th Corps to enfilade the Sheria works on a southeast to northwest axis. The advance at dawn on 6 November proved irresistible, the 60th and 74th Divisions obtaining their set targets that afternoon. That night, elements of both divisions attempted to join hands in a bayonet attack against the large mound of Tel es Sheria. The Turks responded by blowing the Sheria dumps so that bright fires burned all night revealing the EEF maneuvers. At dawn, after consolidation, the 60th went in to secure the mound as the 10th Division captured the Turkish Hareira Redoubt. Allenby now had his 'G' in 'Gap', the cavalryman's dream which throughout the war proved to be so elusive on the Western Front.

▲ An Indian gas sentry of the 58th Vaughan's Rifles (Punjab Frontier Force), 1917.

▶ Right: Lieutenant-General Sir Philip Chetwode commanded the 20th Corps during the flanking of the Gaza–Beersheba Line. Known as the 'Bart' from his inherited baronetcy, Chetwode would in future years become a field marshal and commander-in-chief in India where he became known for radical military reforms. Chetwode was small, suave, spoke in a nasal drawl, and carried an amber cigarette holder.

▶ Far right: The Australian, General Sir Henry George Chauvel, CB. Chauvel commanded the ANZAC Mounted Division from March, 1916 until assuming control of the Desert Column in the spring of 1917 and, finally, the Desert Mounted Corps in the summer of that year.

11

PURSUIT INTO PHILISTIA

ALLENBY'S offensive had caught *Yilderim* in echelon from Aleppo to the Palestine Front. Out of kilter was von Falkenhayn's own planned offensive and there transpired the inevitable recriminations for loss of the line. Djemal Pasha would last a month before resigning, bitterly blaming von Falkenhayn and the time-wasting Baghdad scheme in his passage. Turkish history would blame von Kressenstein as dupe of the 'Haversack Ruse' so that his own days were numbered until a more tranquil situation could safely shift him from Palestine command.

Von Falkenhayn had reached Jerusalem on the evening of 5 November where he had established his headquarters at the German hospice on the Biblical Mount of Olives. His first order was to allow von Kressenstein to evacuate Gaza to the northern side of the *Wadi el Hesi*. Bulfin's 21st Corps troops, moving through Gaza by evening of the 6th, reported it a shell of rubble, a corpse-strewn ghost town.

One of Allenby's maxims was to never let a beaten enemy recuperate. Allenby admonished Chauvel's Desert Mounted Corps to press the Turks 'with the utmost vigour', and to General Barrow – in charge of the temporary force engaged at Khuweilfe on the far right flank – to take 'every

opportunity that may offer of punishing the enemy'.[1] The translation to reality, however, was tricky. Chauvel's forces were scattered and poorly watered. A day was lost when the Turkish 26th Division prevented the British 60th Division from crossing the Wadi Sheria, and in fact was not dislodged till late on 7 November. Then, when the Australian Mounted Division pushed into the fray under cover of darkness, the 60th, in confusion, fired on the Light Horse. By morning of 8 November the dreamed of 'G' in 'Gap' was in danger of closing, as at Arras.

Allenby had given Chauvel instructions to cut a swathe across the Turkish rear via Jemmameh and Huj and ultimately to reach the Mediterranean, or at least join hands with Bulfin's 21st Corps near the sea. Bulfin was ordered to hammer the Turkish far right along the coast where naval support and supply access could keep 21st Corps punching. The three mounted divisions and the 52nd and 75th Divisions had been selected for the pursuit across the Philistine Plain. In order to give the pursuers the best benefit of logistics, transport was hurriedly stripped from the 54th Division at Gaza, and from all of 20th Corps north of Beersheba.

To a staff officer dubious of the extensive goals, Allenby stiffly returned: 'In pursuit you must always stretch possibilities to the limit. Troops having beaten the enemy will want to rest. They must be given as objectives, not those that you think they will reach, but the farthest that they could possibly reach.'[2]

North of Gaza, along the three-mile long Sausage Ridge, the Turkish 7th Division tried to oppose the 52nd Division's march. Sausage Ridge commanded both the rail and road out of Gaza. On 8 November, a well-placed counter attack disrupted the 52nd's progress and fighting gradually devolved into a series of man-to-man grenade and bayonet trade-offs well into the night. Scot and Turk clashed with tenacious blood-lust and Brigadier Hamilton was moved to note that companies and platoons having lost all officers and NCOs nevertheless repeatedly returned to the attack led by privates.[3] In the wee morning hours a fresh flanking move by the 6th Highland Light Infantry finally pushed the Turks off the last spine of the ridge.

Huj

The success of Allenby's pursuit and the fate of the retreating Turks hung in the balance on 7 and 8 November. If von Falkenhayn's counterstroke in the Khuweilfe sector failed in diverting Allenby's attention, it succeeded in forcing the EEF calvary through a constricting gap rather than the more favourable sweep around the flank. On the 7th, rearguard resistance was stiff; the bulk of the Turkish divisions were escaping and it was apparent only the trapped or less resolute were being caught. Chauvel's

troopers played a game known as 'stalking' where small formations watched, followed, then suddenly charged Turkish guns from the rear. The 3rd Light Horse Brigade prided itself in besting this game by taking the most guns and 'claiming' them in chalked letters.

By afternoon of the 8th, contact was established between Chauvel and 21st Corps. They had failed, however, to envelop the Turks who had put up a vicious resistance at the Tank and Atawineh Redoubts. Still, cracks were appearing in the Turkish retirement. Increasingly, valuable equipment was being discarded by an enemy growing more eager to lighten any restricting load.

That afternoon, the 60th Division came under heavy shelling from the rearguard stationed on the ridge in front of Huj. Chauvel's orders had been to break through to Jemmameh and Huj, both being munitions dumps, but Huj being the larger, and also the headquarters of Turkish 8th Army. Explosions in the distance indicated the Turks were destroying Jemmameh.

The rearguard comprised a mixed group of Central Powers personnel – 2,000 Turkish infantry, a battery each of Austrian 75-millimetre and 150-millimetre guns, a battery of German mountain guns, and a complement of machine guns. Major-General Shea, commanding 60th Division, decided an advance by his infantry would be too costly and so requested cavalry assistance. The lot fell to the Warwickshire and Worcestershire Yeomanry currently attached to 5th Brigade, Australian Mounted Division.

Collecting one-and-a-half squadrons of his own Warwickshire and an equal body from the Worcestershire, Lieutenant-Colonel Gray-Cheape prepared a charge ear-

◀ Sergeants three. Regimental Sergeant-Major Bray (centre) and Sergeants Tozer and Tyrell of the Warwickshire Yeomanry.

marked for historical legend. Taking what advantage they could from the rise in the ground in front of the enemy, the Yeomanry slipped unobserved to within 800 yards of the ridge. Ahead was a downhill dip, then a ride up onto higher ground where the Turkish infantry, machine guns, and Austrian 75s were posted on the left and centre, more infantry to the centre and right, the 105 milimetre howitzers to the centre rear, and the mountain guns to the right. The charge would have to be made without the usual fire support of the 18 pounders or Hotchkiss guns, but it would have the brief moment of surprise and determined speed.

The second in command was heard to shout: 'Now then, boys, for the guns!'[4] 'As our cavalry appeared, thundering over the rise, the Turks sprang to their guns and swung them round, firing point-blank into the charging horsemen. The infantry, leaping on the limbers, blazed away with their rifles till they were cut down. There was no thought of surrender; every man stuck to his gun or rifle to the last. The leading troops of the cavalry dashed into the first enemy battery. The following troops, swinging to the right, took the three heavy howitzers almost in their stride, leaving the guns silent, the gun crews dead or dying, and galloped round the hill, to fall upon the mountain battery from the rear, and cut the Turkish gunners to pieces in a few minutes. The third wave, passing the first battery, where a fierce sabre v. bayonet fight was going on between our cavalry and the enemy, raced up the slope at the machine guns. Many saddles were emptied in that few yards, but the charge was irresistible. In a few minutes the enemy guns were silenced, their crews killed, and the whole position was in our hands.'[5]

The numerically superior Turkish infantry had bolted, obviously assuming the crazy charge could only be the vanguard of some larger thundering host. In ten minutes 11 guns, four machine guns, 70 prisoners, and a large number of enemy killed (all from the sabre) fell with the ridge. The rearguard was broken. The ten participating Yeomanry troops had previously been so low in manpower that only 170 troopers had commenced the charge. Out of 12 officers three were killed and six wounded. The 158 troopers lost 26 killed and 40 wounded while of the horses – always an easy 'mass of brown' target – 100 were lost.

The affair at Huj again emphasised the strength of cavalry when handled boldly and at closing speed. Von Kressenstein himself barely escaped being taken in the follow-on action, and communications equipment which the Germans could not replace until the next year was taken, along with a special code book which the Intelligence Branch thenceforth used to decipher *Yilderim* messages. The dump at Huj fell into EEF hands with its rich yield of heavy artillery shells which, ironically, were later fired on their former owners.

Huj notwithstanding, the Turks had evaded the wider net of encirclement. But only just. RFC reports indicated Turkish forces were in an advanced state of disorganisation. On 9 November the RFC bombed the new 8th Army headquarters at El Tineh. Von Kressenstein's memoirs record the

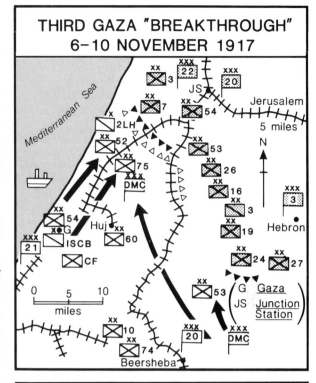

THIRD GAZA "BREAKTHROUGH"
6−10 NOVEMBER 1917

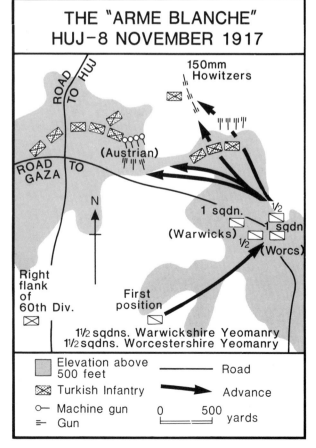

THE "ARME BLANCHE"
HUJ−8 NOVEMBER 1917

panic subsequent to the rumour there had been a cavalry breakthrough at the front. Order was not restored for a day and by then nervous tremors had rippled to Jerusalem.[6]

El Mughar and Junction Station

Pursuit slackened during 10–11 November. The EEF had lost its first wind, but the Turks were in dire straits, possessing at most 15,000 men still in formation, thinly spread over 20 miles. At Ramle, the Turks adopted the desperate if expedient course of collecting 10,000 stragglers, dividing them into lots of 200, parcelling out available officers, and rushing them to shore up widening cracks at the front.

Allenby knew it was now mandatory to gather second wind. From deciphered Turkish messages Allenby knew von Falkenhayn was plotting a blow with 7th Army out of the Judean Hills onto the EEF right. After considering local conditions and the state of the opposing forces, 'The Bull' decided to ignore this threat and gamble events instead on his own next phase set for the morning of 13 November. This was a main blow against the Turkish right, the 52nd and 75th Divisions, prising the Turks away from the coast and moving on Junction Station while the Yeomanry Division and the Imperial Service Cavalry Brigade dashed through the breach toward Ramle and Jaffa. At Junction Station the Beersheba rail joined the Jaffa–Jerusalem line. Occupation would split 7th and 8th Armies, thereby preventing any later Turkish supply or reinforcement.

The weakened Turkish coastal line was tactically toughened by a series of villages crowning rocky hills and surrounded by cactus hedges. Of these natural strongpoints, Katrah and El Mughar were the most prominent, blocking the way to Junction Station. Against the Mughar Ridge, slightly northwest of Junction Station, the 52nd Division had stalled. Cavalry support was requested and tendered by way of Brigadier Godwin's 6th Mounted Brigade, Yeomanry Mounted Division.

Godwin chose his Dorset and Buckinghamshire Yeomanry to execute one of the war's most severe tests of the *arme blanche*. As at Huj, it was a scheme of extreme daring, but unlike Huj the charge was supported by a battery of artillery and a company of machine guns. The Mughar Ridge ran along a north-south axis. The cavalry's approach along the west and southern side crossed open ground sloping gently upward to the ridge. Under cover of the Wadi Jamus the Yeomanry worked to within two miles of the Mughar Ridge's western face.

At 1500 hours the Yeomanry left the wadi in column of squadrons extending to five pace intervals: the Dorsetshires on the front and left, the Buckinghamshires to the rear and right, the Berkshires in reserve. The regiments covered the first mile at a trot, coming immediately into heavy but 'plunging' machine gun fire. At a half mile the pace shifted to canter then a full charge 100 yards from the top. The Buckinghamshire 1st Squadron charged home just north of Mughar village, galloping over the ridge and in ten glorious seconds cleaved through the defenders, the remainder of the Regiment close on their heels. On their left the Dorsetshires had had a longer turning ride over broken

▼ Turkish field artillery battery, Palestine.

ground so that their leading squadron dismounted near the top and went in with the bayonet while the following squadrons rode in at sword's point.

The village fell to the Berkshire Yeomanry coming out of the reserve against the northern side while two battalions of the 52nd Division, personally lead by Brigadier Pollok-M'Call, charged over open ground from the south. At nearly the same hour Katrah village fell to elements of the 52nd who reported the Turks holding their ground to the last.

The Mughar-Katrah Ridge was captured, breaking the spine of Turkish 22nd Corps defence. The exodus of Turks from the ridge made for the village of Aqir, closely followed by leading elements of the East Riding Yeomanry. In the gathering dusk, Corps Commander Refet Bey rallied his slender resources, riding to and fro on a white horse under the deliberate aim of snipers, and bearing a charmed life, succeeded in extricating his survivors.

One thousand prisoners and 400 Turkish killed was the cost for 616 EEF casualties. Mughar had been a classic set-piece battle as well as further tribute to the exploits of the mounted arm. Yeomanry losses were incredibly light — 16 killed, 114 wounded, and 265 horses, or 16 per cent of personnel and 33 per cent of horses.[7]

Early the next morning of 14 November a brigade of the 75th Division with armoured cars entered Junction Station unopposed. Signs of efficiency indicated the Germans had been in control of the station during the preceeding months, but now animal carcasses and discarded items testified to the recent rout. Turkish Colonel Hussein Husni had made arrangements for the demolition of all points of strategic value, but at the last moment those responsible for the engineering had bolted. Thus, the EEF captured intact the steam pumping plant which offered for the first time an unlimited supply of potable water.

Allenby's gamble that the Australian Mounted Division could hold the right of his line against von Falkenhayn's counter attack proved correct. Yilderim marshalled as many of its weakened divisions as possible along 'exterior' lines to hurl against the Desert Mounted Corps as it moved, strung-out and thirsty, northwest to support the Junction Station operation. As a map maneuver it was faultless and indicative of a resourceful and energetic commander. It was excellent strategy, but applied to Palestine realities bad tactics.

Von Falkenhayn's second and third in command, Colonel von Dommes and Colonel Hussein Husni, opposed him, witnessing to the hounding of their men by the superior mobility of the EEF. In their assessment, any attempt to fight using maneuver was a hopeless cause; better to retire to the Jaffa–Jerusalem defensive line. The Turkish infantry were marched to exhaustion so that when they hit the Australian light horse, they could only be reported as 'obviously good and well-disciplined troops, but very tired.'[8] The crack 3rd Cavalry and 19th Divisions additionally failed to coordinate their advance with the rest of his line so that, with a loss of four miles of ground, the Australian Mounted Division weathered the storm. The loss of the Mughar Ridge made final folly of the entire plan. Yilderim was split in half.

▼ Light horsemen of the ANZAC Mounted Division watering at Ain es Sultan, a natural 80° Farenheit spring also known as 'Elisha's Well'.

12

THE AQABA BASE

AQABA was a strategic windfall for the fortune of the Arab Revolt and its cooperation with the Egyptian Expeditionary Force. Aqaba had once been the fabled port of King Solomon. East of the town the ground sloped steeply to a precipitous range of hills and to the 'King Solomon' Mountains. From the Gulf of Aqaba's northern shore the Wadi Araba traversed north into the southern shore of the Dead Sea. Offshore Aqaba, on Faroun Island, stood Godfrey de Bouillon's stone Crusader castle as a mute, crumbled sentry.

Although the slender grove of palms hugging the coast was generous in the offering of fresh water, its branches bore only the evil diurnal fruit of green dates. Aqaba had no indigenous food industry and no way to feed the 700 Turkish prisoners, Lawrence's 500 men, or the 2,000 new tribal allies. For all its future potential Aqaba in July, 1917 was a logistical liability for its new owners.

◄ The British monitor *Humber* off Chatham Pier, Aqaba. The ancient port, while deficient in natural food, held sufficient natural water below the surface of the palm groves along the seashore.

Someone had to inform the British of their new possession and get supplies moving to the new Arab base. As a Bedouin showing up at GHQ would not likely be believed with the message that a huge flank over several hundred miles had been undertaken with a small warband and that 1,200 Turks had been removed from the enemy force pool for the cost of two Arab irregulars, Lawrence had to go himself. In 49 hours Lawrence and a small party crossed the southern Sinai, fed on lumps of boiled camel and broiled dates. They stopped only once for water at the Themed wells.

The desert had already begun to claim the former Canal defence works of Murray's EEF. By hook and crook,

▼ Faroun Island, looking west off Aqaba, 1917. Aqaba was once the fabled port of King Solomon, and lay at the apex of a beautiful turquoise sea inlet fringed by palm trees and coloured coral reefs. Capping the deserted Faroun Island is Godfrey de Bouillon's Crusader castle. Unused for centuries, a collection of mud huts remained at Aqaba, but its position was the needed strategic link between the King of Hejaz' Arab armies and Allenby's EEF.

Lawrence impatiently managed to pole vault the layers of bureaucratic red tape to secure a berth on the train from Suez to Cairo. Suez had been educational. The EEF learned of Aqaba while Lawrence learned Allenby was the new commander of the EEF. While at Suez Lawrence arranged for the dispatch of food to Aqaba via the ship *Dufferin*, which would return laden with the Turkish prisoners.

Lawrence first sighted Allenby on a station platform in Ismailia while bound for Cairo. His impression was of 'a very large and superior general' who caused a 'terrible tension' wherever he strode.[1] Lawrence's first report in Cairo was to Allenby's chief political officer, Brigadier-General Clayton, of the Arab Bureau. Here was drawn £16,000 sterling in gold so that Sherif Nasir might pay the Arab levies in Aqaba. Then, before he could change into uniform (soon that of a major) Allenby sent for him. 'It was a comic interview, for Allenby was physically large and confident, and morally so great that the comprehension of our littleness came slow to him.'[2]

Lawrence expounded on the tribes of eastern Syria and how they might be employed as in the Crusader days of Saladin to threaten Jerusalem. These were welcome ideas for Allenby who planned to break the Gaza–Beersheba Line and present the Prime Minister with Jerusalem for Christmas. As at any first meeting, promise had yet to become fact. Allenby could not be sure how far this sandalled Captain in silken robes could carry his claims, nor could Lawrence ascertain how far to credit Allenby's concurrance of logistical support – now the virtual economic lifeline of the Arab Revolt. If the fears of either were great they were unfounded, for history recorded that July the meeting of two of its champions . . . one a great conventional soldier, and one a master of irregular war. In under 16 months Lawrence's desert marauders would ride through the gates of Damascus alongside Allenby's victorious legions. As for logistics: '. . . we learned gradually that he meant what he said; and that what General Allenby could do was enough for his very greediest servant.'[3]

The Aqaba interlude had produced a change in Lawrence. No longer the shy office clerk protesting unsuitability, he had essentially pushed himself for the Aqaba command. Clayton balked, for the reason of Lawrence's junior rank, but a mutually satisfactory base commandant was agreed in the form of Lieutenant–Colonel P. C. Joyce. Lawrence knew Joyce as a great organiser who would develop the base area while Lawrence was up-country inmeshed in tribal machinations. Colonel Wilson was selected as head of the Military Mission, and Captain Goslett – who had put Wejh in order – as supply officer.

Aqaba was 100 miles off Allenby's right flank and 800 miles from Mecca. Common sense and military logic dictated that the northern Arab forces should now become an army under Feisal and act, in essence, as one of Allenby's own corps. With proper Anglo-Arab permissions, the Arab Northern Army was born. Admiral Wemyss volunteered his own flagship, the *Euryalus*, to anchor off Aqaba for moral support during the early weeks. This was significant encouragement, for the Arabs judged a ship's prowess by the number of its funnels. As the *Euryalus* had

▲ Jafaar Pasha served as a Turkish officer but, as an ethnic Arab from Baghdad, was eager to join the Arab Revolt. Jafaar headed the trained Arab regulars and was Feisal's chief of staff in the Arab Northern Army. He is depicted here in the regular uniform of the King of Hejaz. Ironically, the Germans had given him the Iron Cross for action at Gallipoli, the Turks awarded him the Turkish Crescent for work with the Senussi, and the British made him a Commander of the Order of St. Michael and St. George, which Allenby presented to him in autumn, 1918.

four, it seemed evidence they were on the winning side.

Further evidence came by the stores coming into the ancient port and unloading at the newly constructed pier. Wejh was being shut down as a supply base with the proceeds being transferred to Aqaba. That summer, the armoured car section and flight of aircraft augmenting the Hejaz operations was conveyed to Aqaba.

Aqaba was itself easily defensible. After clearing Turkish sea mines out of the Gulf, the rear was secure. Only the northern and eastern approaches might be threatened by the Turkish base at Maan and nature had gone to some length protecting these. While a northern approach would enjoy sufficient water, it necessitated a 16-mile negotiation of a narrow defile. Throughout, the track was only fit for camels. The eastern approach was still trickier, for an invader would be channeled through the treacherous gorge

▲ Depicted is the interior of the fort at Aqaba dismembered by British naval gunfire during the Turkish occupation. In the foreground are sacks of food and forage landed in support of Feisal's Arab Northern Army.

▼ Amir Zeid arriving by sea at Aqaba with elements of Feisal's Arab Northern Army.

of the Wadi Itm. Lawrence planned four independent yet strategically interlinking posts to guard these approaches: Guweira, 30 miles from Aqaba near the head of the Wadi Itm, the ancient city of Petra, and at Delagha and Batra. The four posts formed a semi-circle around the edge of the Maan highlands, positioned so that a successful attack on one would yet demand a successive reduction of all four.[4]

In August, the regular troops of Jafaar Pasha transferred to Aqaba. Jafaar was an ethnic Arab with former service as a Turkish officer. Enver Pasha had chosen him to organise Sheikh el Senussi's tribal forces during the Senussi Revolt along Egypt's western frontier. He demonstrated tactical ability in two battles before being captured. Incarcerated in Cairo's Citadel, he escaped by means of knotted bedsheets down a wall. Because of his portly size the knotting split and he broke his ankle and was recaptured. When he heard of the Sherifian Revolt he applied for service with the Arabs and Feisal made him commander-in-chief of his own regular Arab troops. Under Feisal he became Chief of Staff in the Arab Northern Army.

Feisal's regular infantry totalled 800. They were divided into a North Regiment of Syrian-Mesopotamians, and a South Regiment of Meccans. For six weeks they trained at Aqaba, along with the 300 Camel Corps and Mule Mounted Regulars and the 150 gunners, while being re-equipped and reclothed from Egypt. The men did not receive their training with either efficiency or enthusiasm, but they did express impatience to get at the Turks.[5]

Sir Reginald Wingate, having replaced McMahon as High Commissioner, was responsible for Arab operations south of Maan (Allenby was responsible north of Maan). 'South of Maan' meant the supply and advisement of the armies of Ali and Abdullah, who had their own hands full besieging Medina, watching Turkish Yemen, and protecting the King of Hejaz and the source of the Arab Revolt. Seaborne supplies and naval support were rendered to both sections by Captain W. H. D. Boyle, commanding the Red Sea Patrol. In November, 1917 the 'Hejaz Operations Staff' was set up in Cairo as an administrative and operational attempt at supervision in both these northern and southern spheres. By practical necessity, it was a loose-leaf central control allowing the widest advisory and operational latitude. If local Arab forces refused to carry out an agenda, attached British officers were to act as far as possible on their own.

Baiting the Hook

In early autumn the liklihood of a Turkish thrust from Maan was feared. Behet Pasha's 1st Composite Force was quartered at Maan with a ration strength of 6,000 men and 16 guns. At the end of August he had pushed 2,000 men forward to the wells of Abu el Lissan which he set about fortifying. At the end of September he was joined by the 7th Cavalry Regiment.

Contrary to predominant opinion, Lawrence was confident of Arab ability to hold Aqaba. Specifically, he *desired* a Turkish attack toward Petra (Feisal's northernmost post in the Wadi Musa), and so set about creating the provocation. Incessant raids were plotted against the Turks on the Maan Plateau. Acting in coordination, the RFC flew long-range missions from the Sinai, bombing Maan once and Abu el Lissan twice.

Meanwhile, Lawrence sought to improve his skill at demolition by experimenting with direct mine firings from an electrical charge. Instead of the 'automatic mine' method which a passing train exploded on contact, the electrical mine with plunger would allow some selectivity as to the moment of firing.

He first chose Mudauwara Station the well of which was the only one in the dry district 80 miles south of Maan. Discovering their party doubly outnumbered by alert Turks, the warband diverted north to blow a train and arched bridge. It took five hours to bury the mine and the tell-tale wires leading to the plunger. The Arabs lined the hills 150 yards from the rail while the Lewis guns and Stokes mortars posted at 300 yards. The experiment worked, derailing the train, and the Arabs surged down the dunes, losing only three men for a kill of 70 Turks, and a captured party of Austrian artillerists come to instruct the use of the new Skoda mountain howitzers.

On 6 October the French Captain Pisani employed a similar technique to blow a supply train and bridge near Maan. Altogether, 17 locomotives were destroyed that autumn by British and Arab experts operating out of Aqaba.

The raids contributed in two ways – to illustrate the unfeasibility of evacuating Medina, and by impairing Turkish reinforcements against Allenby. The demolition of engines and rolling stock had reached critical proportion.

'Travelling became an uncertain terror for the enemy. At Damascus people scrambled for the back seats in trains, even paid extra for them. The engine drivers struck. Civilian traffic nearly ceased; and we extended our threat to Aleppo by the mere posting of a notice one night on Damascus Town Hall, that good Arabs would henceforward travel by the Syrian railway at their own risk.'[6]

Early in October the Arabs raided north from Petra against Shobek. The move jeopardised the Turkish grain belt, occupied the village for several days, and damaged the light railway used for the collection of wood fuel for the Hejaz rail. For the Turks it was the last straw. On 27 October four weak battalions, the 7th Cavalry, and 10 guns sortied from Maan against the Arab Maulud's 350 camel and mule mounted regulars with nearly 200 Bedouin auxiliaries. The ancient

▲ Captain Ismail Abdo and other ranks of the Hejaz Camel Corps, Aqaba, 1917. This unit of regulars belonged to the 'Sherifian Army' which was trained under Moslem officers and under British officer advisement. Costs came out of the monthly gold subsidies sent to the King of the Hejaz whenever the regular camelry, infantry and mule-mounted infantry operated in Hejaz or southern operations against Medina. When units of the Sherifian Army were based out of Aqaba for participation in the Arab Northern Army, costs came out of Feisal's Northern Operations fund. The Corps wore Arab headdress over British uniform.

Palmyran rock city of Petra had given the Romans considerable difficulty – it was not about to be denied repeating history for the Turks.

After an artillery and aerial bombardment the Turks advanced into the narrow channel of the Wadi Musa. Above them, perched in crevasses along the cliffsides, were the old buildings of the ghost city. This was Lawrence's desired trap, although he was not present to see the fish take the

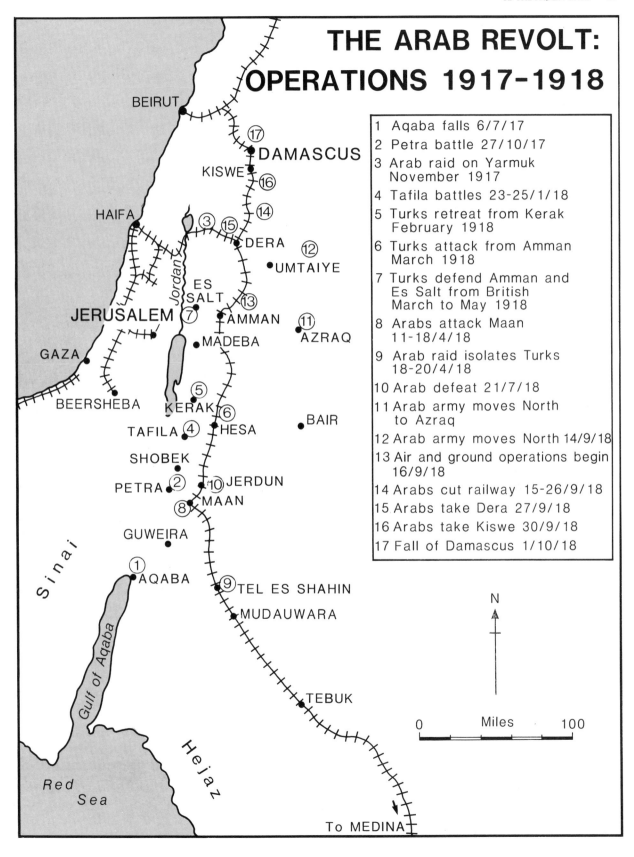

THE ARAB REVOLT: OPERATIONS 1917-1918

1 Aqaba falls 6/7/17
2 Petra battle 27/10/17
3 Arab raid on Yarmuk November 1917
4 Tafila battles 23-25/1/18
5 Turks retreat from Kerak February 1918
6 Turks attack from Amman March 1918
7 Turks defend Amman and Es Salt from British March to May 1918
8 Arabs attack Maan 11-18/4/18
9 Arab raid isolates Turks 18-20/4/18
10 Arab defeat 21/7/18
11 Arab army moves North to Azraq
12 Arab army moves North 14/9/18
13 Air and ground operations begin 16/9/18
14 Arabs cut railway 15-26/9/18
15 Arabs take Dera 27/9/18
16 Arabs take Kiswe 30/9/18
17 Fall of Damascus 1/10/18

BEIRUT
DAMASCUS
KISWE
HAIFA
DERA
UMTAIYE
ES SALT
JERUSALEM
AMMAN
AZRAQ
MADEBA
GAZA
BEERSHEBA
KERAK
BAIR
TAFILA
HESA
SHOBEK
PETRA
JERDUN
MAAN
GUWEIRA
AQABA
TEL ES SHAHIN
MUDAUWARA
TEBUK

Jordan

Sinai

Gulf of Aqaba

Red Sea

Hejaz

To MEDINA

N

0   Miles   100

bait. Maulud held his hand till the Turks were well into the defile, then hit them with frontal and enfilading fire. His irregulars worked along the flanks, sniping. It was the first and last time the Turks attempted attacking the semi-circle of Arab positions.

Bitter Pills

Mid-October had found Lawrence back at Allenby's GHQ learning what could be done to support the breaking of the Gaza-Beersheba Line. Allenby wanted a diversion in the Turkish rear timed five days after the projected fall of Beersheba, or on 5 November. The means were up to Lawrence, so long as the Turks looked behind them with high anxiety.

Obviously, Allenby needed a significant distraction and it put Lawrence in a moral and strategic quandary. He could call out the Syrian, Dead Sea, and North Arabian tribes and stake all . . . 12,000 irregulars would flock to Feisal's colours. But the rainy season was coming and if Allenby's program fell short of its mark the Arab peasantry would be sacrificed to the vengeful Turkish embrace. Feisal's political position would be neutralised and the ace card played.

Faced with two worlds, Lawrence confessed he made half decisions and plumped for a demolition of the Yarmuk Valley Railway, a critical retreat artery for the main Turkish forces. The precipitous river gorge winding from Palestine through the Hauran District to Damascus was crossed by a series of long, arched bridges, the ones at extreme ends being the hardest to replace. The destruction of these would isolate the bulk of the Turkish Army for two weeks.

The plan involved a raiding party of platoon to small company size, traversing 420 miles from east of Aqaba through the oasis of Azraq, and from thence dropping into the Yarmuk. It was a scheme of such unconsidered daring that the Turkish presence was reported as correspondingly slack.

Lawrence's warband consisted of six bodyguards, volunteer Indian machine gunners, a body of Abu Tayi's fierce tribesmen, an English officer engineer named Wood, and a general sprinkling from the tribes. From the outset, the expedition was plagued with problems. The Indians were such camel novices that progress was slowed to 35 miles per day, with the typical meal stops customary to the Indian Cavalry Division from whence they had come. Ominously, after setting out, Feisal sent Lawrence a message that Abd el Kader (grandson of the Algerian anti-French hero) – upon whom the party was depending for Yarmuk connections – was a Turkish spy.

To the west of their march, the party could hear the rumbling guns of Allenby's offensive underway at Beersheba. At Azraq Oasis they encamped in the square castle above the palm grove, once the eastern garrison outpost of Rome. Abd el Kadir escaped to report in to his Turkish paymasters but the party decided to continue. As the final leg of the journey was an 80-mile ride, with a tricky demolition, all in the 13 hours of darkness, and a return of 80 miles under Turkish pursuit, only the best six Indians on the best camels and most of the Arabs were taken – a party

of less than 75 with only one Vickers gun.

Dera was passed in the night, the Yarmuk Valley entered, and the party subsections fanned out to their individual tasks. But as Lawrence and his men examined the *Tel el Shehab* bridge, a dropped rifle alerted a Turkish sentry and an exchange of fire became general. The Serahin porters dropped the explosives into the ravine, and the raiders pulled up stakes in scrambling flight.

On the return to Azrak, they cut telegraph wires to the continued tunes of Allenby's guns. Bad luck continued. A bungled train demolition left Lawrence sitting Arab-fashion beside the tracks of kilometre 172 from Damascus while a Turkish troop train passed with menacing looks, but blissfully ignorant of their new lease on life. A second demolition worked, but its impact stunned Lawrence whose Arabs rushed out to save him, losing seven in the process but rescuing their leader. Five bullet holes had deeply grazed his skin. Unfortunately, the target had been a troop train complete with the commander of the Turkish 8th Corps with 400 able-bodied men. After losing half their party in disengaging, discretion's better part of valour aided their run back to Azraq.

Lawrence and Sherif Ali ibn el Hussein and others decided to winter 1917–1918 at Azraq Castle. In this northernmost outpost of Feisal's army they would remain a physical reminder to such Arab leaders as Nuri es Shalaan who cooperated but still sat the neutral fence. November saw the traffic of local chiefs come to hear Feisal's message. Among these was Talal el Hareidhin, a valiant chief who had slain 23 Turks and became an inspiration to Lawrence's prose.

As Allenby's offensive slowed to the rains, so did the castle's local visitors. Azraq braced for the icy cold onset of winter that wrought climactic terror to both Arabian Arab and his desert camel. Fortified by Malory's *Morte d'Arthur*, the *Oxford Book of English Prose*, and the comedies of Aristophanes, Lawrence fared somewhat better.

Inactivity, however, spurred him to a fateful reconnaissance. Travelling incognito, he walked into Dera, the principal town of the Hauran District, and strategic Turkish centre of communications. Here, a Turkish sergeant cornered him and brought him before Nahi Bey, the Governor. It was not the reward price on Lawrence's head the Bey was after – for Lawrence's cover story and accent as a fair-haired Circassian Turkish subject stuck. The Bey was a notorious and deadly sexual pervert and Lawrence had inspired his fancy. What transpired through the night was a series of wretched beatings and tortures interspersed with sexual assaults by the Bey and his guards.

Later that night Lawrence was given a small room and the last guard whispered that a certain door was not kept locked which lead to a dispensary. Through this, Lawrence stole some clothes and a poison against recapture, and climbed out of a rear window. It was poetic justice that during his escape he discovered a hidden road which would later afford his Arabs the best attacking route into Dera.

Managing an escort back to base from a friendly tribe, Lawrence handed the maintenance of the Azrak position over to Sherif Ali and took leave to Aqaba, struggling to heal mind and body.

13

JERUSALEM BY CHRISTMAS

SINCE the opening of Allenby's offensive the EEF had captured 10,000 prisoners and 100 guns (or a third of the enemy's effective rifles and half his artillery). Over 17 days the front had been advanced 50 miles. It was a great victory, but still short of Jerusalem.

Allenby's soldiers were tired, his communications taut, his 20th Corps lay immobilised 50 miles behind his new front, and he possessed no adequate maps of the hill country through which he must advance. Much of the cavalry had ridden 170 miles during his offensive, while carrying a mean weight of 280–294 pounds of man, tack, and equipment. The horses had averaged a drink only every 36 hours while performing under half reduced grain with no bulk ration. Out of the three regiments of the 5th Mounted Brigade a scant 690 troopers remained in the saddle.[1] Fortunately, half the Corps horses were the Australian-bred Walers, a lighter but hardier breed of horse raised in the outback so that it was uniquely suited for the rigours of a tough campaign.

Allenby struggled over a fundamental question: to consolidate his victorious ground or to proceed against the elements to Jerusalem. The War Office had wired a cautionary telegram about advancing beyond his means, and added the frustrating corollary that he might have to give up troops to other theatres in 1918. Two other sources urged caution – the two books Allenby carried and habitually read – the *Bible*, and the *Historical Geography of the Holy Land*. Both disclosed valuable insights into the precepts of military history through the hundreds of years and the hundreds of conquerors Palestine had seen come and go. They warned of the danger to armies entering the Judean Hills, of the restrictions on space and maneuver, of the qualities of local defence and of the opportunities of sudden ambush. As if these prohibitions were not enough to make Allenby rest on his laurels, the seasonal rains were overdue.

Such a resting, however, was not Allenby's way. He loved the bold thrust based on calculated risk as he hated the allowance of an enemy recovery. If he had problems and concerns, so did the Turks. Von Kressenstein's 8th Army had been driven beyond Jaffa and the Auja River, in the coastal area straddling the Philistine Plains on one side and the Plains of Sharon on the other. Fehvzi Pasha's 7th Army had been pushed into the Judean Hills where it sat amidst the rail spur to Jerusalem. Seventh Army's logistics had to be detrained at Nablus, then carried 40 miles overland to Jerusalem, or alternately detrained at Amman and motored 60 miles via the indifferent road through Jericho. Continued buffeting of *Yilderim*'s shallow positions could keep their line destabilised and from hardening. Given determination and a fair measure of luck Jerusalem could yet be wrapped for Christmas.

The big picture in Allenby's thinking was a holding action opposite 8th Army while propelling 7th Army out of the hills and roads leading to Jerusalem. Three arteries were instrumental to the plan; the Nablus–Jerusalem–Hebron–Beersheba (north-south) road over the 3,000-foot high saddlebacked limestone spine of Judea, the Jaffa-Ramle-Qaryet el Inab–Jerusalem (east-west) road, and the even poorer (east-west) Jaffa–Lydda–Beit Liqya–Jerusalem road, which disintegrated eventually into an animal path.

Water in the plains was found at sea-level, and it decreased in salinity north of Gaza until a natural sweetness was attained near Jaffa. Not for nothing did Jaffa's name mean 'beauty' nor its groves produce the famous harvest of oranges. In the hill country, however, occasional springs supplemented by plaster-lined rock cisterns in villages provided the main water access. During the coming rains, of course, the hills were flushed with streams.

▼ Jerusalem as seen from the Mount of Olives, 1917.

Allenby was not long in waiting; 17 November was a day of rest and the advance resumed the next day. Chosen to hold the plain was the ANZAC Mounted Division and the 54th, newly marched up from Gaza. The rest of the Desert Mounted and 21st Corps were operating against 7th Army. The 75th Division was set trudging along the main Jaffa–Jerusalem road with one brigade of the Australian Mounted Division on its right. This group was to force its way northeast of Bireh before Jerusalem, then act as a right pivot for the 52nd and the Yeomanry turning to their left on *Yilderim* GHQ at Nablus. Jerusalem would be isolated and surrendered without a fight. Allenby was under orders not to fight within six miles of the Holy City and von Falkenhayn was under similar orders not to let Jerusalem become a besieged city.

The human material leading 21st Corps advance into Judea was excellent. The 52nd (Lowland) had been honed in action since Romani, while all of the 75th's battalions had served in India or were actual Indian units — including Gurkhas. The excellence was required . . . immediately, the rains began and the night temperatures radically dropped, becoming a challenge for men still in summer khaki.

Experienced in hill country, the 75th successively outmaneuvered the Turkish-held ridges, halting the end of the first day as a rain-storm with black clouds obscured movement. The going of the 52nd was tougher as the road played out to a goat track strewn with boulders that ripped boots and cut the feet of camels. Pack animals slipped in the wet and toppled into ravines. Night halt for them was four hours with no tent or blanket being issued. In the early hours of 18/19 November the Yeomanry crossed in front of the 52nd to guard their left flank. One of its brigades bogged down into a six mile single-file snake which stopped then started in frustration every time a transport beast dropped from exhaustion.

The rains were no more graceful on the plains. Communications arteries choked and disintegrated into quagmires. On the Palestine frontier the Wadi Ghazi flooded and demolished the EEF rail line. Artillery could not move off the main road. By 20 November the operations were in jeopardy as much from the weather as from the Turks.

Allenby and Bulfin were increasingly convinced von Falkenhayn was planning a counterstroke because thus far only rearguards had been encountered. The Yeomanry became stalled against the Zeitun Ridge, then the 52nd, neither being able to reach Bireh and cut the Nablus–Jerusalem road. As the 75th turned off the main Jaffa–Jerusalem road on 21 November to shift northeast on Bireh, the Turks were discovered in a high blocking position at Nabi Samweil.

Nabi Samweil was the burial place of the Prophet Samuel over which lay a crowning mosque, picturesque in silhouette upon sky and mountain. It was the 'key' to Jerusalem, and the place where Richard the Lionheart had halted and turned his face in remorse from the prize of the Third Crusade. That evening, the 75th Division attacked uphill in the failing light and took the summit by midnight. This proved the high water tide of the first gamble for Jerusalem and henceforward the 75th — the last British

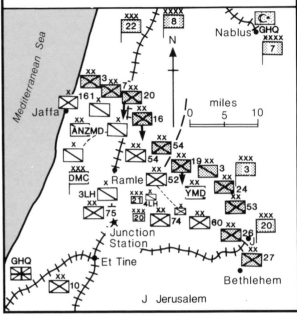

Division formed during the First World War — adapted a heraldic 'key' for their divisional badge.

Meanwhile, in order to assist the assault on Nabi Samweil, the 52nd had made demonstrations while the dismounted Yeomanry attacked — then lost — the Zeitun Ridge. For the next two days the infantry expended themselves on El Jib in a futile effort to extend ground north of Nabi Samweil. Simultaneously, the Turks thrice counterattacked Nabi Samweil, the mosque and summit of which was held by the 3/3rd Gurkhas. As the machine guns in the minaret chattered over the valleys the Turks closed, bayonet to *kukri*, hand bomb exchanged for bomb. Against the last bitter wave the Gurkhas rolled boulders down the slopes as if reliving some primeval siege of cave. Fifty per cent of the Gurkhas, 2/4th Hampshires, and the overall immediate area defensive forces fell casualties, the Gurkhas with only one officer and 16 men unhurt. The scene was grim. Bulfin informed Allenby at his new field GHQ near Junction Station that 21st Corps could not proceed without preparation and reinforcement.

On the EEF left flank Allenby's holding attack in the northern plains of Philistia worked, but received an offensive check. For 18 miles, from the coast to the Shephaleh hills leading into Judea, the front was held by the ANZAC Mounted Division, the 54th, the 7th Mounted Brigade, and the Imperial Camel Brigade. Behind this line, the EEF reshuffled forward in stages. As repair of the Turkish rails progressed, the 60th Division moved up to Junction Station, the Australian Mounted was withdrawn so its transport could be stripped and given to the Yeomanry in the hills, and the 74th (dismounted Yeomanry) was ordered up from Gaza.

Turkish lancers in Arab headdress with goggles.

▶

Tactically, Allenby wished a bridgehead across the Nahr el Auja River. Elements of the New Zealand Mounted Rifle Brigade and the Essex Regiment crossed the 40-foot wide Auja in the shallows where it emptied into the Mediterranean Sea. At first the plan went well enough but the invaders were too weak to establish any bridgehead of breadth. The maneuver was premature and catalised a stiff riposte from Turkish 3rd and 7th Divisions.

The weather and delaying set backs on both flanks thus caused Allenby to eye the calender with concern. Then, in the closing November days, von Falkenhayn conspired to do his worst.

The Yilderim Counteroffensive

Von Falkenhayn had relocated his headquarters from Jerusalem rearward to Nablus so that his staff might be free from the front line anxiety previously suffered by von Kressenstein's staff at Huj. His orders were for 8th Army to hold the plains as 7th Army delayed the EEF push on Jerusalem. Von Falkenhayn appointed Ali Faud commander of 20th Corps, coming to defend the environs of the Holy City. Ali Faud, however, seemed to have other ideas, protesting that in a prophetic dream he saw himself marked by posterity as the man who lost Jerusalem. To sweeten his distress, von Falkenhayn ordered him to his post, and raised him in rank to major-general which in Turkey bore the additional accolade of 'pasha'.

Von Falkenhayn considered the fate of Jerusalem a question of time. Allenby had seriously upset his timetable for the arrival of the Yilderim divisions. The 1st and 20th Divisions and the Caucasian Cavalry Brigade were nearing

his front and the Asien Korps was in transit south from Aleppo. Across the Jordan the 150th Regiment and 7th Cavalry Regiment were being mustered for transfer to his command. If enough time were purchased, Allenby could be stopped.

Von Falkenhayn was not a general to wait for his time; he determined to create it. Regular forces normally become strung out in hill operations, and the EEF made no exception to the rule. A five-mile gap emerged between the EEF units in the Shephaleh Hills and those in the Judean Range. Behind this gap was the communication and supply of the Yeomanry Mounted Division, now a weary body of men with no reserves. Von Falkenhayn knew that effective penetration at this juncture could abort the Jerusalem enterprise.

On 27 November he thrust the crack 19th (Anatolian) Division into this gap. Part of the 19th crashed into Nabi Samweil with no effect, but a wedge was driven into the Yeomanry. A farce ensued the next dawn as the 7th Mounted Brigade moved up to plug the gap, and passed under the Turkish rifles on the ridge, neither side cognisant of the of the other. At last, as tea was up, someone on the Turkish side looked down and machine guns began tearing into the Yeomanry horses. It was a hasty breakfast.

For 36 hours the Lincolnshire Yeomanry, Sherwood Foresters, and South Nottinghamshire Hussars held the line, flanked by their sister Yeomanry brigades until the 4th Light Horse Brigade marched up in relief. At one critically dangerous point the Turks had only been opposed by one armoured car, personally sent up by General Chauvel. Late on the afternoon of 28 November the retirement of the 22nd Yeomanry Brigade was aided by a mysterious

▲ 'The New Crusader's first sight of Jerusalem'. Cartoon by Raemaeker.

phenomenon. As the sun had once 'stood still' in the Biblical Vale of Ajalon, so it did again that night in the same location. The setting sun caused a reddish glow throughout the Turkish positions while rendering a peaceful Yeomanry retreat through the shadows on the hillsides of the rising moon. All through the 'false day' the brigade maintained contact via heliograph.

The *Yilderim* counterattack had meant to give double injury by punching in the plains south along the railway on Ramle. The attack of the 16th and 20th Turkish divisions was aimed to hit the western elements of the 54th near Wilhelmina, one of the German civilian colonies in Palestine. On 27 November the Northamptonshires fought a brisk engagement, halting 2,000 Turks coming in at dusk with the bayonet over open ground. The bulk of the 20th Division had had a long approach march so that its supporting attack ended striking *en l'air*.

The highwater mark of *Yilderim*'s ploy had passed. Inferior in numbers overall, their moment of local superiority along selected axes of attack was expended. EEF reserves rapidly reinforced all threatened sectors. Fighting degenerated over the next week into less critical, if bloody, actions.

On 1 December Second Lieutenant S. Boughy was awarded a posthumous Victoria Cross for action during a Turkish night raid against the Royal Scots Fusiliers. Incensed over loss of sleep, Boughy surged ahead of his men hurling bombs and taking 25 prisoners. Before being mortally wounded Boughy was heard to yell:

'They mairched us a hunder miles! (Tak' that, ya . . .!)
An' we've been in five fechts! (Anither yin, ya . . .!)
And they said we wur relieved! (Tak' that, ya . . .!)
And we're oot oor beds anither nicht! (Swalla that, ya . . .!).'[2]

The same morning and locale also witnessed the death of an elite Turkish formation – the Storm Battalion of the 19th (Anatolian) Division. Equipped with new 1917 Mausers and steel pattern helmets, the 600-man unit drove too far into EEF lines and their gallantry wrought their undoing. The machine guns of the 3rd Light Horse Brigade so barred their retreat that at dawn only 112 were alive to surrender. The complete 'disappearance' of this fine unit was to puzzle *Yilderim* for some time.

End Run

A consequence of von Falkenhayn's probing 'storm troop' tactics was an unfortunate high wastage among his remaining dependable men. Allenby had meanwhile relieved his 52nd (Lowland) Division with the 10th (Irish). Three fresh divisions of Chetwode's 20th Corps had been introduced into the Judean Hills to relieve Bulfin's stretched 21st Corps, which assumed its primary position west in the plains. The Australian Mounted Division slotted into the juncture of both Corps in the foothills.

With his force back together after the pursuit through Philistia, Allenby decided to renew his offensive. The first try for Jerusalem had been deprived of artillery owing to weather and the need of off-road movement. Conversely, the Turks had been able to defy the rains and reinforce most parts of their line because of their control of the north-south Nablus to Jerusalem road. Bulfin had attempted to pivot left, but Chetwode's 20th Corps intended to reverse this strategy by pivoting right and thereby sweep the western outskirts of Jerusalem and overlap the Nablus road to the north.

Chetwode's offensive involved a punching blow by the 60th and 74th Divisions up the Jaffa–Jerusalem road, backed by maximum artillery support, while the 53rd moved north up the Hebron road to protect the right flank and to envelop Jerusalem on the east. The 20th Corps Cavalry Regiment (Worcestershire Yeomanry) and 10th Light Horse were picked to liaise between the 60th and the 53rd.

The selection of the main good road as the axis of advance allowed participation of the divisional artilleries with an additional three mountain batteries, three 6-inch howitzer batteries, and one-and-a-half batteries of 60 pounders. And since by 5 December the Turkish railway had been repaired as far as Ramle, supply trains could for the first time unload directly onto the Jaffa–Jerusalem road.

Despite the railway, camel and lorry columns were the backbone of the offensive logistics. Any day a resumption of the rains was expected so that with the troop and supply traffic the thinly metalled Turkish roads took a hefty battering. The cold and wet was a severe handicap for the camels . . . time and again the burdened beasts were seen to stumble, legs splayed out so that limbs cracked and split from the bodies. A good measure of assistance was given by the 2,000 Egyptian donkeys of the first company of the 'Donkey Corps', which administrative foresight had begun after the fall of Beersheba.

Twentieth Corps inched forward into positions from 4–6 December, preparing for the opening moves against the

15,500 men of 7th Army. Rainfall became constant on 7 December, continuing into the early morning hours. At 0200 hours, protected by night and cloaked in mist, the 60th and 74th Divisions moved south from Nabi Samweil. Allenby again demonstrated the superiority of a 'bolt from the blue' over a long preparatory bombardment. The Turks had shown a sluggishness in the dark, and that early morning it was no exception as the EEF, with complete surprise, penetrated four-and-a-half miles of the Turkish front trench-line. Part of the 74th, with the steepest climb, received Turkish artillery fire, but just before dawn of 8 December the 60th signalled the success of the first phase with red flares.

At dawn the main attack commenced under the blanket of rain and mist. The Turkish positions had been constructed in 1916 and developed over the next year to project three tiers of fire. Chiseled out of hillsides they should have made dangerous going; the succession of retreats, however, and the burning of the last dependable reserves had shaken 7th Army morale. Nevertheless, the advance in face of the elements was laborious. The 74th secured the Beit Iksa Ridge but became stalled against the lower slopes of Nabi Samweil. The 60th continued up the Jaffa road toward the Jerusalem suburbs, but its right flank became exposed as

the 53rd Division had not yet joined from the south. That afternoon the pivot over the Nablus road had to be postponed till the anticipated juncture.

'Motts' Detachment', consisting of two cavalry regiments and the 53rd, had been delayed along the Hebron road by fog and had not yet converged on Bethlehem to the south of Jerusalem. Twentieth Corps was thus ordered to consolidate and await a further coordinated advance the next day. But at dawn of 9 December it was discovered that the Turks had thrown in a surprise of their own. During the night they had pulled up stakes and were everywhere in retreat. Jerusalem was an open city.

Occupation

It was von Falkenhayn's bitter irony that his 3rd Corps — having irresolutely fought at Beersheba, resolutely defended the Nablus road while his 20th Corps — specifically picked over 3rd Corps for the defence of Jerusalem, should melt away after preliminary engagements. True to his own prophecy, Ali Faud became marked by history as the man to surrender 400 years of Ottoman rule in the Holy City, while Allenby inscribed his name upon the honour role of

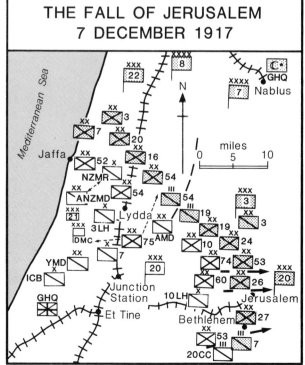

◀ Colours and decorated guards of a crack Turkish (Anatolian) Regiment. The new green khaki cloth uniform was adopted shortly after the 1908 Revolution and was of traditional European cut with puttees and boots. The grey service cap was an unusual creative concoction of German helmet and Turkish turban, intended to carry a religious and traditional purpose in conjunction with modern practicality. It was nicknamed the 'enverieh' in honour of its designer, Enver Pasha, who purportedly made a fortune from its patent.

THE FALL OF JERUSALEM 7 DECEMBER 1917

Jerusalem's 34 conquerors alongside such redoubtables as David, Nebuchadnezzer, Alexander, Antiochus the Great, Judas Maccabeus, Pompey, Herod, Titus, Omar, Godfrey de Bouillon, and Saladin.

But the symbolic surrender was not as easy as might be seemed. The Turkish Mayor spent most of his morning simply trying to find someone to whom to hand over the keys of the city. His first appeal was to two mess cooks of the 2/20th London who – having been lost in the night – blundered into Jerusalem in search of water. Flattered, but feeling unequal to the honour, the cooks declined. The Mayor's next try was to Sergeants F. G. Harcomb and J. Sedgewick of the 2/19th London . . . then to two officers of 60th Division artillery . . . then to Lieutenant-Colonel Bayley of the 303rd Brigade, RFA . . . whereupon Bayley contacted Brigadier Watson of the 180th Brigade . . . who contacted Lieutenant-General Chetwode . . . who sent Major-General Shea of 60th Division to accept the surrender . . . on behalf of General Allenby. Confused, but undaunted, the occupation continued.

Sir Edmund Allenby made his official entry into Jerusalem via the Jaffa Gate at high noon on 11 December. Reflecting on the city's emotive sway to the Christian, Jewish and Moslem religions, Allenby entered at the head of his procession, humbly, on foot. Representatives of all the EEF and Allied nationalities which could be present were so present. Behind Allenby marched Major-General L. J. Bols, his Chief of Staff, Brigadier G. P. Dawnay, his Deputy Chief of Staff, *Monsieur* Picot, the French High Commissioner, the commanders of the French and Italian contingents, his Chief Political Officer, Brigadier Clayton, and Major T. E. Lawrence

Above left: The Kaiser and Sultan Mohammed V being cast out as lepers from Jerusalem. Cartoon by Raemaeker.

Left: 'The Surrender of Jerusalem, 9th December 1917. Sergeants Harcombe (right) and Sedgwick (left) of the 1/19th Londons, 60th Division, with the Mayor and White Flag Party on the Lifta–Jerusalem Road, shortly before 9 am.'

▶

General Sir Edmund H. H. Allenby's official triumphal entry through the Jaffa Gate into Jerusalem, 11 December, 1917. With the right of a conqueror, Allenby chose, as a gesture of humility and out of respect for the religions to which the Holy City was sacred, to enter Jerusalem on foot. For this act, the Arabs called him 'The Pilgrim'. In Arabic *Alla-nebi* means 'The Prophet of God' Read backwards, the name implies 'Servant of Allah'.* The Turkish soldiers inferred from Allenby's of Arabia — recently from the Yarmuk Valley raid who had come in to report on the Arab Revolt. In honour of the Holy City no flags were flown.

Anticipating the fall of Jerusalem, H.M. Government had forwarded the text of Allenby's victory proclamation to be read in English, Arabic, Hebrew, French, Italian, Greek, and Russian.[3]

'To the inhabitants of Jerusalem the Blessed and the people dwelling in its vicinity.

'The defeat inflicted upon the Turks by the troops under my command has resulted in the occupation of your city by my forces. I therefore here and now proclaim it to be under martial law, under which form of administration it will remain so long as military considerations make it necessary.

'However, lest any of you should be alarmed by reason of your experience at the hands of the enemy who has retired, I hereby inform you that it is my desire that every person should pursue his lawful business without fear of interruption. Furthermore, since your city is regarded with affection by adherents of three of the great religions of mankind, and its soil has been consecrated by the prayers and pilgrimages of multitudes of devout people of these three religions for many centuries, therefore do I make known to you that every sacred building, monument, Holy spot, shrine, traditional site, endowment, pious bequest, or customary place of prayer, of whatsoever form of the three religions, will be maintained and protected according to the existing customs and beliefs of those to whose faiths they are sacred.'

Allenby had tactfully dodged sensationalist press references to a 'crusade'. If a crusade, it was the 'Last Crusade —

accomplished with the assistance of thousands of Moslem soldiers and labourers. With similar acumen, Sir Mark Sykes (H.M. Government's Political Representative) manipulated the posting of Moslem guards at the Dome of the Rock. When Caliph Omar captured Jerusalem from the Byzantines in AD 637 he had established the 'Wakf', or hereditary custodianship, which symbolically preserved Christian rights.[4] Once again, as a gesture of religious tolerance and solidarity, this tradition was returned.

The Palestine Campaign in autumn, 1917, dealt the restoration of Turkey a critical blow. The vaunted joint German–Turkish *Yilderim* scheme was kicked into disarray. Many of von Falkenhayn's units were still struggling to reach the front; those that had had been disrupted or had received heavy losses. Any danger to British forces in Mesopotamia had been removed and key Palestinian areas lost. With Mecca, Baghdad, and Jerusalem in enemy hands and Medina under siege, Turkey was forfeiting both her religious appeal to and her political grip on the Arab World.

As Allenby summarised in his 15 December special order:

'In forty days many strong Turkish positions have been captured, and the Force has advanced some sixty miles on a front of thirty miles.

'The enemy had been heavily defeated, only the nature of the country saving his forces from complete destruction. Over twelve thousand prisoners and more than one hundred guns had been taken, and the Turkish casualties for the period were approximately 25,000, almost half as many again as the British, which were about 18,000. Jerusalem had been captured without damage to a single sacred building.'[5]

name that the EEF was commanded by a larger than life man known as 'Allah Bey'.† Assisting these mystical interpretations was the EEF pipeline which had reached Gaza and Beersheba, for as the prophecy ran — 'when the waters of the Nile come to Palestine, Jerusalem will be retaken from the Turks.'‡

*Hogue, *The Cameliers*, p. 202
†Inchbald, *Camels and Others*, p. 79
‡Wavell, *The Palestine Campaigns*, p. 62

For the Allies, the news was an opportune switch from the bleak reversals of 1917. America had entered the war, but it was still too soon for her vast legions to muster and sail to Europe. Allied Russia had collapsed under the Bolshevik Revolution and had fallen into the throes of bitter civil war, Allied Italy had suffered a great reverse at Caporetto and the Germans had recently begun a counter-offensive at Cambrai. Only the news from Palestine was encouraging. The Prime Minister had his Christmas gift for the British and Allied peoples.

Yilderim Strikes Back

The days during and directly after the occupation were spent by 20th Corps cleaning up snipers and consolidating the cordon around Jerusalem. The RFC dropped 100 bombs on 7th Army columns north along the Nablus road and east toward Jericho, scoring 20 direct hits. Twenty-First Corps had meanwhile planned a bridging and rafting penetration of the Auja River with three brigades at selected points where Turkish vigilance seemed slack. Again, surprise over bombardment was chosen, and again, the technique paid off, the 52nd Division landing virtually unopposed. By 22 December 21st Corps had expanded a bridgehead eight miles north of Jaffa's famous orange groves.

Given the confusion of 7th Army, Allenby ordered 20th Corps to develop the Jerusalem enclave northward. Down-

pours, however, caused the postponement of the planned advance and created six inches of mud on the 'roads'. There was little Christmas cheer for the men in the soaking fields.

During these days, Turkish prisoners, secret agents, and wireless messages deciphered from the Huj codebook disclosed *Yilderim* was plotting a counter offensive for Jerusalem. Always a proponent of maneuver, von Falkenhayn was hoping to capitalise on several conditions. He reasoned that 7th Army's right flank would be secure because of the difficult lie of the land and that Chetwode's 20th Corps would be disorganised. In line from its right to left, 7th Army had the 3rd Cavalry, the 1st, 24th, 19th, 53rd, 26th divisions, then the 7th Cavalry Regiment (from 3rd

Above: Personnel of No. 113 Squadron with an RE 8 aircraft.

Left: Sketch from the *Illustrated London News*. The RFC bombed Turkish 7th Army elements retreating from Jerusalem north up the Nablus road.

Cavalry Division). The 1st Division and the strong 61st Regiment were newly arrived, but the *Asien Korps* and many more units were still in transit. In total, the ration strength of 7th Army was less than 30,000 with a combat strength of less than 20,000.

As Chetwode opposed von Falkenhayn with 33,000 rifles, the offensive was a desperate adventure. Chetwode used his 53rd and 60th Divisions to hold 7th Army's attack in front of Jerusalem even as his left wing (74th and 10th Divisions) commenced the British advance. Soon after midnight on 27 December, the first waves of Turkish infantry from the gallant 19th charged, hurling hand bombs under the illuminating red glow of British flares descending

weeks nor their eternal gratitude owed to the veterinary services.

The largest casualty of autumn, 1917 was *Yilderim's* own plan for the regeneration of Turkey. For too long indecision had been the handmaiden of disaster. Quarrels within the Turkish High Command first halted the Baghdad scheme, then paralised *Yilderim* for precious summer weeks, delaying expeditious movement to Palestine. Allenby's first offensive option ensured him crushing local superiority followed with an impressive cavalry pursuit. With further daring against an increasingly demoralised and hustled enemy, Allenby had been able to breach the defensible Judean Hills and capture Jerusalem before the seasonal

in the early morning dank. The 60th's divisional artillery blasted flashes of light into the coming waves as the Turkish infantry was mowed down by small arms at close quarters. Turkish artillery rumbled in return as the infantry came again at 0330 hours, concentrating against Tel el Ful and the Khadase Ridge, which dominated the surrounding country down to Jerusalem. At 0530 hours, and later in the early afternoon, further attacks were beaten off, the Turks having assaulted with courage but with little tactical skill.

Chetwode's left flank had hit the Turkish 1st Division hard, bowing them back-two-and-a-half miles deep over a front of six miles. On 28 December the entire 20th Corps went over to the offensive, the Turks resisting stubbornly and causing substantial damage from concealed machine gun nests. In two days 7th Army had fallen back in a wide arc from Jerusalem. *Yilderim's* offensive had cost 1,558 casualties for an infliction of 1,360. From 31 October the campaigns had accrued 21,000 EEF casualties for over 28,000 of *Yilderim*.

The camelry had suffered most of all. Stricken with a virulent mange, many had wound cavities in their flesh the size of cricket balls. In order to save part of the Imperial Camel Brigade, which was withdrawn in quarantine near the Mediterranean, only the worst cases were saddled and used to collapse. To their horror, the camel troopers discovered the mange was catching. Few forgot the next

▲ Turkish (Anatolian) infantry 'go over the top' of a shallow trench in Palestine.

rains could put paid to his operations. What reinforcements did reach *Yilderim* in the interim were mere replacements for units chewed up by Allenby's offensive. The redoubtable von Falkenhayn never regained equilibrium.

Yilderim had also failed on a more subtle level. After joint German–Turkish conception, the project rapidly became German led. The senior staff was almost entirely German, and composed of officers who, while exceptionally qualified, brought with them experiences from other inapplicable theatres. As most were direct importations without local acclimitisation and were deprived of necessary joint Turkish leadership, matters at all levels quickly went awry.

Orders were not necessarily carried out. *If* carried out, the results were often different, indeed, *indifferent*. Conversely, the Turks distrusted German time schedules and efficiency. Supply was an ever irritating controversy. Turkish central stores acquiesced in all the Germans asked, for 'the Turk considered a direct refusal impolite; but the keeping of the promise was a different matter.'[6] Passive Turkish resistance permeated like grains of sand all cogs of the German war machine. As if prophetic, even as *Yilderim* inched out of Constantinople bound for Palestine early that September, British secret agents blew up its main supply dump at Haider Pasha, just outside the capital itself!

The cavalryman's campaign: Above, Turkish lancers at the charge, Palestine. Below: 'C' Squadron, 12th Australian Light Horse, Syria.

PART 4
THE LAST CRUSADE
January to November 1918

'So fierce was his onset this day that the Turks very soon all
turned off from his irresistible attack, and left a free passage
to our army. Thus at last, despite their wounds, our men
reached the Standard, the ranks were formed again and the
host proceeded to Arsuf, outside which town it pitched its
tents.'

– King Richard I, the Lionheart,
1 September 1191 in *Itinerarium Regis Ricaldi*

14

THE DEAD SEA CAMPAIGN

IN December, 1917 Allenby transmitted his appreciation of current and future events to the Imperial General Staff. Robertson attached his own considerations and sent the 1918 Palestine assessments to the War Cabinet. On 21 January, 1918, the military representatives to the Supreme War Council at Versailles established the foundation of Allenby's future campaigns in Joint Note 12. The Note was endorsed by Sir Henry Wilson (Britain), M. Weygand (France), and L. Cadorna (Italy). In brief, the representatives did not believe either the Allies or the Central Powers could force a decision on the Western Front in 1918. In 1919 America's legions would be in place in France and the Allies could expect a victorious offensive if not the end of the war.

The question was what could be achieved in 1918. Only against Turkey in the Palestine–Arabian theatre did prospects appear bright. If Turkey were eliminated, the opening of the Dardanelles would allow supplies to flow to remaining Allied friends in Russia and Rumania. Pressure on the Turks would either collapse Germany's southern ally, or force Germany into stepping-up aid, in either case having a direct impact on Germany and the Western Front.[1]

In Britain, this appreciation provoked another 'Easterner' versus 'Westerner' debate, with Lloyd-George and Wilson on the 'Easterner' floor and Robertson and Haig on the 'Westerner' floor. The common hall to both these floors was that the ultimate security of the Western Front was paramount . . . contention lay in the design and distribution of the house furnishings. Finally, the controversy settled to the Prime Minister's satisfaction and General Smuts was sent to Palestine in early February to acquaint General Allenby with the War Cabinet's proposals.

Including attached Germans and Austrians, the General Staff calculated the total Turkish force at some 250–300,000 men. Theoretically, a maximum of 180,000 might be allotted to Palestine, but, recognising problems of communications and logistics, probably only 80–100,000 would be seen. In their 11 divisions sitting on the Jaffa–Jerusalem line, the Turks had 39,000 and this could be augmented by two divisions south of Damascus, three near Aleppo, one from the Hejaz, and four from Turkey and Rumania. A further 15–20,000 were shut up in Medina.

Allenby's EEF comprised 112,000 combatants in seven infantry and three cavalry divisions, and Smuts brought news the War Cabinet intended to reinforce Palestine with three infantry divisions from Mesopotamia and at least one Indian cavalry division from France. The need for railway materials and technicians was understood along with continual local air superiority, which confers a unique advantage on the possessor in less 'civilised' regions where 'communications are limited, concealment difficult and anti-aircraft arrangements defective.' And also the necessity of a 'definite, coordinated and vigorous political offensive both

▲ General Sir William Robertson was Murray's successor as Chief of the Imperial General Staff in January, 1916. As a 'Westerner' Robertson opposed Lloyd-George's increasing commitment to the Eastern theatre.

among the non-Turkish races of the Ottoman Empire and among the Turks themselves. And, finally, that 'the Allies should undertake a decisive offensive against Turkey with a view to the annihilation of the Turkish armies and the collapse of Turkish resistance.'[2]

Unlike some senior commanders, Allenby never promised more than he could deliver, and he usually delivered more than he would promise. Nor could political pressure jog him into conclusions with insufficient troops or unprepared conditions. Such had been Murray's mistake. Allenby knew a period of consolidation was in order.

The broad gauge rail was constructed to Allenby's GHQ at Bir Salem just southwest of Ramle. The Sinai railway had been doubled to El Arish, and by 28 January the captured Turkish rail was put in working order from Junction Station to Jerusalem. The Director-General of military railways called for '220 miles of track, 35 locomotives, 1,000 wagons, and 1,000 additional railway personnel.'[3] The Force in Egypt concept was resurrected for the practical reason the bulk of the EEF was too far east from Egypt for any other solution. Brigadier H. D. Watson was promoted to head the Force in Egypt while two other Brigadiers were delegated the sub-commands of the 'Delta and Western Force' (including the Southern Canal Section) and the 'Alexandria District.'

Egypt itself had long been indifferent to the military outcome in the Middle East; she had no natural reason to desire the occupation of either Turkey or Britain. By 1918, the drain of material for the British war and the daily effects of occupation caused the stirrings of unrest which, in 1919, exploded into civil insurrection. Sir Reginald Wingate put his immense reputation and experience to work to keep the populace pacific at least until conclusions could forced with the Turks. Sir Ronald Storrs undertook a similar responsibility in Jerusalem which was always a fulcrum of religious strife.

Allenby chose four military governors to preside with martial law over the districts of Majdal, Jaffa, Beersheba, and Jerusalem. Brigadier-General Clayton acted as overall administrator until Major-General Sir A. W. Money took charge in April. A market system was built coincident with reopened school and postal functions. Agriculture was rehabilitated by importation of livestock and seed grains with a deferred payment option, and later a loan of £500,000 sterling. Egyptian currency was introduced and Palestinian goods were sent south on returning military trains. Much of the administrative groundwork of 1918 survived for the next ten years.

The Lions in Winter

After the official entry into Jerusalem, Lawrence was at Allenby's GHQ to discuss future campaign collusion. Allenby had not completely formulated the details of his 1918 campaigns but he desired a spring advance east into Jericho, a crossing of the Jordan River Valley, and a clearance of the enemy from the northern shores of the Dead Sea. Lawrence was asked to obtain Feisal's consent for an Arab extension through the highlands north of Aqaba to Shobek, Tafila and Kerak, three small towns spaced in a row at intervals running north to the southern shore of the Dead Sea. Successful deployment would terminate grain and wood shipments valuable to the Turks, and be preparatory to a junction of the EEF with the Arab Northern Army northeast of the Dead Sea at Madeba. If these plans worked, Jericho would supersede Aqaba as the new Arab logistical base and receive the daily 50 tons of supplies. Brigadier Clayton reported on the contributions the Arab Revolt had made to date for the Allied effort. In manpower the revolt was tying down 23,000 Turks of the 1st and 2nd Composite Forces and the Hejaz Expeditionary Force. Racially, they were 80–90 per cent of Anatolian stock of the most reliable Turkish material. In terms of casualties, illness and prisoners the rebellion had already cost the Turks the equivalent of a full British division. These losses were a running sore resulting in steady replacements which would otherwise have appeared against the EEF. Economically, the rail ruptures, destruction of bridges, engines, and rolling stock, and the tribal threatening of the Hauran's wood and corn belt

▲ Cairo's oldest fortress was the Citadel, home of the Egyptian Army's ordnance workshops. The Citadel cleaned and repaired small arms, machine guns, and equipment for the EEF.

▲ Arab soldier sporting Turkish belt equipment and a military tunic underneath his frock. Note unusual collar insignia.

A mule-mounted Vickers machine gun section near Aqaba. Most of the mule-mounted 'regulars' in British uniform and Arab headdress were lead by the fiery Maulud. ◀

became such a burden that materials and manpower resources were strained to the limit. The mere extension from Aqaba to the Wadi Musa at Petra had severed the pro-Turkish Sinai Bedouin from their mentors, and promoted dissension within the Syrian tribes astride the Turkish lines of communications.[4]

By Christmas, Lawrence had returned to Aqaba in session with Colonel Joyce. The Arab regulars had been trained and reinforced to 3,000 and under the astute and fervid leadership of Maulud, had pushed the Turks back to Abu el Lissan, and were harrying the 1st Composite Force north of Maan. On 7 January 1918 he boldly cut up a Turkish battalion and pushed the Composite Force to within three miles of their Maan defences.

South of Maan, Arab raiding parties independently and with British advisors were falling upon Turkish assets. The Armoured Car Section's new home was at Guweira where it had moved up the line from Aqaba after engineers had completed the road through the Wadi Itm. The eight cars consisted of six Talbots, two of which carried ten-pounder guns, and two Rolls Royce tenders. Joyce and Lawrence took the cars on reconnaissance toward Mudauwara Station, ripping across the mud flats at 60 miles per hour. An exchange of fire at the station failed to dislodge the garrison but showed that at the selected moment the station and Hajaz Railway in this quadrant could be captured in one day out from Guweira. Medina could be irrevocably isolated at will.

The historian Liddell Hart deemed Lawrence a generation ahead of his time in the perceptive use of fire mobility and armoured cars. Lawrence knew that Britain had the industrial capacity to churn out masses of armoured cars with which he could dominate Arabia–Syria–Palestine. Cars were a deadly scourge to infantry caught indefensibly in the open. With a few more armoured car sections he believed he could have quarantined the Turks into huddled pockets. To some extent, Lawrence compensated with horses, camels, and light machine guns. He considered one Lewis or Hotchkiss light machine gun per two mounted men as the ideal, and kitted out his bodyguard accordingly. 'He exploited the mobile possibilities of the light machine-gun to a greater extent than any other leader, or in any other army. In his next campaign he introduced the probing attack by light automatic 'fingers' – two months before the Germans pierced the British front in France with the aid of similar but less economic "infiltration" tactics. In his way of using machine-guns with crews of only two men and mounted on camels – they were even fired from the saddle occasionally – he foreshadowed that post-war development, the mechanized machine-gun carrier.'[5]

The formation of a substantial bodyguard of hüscarles, variously totalling 40–100 troopers, had been undertaken in response to the governor's brutality in Dera and the German–Turkish fixation of a £50,000 sterling reward 'dead or alive' on Lawrence's head. Basic training consisted of leaping onto the saddle of a trotting camel while holding a rifle in one hand. It took Lawrence's fancy to take on desperate characters as well as renowned fighters of which Abdullah – one of his two officers – set a good example by his substantiated boast that he had served all of the great desert princes and had been imprisoned by each of them in turn.

Competition to join *Sidi* (Lord) Lawrence's band was high, for news of the everpresent adventures, hard riding, and attendant booty travelled fast in a society respecting such virtues in manhood. To whet incentive, Lawrence offered a higher salary than in other Arab units and an allowance for clothes. Lawrence knew psychology and modern methods of advertising: invariably his bodyguard caparisoned themselves in the most colourful vestments of every rainbow hue. Gaily, his buccaneers used khol around their eyes while their hair hung in greased and perfumed ringlets – their swagger was known even to Cairo and in British circles they were nicknamed the '40 Thieves'.

This was not vanity or cheap gimmickry but a practical assessment of local conditions. In Lawrence's own words: 'In the desert I shaved regularly. My burnt-red face, clean-shaven and startling with my blue eyes against white headcloth and robes, became notorious in the desert. Tribesmen or peasants who had never set eyes on me before would instantly know me, by the report. So my Arab "disguise" was actually an advertisement. It gave me away instantly, as myself, to all the desert: and to be instantly known was safety in ninety-nine cases out of the hundred.'[6]

In Arabia, a great person, as in feudal times, marched with his own entourage of retainers; Lawrence's were not only among the best, but were certainly the best armed, for collectively, their firepower equalled that of a battalion. The '40 Thieves' were 'pan-Arab' in outlook, with no more than two accepted from any one tribe. This assured their highest loyalty was to Lawrence, if not to the Arab movement as a whole, and reduced undue tribal influence. It also gave Lawrence potential spies and influence in almost any Arab camp. Always either behind the lines or galloping with their master on a daring exploit, the bodyguard earned their pay and their right of singing, jesting unruliness for which they were infamous. Sixty died in the service, proportionately, by far, the highest casualty rate in the Arab Northern Army.

Tafila

Sherif Nasir opened the Dead Sea campaign by descending onto the Maan Plateau and working north to Jurf Station which he captured after a brilliant maneuver and charge. It was a good opening: for three days the Bedouin feasted on seven rail trucks of delicacies intended for the palate of Turkish officers at Medina. Included in the capture was the entire tobacco shipment. Through spies, Feisal soon learned that the Medina garrison was in such a plight over their nicotine-less fortune that (being himself a confirmed smoker) he took pity and with chivalric *beau geste* sent cheap cigarettes to them through the siege lines!

Jurf Station was poised east of Shobek and Tafila. Its fall was the signal for Sherif Abd el Mayin's warband to set out across the spine of hills from Petra through the forests to

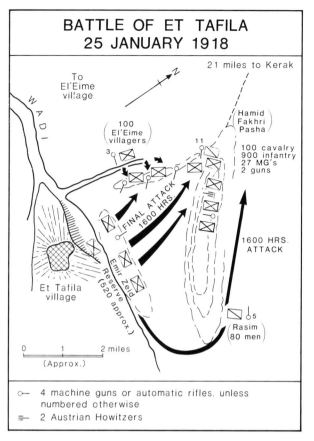

BATTLE OF ET TAFILA 25 JANUARY 1918

21 miles to Kerak

To El'Eime village

100 El'Eime villagers

100 El'Eime villagers

Hamid Fakhri Pasha

100 cavalry 900 infantry 27 MG's 2 guns

FINAL ATTACK 1600 HRS

Emir Zeid (Reserve 520 approx.)

Et Tafila village

1600 HRS. ATTACK

Rasim (80 men)

0   1   2 miles
(Approx.)

o—   4 machine guns or automatic rifles, unless numbered otherwise

≡—   2 Austrian Howitzers

Shobek. The highland forests hung heavy with ice and hoarfrost. For the Arabian Arab the cold was an unaccustomed challenge; even the camels trod hesitatingly through the uncertain elements and plucked at the fallen snow with anguished curiosity. Surprised, the tiny Turkish garrison and the old Crusader castle of Monreale surrendered to the Arabs.

The original plan for Tafila had involved three converging groups from the west, south, and east. Before Abd el Mayin or Mastur with his Motalga horse could arrive, however, Sherif Nasir entered the outskirts of Tafila on 16 January. The Turks were only 180 men, but were supported by a belligerent peasant clan which was by circumstance tributary to the Abu Tayi Howeitat. Enraged at such a chilly reception from his thralls, Auda Abu Tayi rode up in full view of the village shouting convincingly, if not endearingly – 'Dogs, do you not know Auda?' Whereupon the Turkish governor and his men suddenly found themselves on the unpleasant ends of their rifles.

Feisal had delegated technical authority for the Dead Sea Campaign to his younger half-brother, the Amir Zeid. Zeid's competent advisor was Jafaar Pasha, but, unfortunately, the food situation in the highlands prevented Jafaar's regular Arab forces from traversing north of Petra. The inexperienced Zeid was unable to prevent feuds between the Motalga horse and Auda's clan. Because the abu Tayi were locally only half the Motalga strength, Zeid, perhaps foolishly, paid off Auda's men and temporarily dismissed them. Then he set about with lavish display of gold, organising the Tafila defences. Before he had finished, the Turks hit with lightening surprise.

Hamid Fakhri Pasha had organised three battalions of a total 900 men of the 48th Division, 100 cavalry, two mountain howitzers, and 27 machine guns south of Amman, and had advanced to Kerak. There he collected transport and the cadres of a new civil administration he intended to re-establish in Tafila. Setting out from Kerak on 23 January, the expedition ambushed the Arab piquet in the Wadi Hesa the next day. The Wadi was the last obstacle between Kerak and Tafila.

Lawrence was incredulous at this Turkish diversion of any assets away from Allenby's front, and more, for an obscure mountain village. It was obviously a punitive expedition to reassert authority, and an indication of Turkish sensitivity to being rolled back in this economically important district. From their very speed Lawrence divined this was a small regular column unsupported by immediate reinforcements. He decided to give the Turks the conventional battle they sought, albeit on his own terms.

Tactfully, Lawrence managed to sidestep the less able plans of Zeid and Jafaar and assert area control. After collaboration with the Arabs, the Tafila villagers were terrified of a Turkish return. Hastily, Lawrence sent them two machine guns so that with the Motalga horse they threw the advanced Turkish cavalry back two miles across a plateau to a ridge of hills, through which the main Turkish column was deploying off the track from Kerak. In effect, this end was the northern tip of a triangular plateau. At the base, or southern end of this natural triangle, Lawrence gathered the disparate forces of his central reserve. The reserve was also his central firing line, set on a 60-foot ridge in front of the wadi and Tafila village. The northern sides of the triangle were low ridges over which the Turks were laterally deploying from their debouchment point off the Kerak track.

After a brisk engagement, the Turks ousted the villagers and Motalga off the western ridge who quickly fell back on the central reserve which had now accumulated nearly 520 men. From this, Lawrence detached Rasim with 80 mounted men to work around the Turkish left on the eastern ridge. Meanwhile, 100 villagers from El Eime with three machine guns crawled toward the rear of the Turkish-held western ridge.

The Turks soon found their ridge positions inhospitable. Despite a two-fold machine gun superiority and an advantage of ten to seven in men, the Arab central reserve had their range and was laying down a carpet of fire which richochetted terribly off the flinty rock. Not only was the ground impossible to entrench, the observing Turkish aircraft circling overhead failed to spot the El Eime villagers. Experts on every cranny of their home turf, the villagers surprised and routed the western ridge.

This was the signal for Rasim to press his mounted men against the flank and rear of the eastern ridge as Lawrence launched the central reserve in a headlong charge. *En masse*, and with banners unfurled, the Arab reserve raced across the plateau to press the Turkish centre. The Turkish

fire, now ragged, began to crumble. Desperately, Hamid Fakhri Pasha addressed his headquarter staff: 'I have been forty years a soldier, but never saw I rebels fight like these. Enter the ranks.'[7]

It was a token too late expended. The Turks were now pouring off the broken flanks onto the confused centre as the infantry jammed the track to Kerak. Behind them the Arabs fired and cut out the hindmost in massacre. All artillery and machine guns were left behind with 250 prisoners and 300 dead including Hamid Fakhri Pasha. Only the Turkish cavalry and the precipitous Wadi Hesa prevented further slaughter.

Tafila was Lawrence's crowning chesspiece conventional battle which drew praise even from his most orthodox critics. Only 25 Arabs had been killed with 40 wounded. Allenby later presented Lawrence with the Distinguished Service Order for Tafila.

On 28 January the Arabs followed their victorious run down from the highlands onto the Dead Sea port of El Mezra. At anchor lay berthed seven craft of the German–Turkish Dead Sea Fleet with a grain shipment and 60 personnel. Surprised by the wild-eyed apparitions thundering down from the snowy heights, the flotilla surrendered – in perhaps the only case in history where a navy capitulated to cavalry.

The Walls of Jericho

Allenby's fulfillment of his agenda in the Dead Sea Campaign as well as his preliminary move in the spring, 1918 Trans Jordan operations, necessitated the capture of Jericho. The plan was for the 60th (London) Division to bear east on Jericho while the ANZAC Mounted Division worked around the Turkish left, entered the Jordan Valley at Nebi Musa, and interposed itself as a buffer between the town and main Turkish units of 4th Army while the infantry digested Jericho.

On 19 February the units started down the east side of the Judean Range into such bleak areas known as the Wilderness. Although low in height, the hills were described in official reports as presenting a 'savage and melancholy grandeur'. In the first twelve miles of march the ground fell away 2,000 feet in a series of steep, narrow valleys and rocky ridges. The descent off the biting hill country brought the troops into the famous warming weather which from February to May had inspired the Romans to treat Jericho as a winter resort.

The steep rate of descent, however, inflicted inordinate delays and at one point the 2/13th London Battalion used the mens' puttees as ropes down which to pass a sharp, blocking drop-off. The delays allowed the Turks to evade the intended trap so that Jericho was found vacant of troops and stores on the morning of 21 February.

An RFC hydroplane was transported by lorry to the northern shore of the deep blue Dead Sea and launched on 1 March in an attempt to cut off the German-Turkish grain flotilla. It was a risky adventure, and immediately after setting out a broken rudder caused the craft to beach. Ingeniously, the crew constructed two boats from the floats

▲ Amir Zeid with Austrian howitzers captured in January, 1918 after Lawrence's chess-piece victory at Tafileh.

▼ German advisors and Turkish personnel of the Dead Sea Fleet. The flotilla was an assemblage of smaller craft with light guns. Their mission was to help protect valuable grains and wood coming from the economic Hauran District south and east of the Dead Sea.

and sailed to the eastern shore, finally abandoning the quixotic quest in early March.

After the Jerusalem Campaign the shortage of remounts and the debilitating effects of the long marches demanded a recuperation for the Desert Mounted Corps. Thus, Allenby had withdrawn them to Deir el Balah, and rotated one division at a time between rest and the six mile long gap between his two infantry corps. In 20th Corps area the 74th Division had also been drawn into reserve.

The next step of Allenby's program was the purchase of maneuvering room for the Trans Jordan operations by an extension of his right flank to the banks of the Wadi el Auja. The key position in 20th Corps realignment was north of Jerusalem at Tel Asur – the highest elevation in Judea. Not surprisingly, here again were significant delays as the men traversed the rough heights: 'so steep were many of the gorges and ridges that men could cross them only by their fellows lying down and lowering or hoisting them up on their shoulders'.[8]

Under the blanket of heavy artillery the 5/Royal Welch Fusiliers captured the mountain on the morning of 9 March. From Tel Asur the Welsh could see, 90 miles to the north, a snow-capped Mount Hermon and the hills of Galilee, to the east and southeast – Gilead, Moab, and the Dead Sea, to the south – the Mount of Olives, and the hills around Hebron, and the Mediterranean to the west. Despite five counter-attacks over five hours, Tel Asur held.

Over the next days, 20th Corps consolidated its five-mile deep, 14-mile wide frontage astride the Nablus Road. The terrain so treacherously concealed Turkish machine gun nests that operations were normally practised only at night. Broken or sprained limbs were the lot of many in the 53rd and 74th Divisions who, with 10th Division suffered 1,300 casualties and considerably more than the enemy. On the Lisane Ridge, Private Whitfield of the 10/Shropshire won the Victoria Cross by seizing a machine gun nest single-handedly and further preventing an enemy bombing attack. For the first time, contact was made with the German 702nd Battalion, *Asien Korps*.

Simultaneously, 21st Corps was able to enfilade and remove part of the Turkish coastal line which had been created by the previous crossing of the Nahr el Auja. This adjustment reduced the gaps between Allenby's two corps to three-and-a-half miles which were patrolled by the Corps cavalry regiment. Twenty-first Corps thus stretched from the old coastal crusading site of Arsuf into the Shephaleh Hills, which remained its line throughout summer.

The recent hill fighting confirmed Allenby in his increasing belief that only a hammer blow against the Turks in the Plain of Esdraelon could yield the sort of comprehensive victory demanded by his superiors. Of course, *Yilderim* must be led to believe the main blow would come against its opposite flank. Fortunately, Allenby knew he could play on *Yilderim*'s fear for Dera – the confluence of the Hejaz, Palestine, and Syrian railways . . . in short, *Yilderim*'s communications nerve centre. In order to adequately menace Dera Allenby needed Arab support. His Trans Jordan operations were conceived both to encourage the Arab Revolt into growing virility northward and to so distract Turkish attention that when his moment of critical concentration came, enemy attention would be rivetted in the wrong sector.

The Arab Northern Army, however, was huddled indoors away from the ferocious winds and with a burgeoning cash problem. The Amir Zeid had overspent. Travelling with a small escort, Lawrence rode from Tafila to Guweira to receive of Colonel Joyce £30,000 sterling. The money came in 30 bags each weighing 22 pounds and these bags hung each side of a camel.

During his return Lawrence kept his escort from viewing the pitiable sight of Maulud's 500 mule troopers encamped in the 4,000 foot wind-swept highlands west of Maan. Dressed in only British summer-weight khaki and with nothing but wormwood to burn for fuel, half would be incapacitated or dead before the end of their three month winter *travail*. Many no doubt would have died bitterly in the knowledge that some of Lawrence's requests for winter clothing had been turned down by British supply clerks, one of whom had haughtily reminded Lawrence that Arabia was a warm country!

Lawrence passed through Tafila, dropped off the funds to Zeid, then ventured on to Kerak – the last town before the possible linking of the Arab Northern Army with the EEF. Returning, Lawrence discovered Zeid had already farmed out the monies to pressing tribal claimants. The northern campaign strategy had been to keep a solid corps of regulars in uniform, then, by use of finance, to call out local irregulars to flesh out the Arab Northern Army whenever and wherever it needed men. Zeid's fiscal irresponsibility had ruined the plan.

Disgusted, despoiled, and tired in body, and torn between the conflicting demands of two worlds, each to whom he could be but half true, Lawrence tendered his resignation to Colonel Joyce then rode to Beersheba to ask Allenby for some minor post. The Ides, however, bore different signs . . . and Lawrence was like a fly drawn into the spider's web. Clayton and Hogarth listened to his grievances patiently, but with no intention of letting him escape. The Prime Minister was calling for at least Damascus, if not Aleppo, at the earliest possible moment. The Arab Army was needed against the Turkish left to waste their resources, threaten Dera, to help convince *Yilderim* that the major offensive would fall in the Trans Jordan, and finally – once *Yilderim* discovered its mistake – to prevent 4th Army's transfer of forces to its jeopardised right flank. No one could exert influence with the tribes as Lawrence could.

If they determined on their pound of flesh, Lawrence demanded to set the price. Any northern advance must entail the reduction of Maan. For that, the Arabs would need guns, machine guns, baggage camels, money, and security against a Turkish counter-offensive from Amman. Previously, Feisal's army had worked its prodigies with 550 Meccan transport camels which had shuttled over a 50 mile line of posts variously at a range of 60–120 miles out of the seabase at Aqaba.[9] Incredibly, none of the 30 companies of Arab regulars had possessed first line transport. The two companies of the Camel Transport Corps Allenby now presented them were indeed a handsome gift, for they endowed the 4,000 regulars with an 80 mile radius. Allenby promised additional hardware and reckoned that his crossing the Jordan River, occupying Es Salt, and destroying rail tracks around Amman would certainly engross enemy attention.

Flying back to Aqaba with the £300,000 sterling Allenby had advanced him, Lawrence met Joyce and Jafaar Pasha and laid the timetables for the siege of Maan. Logistical planning for Arab regulars was a different proposition than that for the lightly loaded Bedouin. Assuming water and forage were handy, three pounds of stuffs per man and eight per animal were calculated. Meanwhile, Feisal set about restructuring the finances of the Arab Northern Army, and sent word to Zeid that Lawrence's intelligence believed the Turks would attack within the week at Tafila.

Attack they did, and under von Falkenhayn's conception the affair was executed along entirely different lines, this time by 8th Corps Mobile Column consisting of one German infantry company, three Turkish battalions, two mule mounted squadrons, an artillery battery and one each German and Turkish machine gun companies.[10]

Travelling south from Amman, the group detrained in two columns 35 miles northeast and 17 miles southeast of Tafila. Zeid evacuated the village on 6 March only to be caught and defeated on the Shobek road. The punitive expedition in the end was but an angry wind; upon its withdrawal, the Arabs reoccupied Tafila on 18 March.

THE TRANS JORDAN OPERATIONS

How wilt thou do in the swelling of Jordan? — *Jeremiah 12:5*

ALLENBY placed Major-General Shea in charge of the First Trans Jordan Operation. 'Shea's Force' contained the 60th (London) Division, the ANZAC Mounted Division, the Imperial Camel Brigade, a heavy battery, a mountain artillery brigade, and bridging and pontoon units. It was a good mixed mobile group, but a group off to a bad start. Unusually heavy March rains raised the Jordan River to a swollen torrent so that the mission was delayed. A new start date was set for 21 March, then local conditions stalled the crossing of the Jordan at Ghoraniye for two more days.

Although the initial Turkish positions were driven in, it soon was apparent how costly were the delays. German–Turkish units, though small and mixed, were already reinforcing Amman. The infantry, with flanking cavalry, quickly overcame minor resistance at the strong-point of Shunet Nimrin, then marched over the crescent of hills directly by the track to Es Salt. By midnight, the cavalry and part of the infantry entered Es Salt, an old town spectacularly perched on a hill rising 4,000 feet above the Jordan. Before the war the town held 10,000 persons, half of them Christians. Oddly, no resistance had been met save the punishing effect of rain and sleet.

Chaytor's ANZACs were unable to move east on Amman until morning of the 27th. Trudging boggy tracks, the New Zealand Mounted Brigade approached Amman from the southwest (coming up opposite Hill 3039), the Imperial Camel Brigade from the west, and the 2nd Light Horse Brigade from the northwest. To Shea's chagrin, it was soon discovered the machine guns in the old Turkish Citadel were in perfect line to enfilade the Camel Brigade.

Meanwhile, the leading brigade of the 60th had been held up on the eastern side of Es Salt by an armed feud between Christians and Circassians. When the brigade negotiated its way through the turmoil and attained the outskirts of Amman it was 28 March and apparent that the advance on Amman had stalled. The Citadel was in full dominance of the western approaches. Worse, 13 German aircraft bombed the Camel Transport Corps into disruption at Shunet Nimrin. The Jordan River had risen higher, wiping out all crossings except the Ghoraniye bridge.

On the 29th, more Turkish battalions arrived from Dera. The next afternoon Chetwode's 20th Corps headquarters gave Shea permission to retreat across the Jordan, with the stipulation that he leave a strong post at the Ghoraniye crossing. The raid, at least in a tactical sense, had been a failure. Shea's Force accrued 1,348 casualties but took 925 Turks and 61 Germans prisoner, not counting enemy battle losses. The expedition did succeed in drawing off Turkish troops from the siege lines at Maan and so helped the EEF Arab allies. Yet, being the first real EEF defeat since 2nd Gaza, it breathed some fresh hope into a dispirited enemy.

The coordinated Arab operations had been conceived along three columns of activity. In the centre, Jafaar and the regulars invested Maan, Joyce with the armoured cars swung southeast to tackle Mudauwara Station in the hope of finally isolating Medina, and Lawrence with his bodyguard, Mirzuk's Ageyl tribesmen, and 2,000 camels, set off north to link with Shea's Force at Es Salt on 30 March. Here, too, the best laid plans of mice and men went astray. Before

▼ Egyptian Expeditionary Force engineers and barrel bridge.

contact, Lawrence's party learned the EEF had fallen back not only from Amman, but from Es Salt as well and that the vengeful Turks were already hanging Arab collaborators.

At least their journey was not without an element of mischievous sport . . . dressing incognito as Syrian gypsy women, Lawrence and four bodyguards entered Amman on a spying mission. Their calculations were cut humourously short when amourous Turkish soldiers pressed them for favours. Unable to shake off their paramours the group sought refuge in flight, running, to the Turks' bewilderment, considerably faster than gypsy women were thought to run. Thereafter, Lawrence vowed to return to his more usual practice of spying in a British private soldier's uniform which was too brazen to be suspect.[1]

Yilderim in Transition

The punitive expedition to Tafila had been von Falkenhayn's Parthian shot, and a brief, victorious shot taken, in fact, after his departure. On 27 February he had received a telegram advising his handover of the Yilderim command to Marshal Liman von Sanders on 1 March 1918. The German grandmaster was now headed for a quiet army sector command on the Eastern Front. As he departed from the Palestine Front by train he sorrowfully commented to his former Chief of Staff, 'I had not bargained for this!' Von Falkenhayn had everywhere made a respectful and genial impression on those he had personally met; Colonel Hussein Husni shook his hand then jotted in his records, 'He did not deserve this fate.'[2]

Von Sanders was a German cavalry general, a hero noted for his tough, static defence lines at Gallipoli, and the head of the German Military Mission in Turkey since 1913. Thus experienced in theatre matters, von Sanders substituted numbers of his German staff for Turkish personnel and increased staff work in the native language. At Semakh Station he met with 7th Army's Chief of Staff, Major von Falkenhausen, and received a first-hand conference on the Palestine Front's morale; von Falkenhausen asserted Allenby was so strong that he could break the Turkish line wherever he chose.

Von Sanders inspected his front troops and qualified von Falkenhausen's statement. Certainly at any one massed point the EEF could break through. 'The Turkish battalions which I saw at the front numbered 120–150 rifles. According to a written report the 8th Army had 3,902 rifles available for the defense of the left sector with a front of twenty-eight kilometers.'[3] It was too thin a crust on the Turkish pie so he set about thickening the dough by kneading his battle lines.

Knowing the EEF could read his cipher codes, von Sanders 'leaked' disinformation of the arrival of substantial reinforcements. Then, when EEF aeroplanes flew over to substantiate the reports, he ensured they photographed prearranged movements of mounted and supply columns. Cavalry was transferred to the more open positions near the Jordan.

Simultaneously, the General Staff sought to augment manpower by cleaning up inefficiencies in the rear. One

▲ German General of Cavalry and Marshal of the Turkish Army, Liman von Sanders. Von Sanders headed the German Military Mission in Turkey from 1913–1918. His stubborn, static defence of Gallipoli made him a Turkish national hero. On 1 March 1918, von Sanders replaced von Falkenhayn as commander of Yilderim.

'company' in Damascus had attracted 1,200 soldiers who were drawing subsistence supplies yet were idle, without orders, and hitherto undiscovered. At Affule Station another 700 were rounded up. Artillery inspected in rear areas often lacked either men or horses or even guns. His only reserve was the 24th Division. The 11th Division, newly arrived from the Caucasus, was rushed south of Nablus to help slow EEF operations north of Jerusalem.

Von Sanders requested permission to obtain the recall and relocation of the Medina garrison. The question was an old sore wound between the Turks and their German advisors. Temporarily moved to countenance such a withdrawal in 1917, Enver Pasha in 1918 denied permission on political and religious grounds; indeed, three weak Turkish divisions were uselessly serving as far south as Yemen and Aden! The refusal put additional emphasis on the vital importance of Dera's security, which not only serviced the primary retreat avenue of 4th, 7th, and even 8th Armies, but for these forces as well. The loss or rupture of Amman or its railway would also doom these southern troops. It was an insecurity which played directly into Allenby's diversionary plans for the Trans Jordan, and into his strategic plans for the primary 1918 offensive.

The change of command had been a splendid opportunity to improve the southern theatre's cumbersome command apparatus. Sadly, opportunity's knock was left unanswered. Von Sanders retained only 7th and 8th Armies under his unconditional orders. Second Army, headquartered at Aleppo, was on his rear line of communications and was responsible for coastal defence. Fourth Army was in charge of his supply and lines of communication, and for the supply of 6th Army in Mesopotamia and Turkish units engaged in the Arab Revolt. From the point of view of the commander of the Palestine Front, this placed an unsatisfactory reliance on others.

Militarily, the 8th Army of Djevad Pasha and the 7th Army of Fevzi Pasha occupied a 45 mile frontage from the Mediterranean to the Jordan River. Here, some overlap occurred between 7th and 4th Armies, but the Trans Jordan in principal and fact was the ward of 4th Army whose only large formation was 8th Corps, its other assets being scattered over a divergent range of responsibility. From the beginning von Sanders de-emphasised von Falkenhayn's reliance on an elastic front based on strong points and reserves, and tightened his line into a more continuous, harder front. This strategic alteration was motivated from the 'traditional' Turkish strength in defence and from belief that a shaken line would receive moral strength from a shoulder-to-shoulder stability. These were the precepts that had won him Gallipoli.

Enver Pasha was not the least of von Sander's worries. Enver was prone to deliver orders directly to 7th and 8th

▲ A German medical team in caps and neckcloths and medical armband in a Palestinian town, 1917–1918. The unique stretcher system of a camel carrying a casualty on each side is known as a *cacolet*, and was used by Germans and British alike.

Armies over von Sander's head, or when it was deemed 'the Germans' should be the last to know. One instance was Enver's order to transfer all Jewish soldiers from the Palestinian to the Caucasian Front; von Sanders was barely able to scratch the order in time. Similarly frustrating was Enver's tampering with German formations in-country. This became especially acute with the military mission in Constantinople, over which von Sanders remained the technical head. Berlin aggravated the problem by communicating directly to the Chief of Staff, General von Lenthe, again, over von Sanders' head. This impossible situation had resulted in an April political crisis wherein Ludendorff was challenged to solve the problem or von Sanders' resignation would appear on Kaiser Wilhelm's desk. Enver Pasha retracted his interference.

Von Sanders rapidly demonstrated his style of leadership in the first Trans Jordan Operation. Djemal Pasha 'Kuchuk', a proven officer in the Trans Jordan region, was placed in charge of the 4th Army at Amman and was forbidden to retreat in the face of 'Shea's Force'. Von Sanders had seen that the German 703rd Battalion had detrained in Amman soon enough to participate in his 30 March counterattack. He had also detached several squadrons of the 3rd Cavalry Division, under the valiant Essad Bey, to menace Shea's position at Es Salt.

Left: Number 205 Pioneer Company, German *Asien Korps* rafting across the Jordan, 1918.
◀

Left: No. 21 Balloon Company, RAF, on the Jerusalem Road.
◀

Left: An Arab mock-fires the machine gun of a Bristol F2 B. 'X' Flight arrived at Aqaba in September, 1917 to support Arab operations and to conduct reconnaissance and bombing in the vicinity of Maan on the Hejaz Railway. Although an independent and self-contained unit of air headquarters in Egypt, it flew under the operational orders of Lieutenant-Colonel P. C. Joyce. Joyce is standing in Arab headdress at the 'one o'clock' position of the British roundel insignia. The Flight variously flew three BE 12s, two BE 2es, and one DH 2, and later in 1918, two Nieuport Scouts.
◀

▶
Right: Lieutenant-Colonel P. C. Joyce was seconded from the Connaught Rangers to act as Base Commandant at Aqaba. As advisor to Feisal's trained Arab regulars, Joyce is shown here in appropriately tactful headdress. The six-foot three-inch Irishman held a previous service record in the Boer War, Egypt, and the Sudan, and spoke Arabic. His style of leadership was relaxed in regard to outward formalities so that his band of experts could more freely perform as the élite technicians they were. Not to be outdone by the derring-do of junior officers, Joyce went on the occasional raid – once blowing 2,000 rails and seven small bridges.

The Siege of Maan

The Arab Northern Army as a formation was complete by March 1918, and except for irregular attachments remained as delineated below throughout the year:

Arab Regular Army – Jafaar Pasha el Askeri
Brigade of Infantry
One battalion Camel Corps
One battalion Mule Mounted Infantry
Eight guns

British Section – Lieutenant-Colonel P.C. Joyce
Hejaz Armoured Car Battery
One 'X' Flight Aircraft
One company Egyptian Camel Corps
200 Egyptian infantry and medical corps (Aqaba)
Indian Army machine gun detachment
Wireless station (Aqaba)
Transport Labour Corps

French Detachment – Captain Pisani
Two mountain guns
14 machine guns and automatic rifles

This army was cemented by the complementary talents of its leaders – Feisal as the political chief, Jafaar in the tactical and technical matters of Arab–Turkish soldiery, Joyce as the efficient organiser and liaison-procurer, and Lawrence as the recruiter and coordinator of the tribal irregulars attached to and swelling the Arab Northern Army. In the ranks there was no formality of discipline or of prescribed correctional punishment. Service being vol-

untary, and for an ideal, the threat of imminent attack combined to preserve army integrity under loose conditions which would have promoted the deterioration of a peace-time formation. As it happened, there was some sin in this looseness. In early April, the regular Arab officers nearly mutinied over their insistence that they be allowed to assault Maan directly to show the Turks their prowess in conventional war. Feisal had sagely broken the impasse by reluctantly tendering permission to do so.

The Arab investment of Maan had been planned by Lieutenant-Colonel Alan Dawnay, the younger brother of Guy Dawnay, Allenby's Deputy Chief of Staff. The plan called for three columns: Maulud's regulars with Auda abu Tayi's irregular cavalry in the centre, Jafaar's regulars in the northern column, and a southern column of armoured cars, Bedouin, and Egyptian camelry under Dawnay himself.

During 11–13 April Maulud's centre took the rail station south of Maan, while Jafaar's column took the station north of the town. Jafaar, Maulud, and Auda then captured Jebel Semna which overlooked Maan to the southwest. On the 17th Jafaar directed the desired attack on Maan itself. Nuri Said boldly led the Arabs in to the main station before Captain Pisani's Algerian artillery ran out of shells and the Arabs were driven back with loss. The 'mutinous' aspirations of the regulars were thus sated, albeit in blood, but at least they had proved their men's courage, their ability to utilise terrain, and their propensity to absorb casualties.

Coincidentally, Jafaar discovered his Turkish opposite in Maan was an old college friend. This amusement inspired him to pen a request for an amiable surrender. The Maan Commandant replied hopefully, but added his orders bound his honour to hold to the last cartridge. Pragmatically, Jafaar suggested this technicality could be removed by the Turks shooting their ammunition into the air. During the hours of pondering indecision the resourceful new head of 4th Army, Djemal Pasha 'Kuchuk' speeded a column with supplies south, breaking the Arab cordon and relieving Maan.

Lawrence had joined Dawnay's party set to take out the elusive and surviving Mudauwara Station. The initial mistake was ironically the very strength of their success at Shahm Station en route. Such loot was to be acquired for the having that four-fifths of the tribesmen made off with their gains. The emasculated party continued down the line to Ramleh where they found a much deserted and much booby trapped station. After a reconnaissance revealed the Turks in alert at Mudauwara, the warband salved its frustration by venting a 'permanent' break on the line at Ramleh. Feisal simultaneously dispatched tribesmen against all seven of the Hejaz stations posted in the 80 mile length between Ramleh and Maan. Thenceforth, Medina's Turkish garrison received no material succour from its countrymen, and Medina lay irretrievably isolated by the southern Arab armies of Ali and Abdullah for the duration of the war.

The Second Trans Jordan Operation

On the same day that Allenby had sent Shea's Force into the Trans Jordan, the Germans opened their stunning spring offensives on the Western Front. As the British lines were forced back in depth, Allenby was notified within the week that his Palestine stance must be on the defensive and that the War Office would commence subtracting his divisions to meet the mounting crisis. Within three weeks he had been shorn of the 52nd and 74th Divisions, nine Yeomanry regiments, nine British battalions, five-and-a-half siege batteries and five machine gun companies. Fourteen more British battalions were earmarked for a May debarkation. As partial compensation the 3rd and 7th Indian Divisions from Mesopotamia were in or due in theatre, and Indian cavalry units to replace the Yeomanry were sailing from France. The 24 British battalions, however, were replaced only gradually over the next months by Indian units from India. Their lack of training and war experience and the massive transfer of forces meant a dislocation and delay of Allenby's plans.

Nevertheless, Allenby proceded with a preplanned extension of 21st Corps' right flank on 9–11 April. The objective was Berukin in the coastal plain, the target a Turkish 8th Army salient which had its back to considerable marshes. If Et Tire could be stormed and the marshes subjected to interdicting naval gunfire, significant enemy forces around Berukin would be trapped. Unfortunately, on the first day of attacks the Turks captured secret EEF documents exposing the gameplan. The Turkish 16th Division dug in its heels as the German 701st and 702nd *Asien Korps* Battalions counterattacked and thwarted the operation.

The Turks countered with attacks of their own on the EEF Jordan bridgeheads at Ghoraniyeh and Musallabeh on 11 April. The objectives were to shorten the Turkish front on the Wadi el Auja and to discourage another Trans Jordan raid. The night attack at Ghoraniyeh was bungled because of a delayed start, but the Turks coming out of the grey dawn in the Jordan sector were still an unexpected surprise. Both EEF bridgeheads held.

Also, from 11 April, Allenby ordered Chaytor's ANZAC Mounted Division and the 180th Brigade to feint in the Jordan Valley, to divert attention from the Arab siege of Maan. The Turks, however, were discovered tenaciously alert. In the end, this small gesture toward their nerve centre hardened the Turks in anticipation of the next Trans Jordan adventure.

Allenby had intended the next show to begin in the middle of May. During the last week of April, envoys from the powerful Beni Sakr tribe announced that 20,000 of their warriors, encamped 19 miles southeast of Ghoraniyeh, would cooperate in cutting off the Turkish strongpoint of Shunet Nimrin. The stipulation was that Allenby moved before 4 May when the tribe's dwindling supplies would force them to disperse. This promise, given to a man of his own word and to an officer of 'regular' training appeared a godsend, and Allenby prepared the new operation for 30 April.

General Chauvel was appointed to lead the ANZAC and Australian Mounted Divisions, the Imperial Service (Indian) Cavalry and Infantry Brigades, and the 60th (London) Division. Blocking his way was the array of 8th Corps along Shunet Nimrin and the brief range of hills. Over a five-day period from 30 April to 5 May Chauvel was to learn the

Turks had thrown all they had into the defence of the Trans Jordan.

Ruthlessly, von Sanders had scoured the hospitals for fit wounded cases and had levied extra Arabs from the populace. Willingness to deploy the distrusted and surly Arabs was proof of the desperate measures taken to fill 4th Army's ranks. On the right of the Nimrim positions and in the juncture of 4th and 7th Armies, von Sanders pushed the arriving elements of the German 146th (Masurian) Regiment, the German Pioneer Company Number 205, a German machine gun company, and the Turkish 3rd Cavalry Division and Caucasian Cavalry Brigade.

Chaytor advanced on 30 April with the ANZAC Mounted Division and two brigades of the 60th Division. Velocity propelled them through the first line of the Turkish Nimrin defences but they were stalled against the second line. Meanwhile, the Australian Mounted Division lapped around the Turks to eject 4th Army Headquarters from Es Salt.

Unhappily, there was no sign of the Beni Sakr tribe. Lawrence had just reached Allenby's GHQ, personally shocked, and with the explanation. Lawrence knew that Fahad, the chief envoy, could only speak for 400 warriors at the most and that this mere sub group of the Beni Sakr had no possibility of influencing the other promised 19,600. In fact, those of the Beni Sakr who intended to fight at all had already gone south to assist in the Arab Maan operations. The imbroglio was partially due to a momentary rupture in the higher EEF planning staff. Guy Dawnay, experienced in Arabian affairs, had been shipped to France, Bartholomew had not yet been brought in by Allenby, and Bols, Allenby's former chief of staff in France, and currently the same in Palestine, was too inexperienced in local matters to smell a rat.

Chauvel had clearly run out of steam while von Sanders had been stoking his in anticipation. The concentration von Sanders collected, for the reason of once more trying an advance to shorten his front, could now effectively be employed to double purpose. Two regiments of Colonel Böhme's 24th Division, a storm battalion, a pioneer company and Essad Bey's 3rd Cavalry Division poured across a Jordan pontoon bridge undetected by British Intelligence. The Australians reported the disciplined Turkish advance was executed 'as though on parade ground'.[4]

The second of May was the critical day. Von Sanders knew the tired state of his men and so executed a subtle strategem of hitting Es Salt on three sides, deliberately permitting the Australians a retreat lane down the southwestern road. The next day Allenby issued permission for just such a retreat. By evening of 4 May Chauvel's men had recrossed the Jordan. Lacking, as always, sufficient cavalry, the Turks could follow, but not pursue.

Tactically an EEF defeat, the Second Trans Jordan Operation at least cost the Turks more casualties – 2,000 against 1,600. After watching the EEF criss-cross the Jordan, most of the Beni Sakr tribe decided neutrality was the better part of valour. Allenby succeeded in one important sense . . . the raids confirmed Turkish paranoia in the Dera-Amman sector. Fully one-third of the German–Turkish assets were relegated to the Trans Jordan.

16

ALLENBY'S NEW MODEL

ON the Western Front, the German spring offensive which had driven a wedge into the Somme had stopped; the month's butcher bill of British Commonwealth lives numbered 225,000. The Germans, with their startlingly innovative *stosstruppen* tactics now aimed a second hammer blow in the Lys, seemingly at the Channel Ports. As fresh divisions were released from the Eastern Front where Russian Bolshevik leaders had concluded the peace of Brest-Litovsk, it became a race of space and time for the Germans to shatter the Western Front before arriving American forces could tip the scales.

Allenby had rotated 60,000 of his EEF as contributions for this emergency. It was a monumental depletion of his experienced force. Fortunately, over the course of the summer the cavalry came out of the wash clean. The Imperial Camel Brigade, largely an anachorism after leaving the desert, exchanged its camels for horses, and was converted into the 5th Light Horse Brigade. The Brigade was then attached to the Australian Mounted Division; its six British camel companies being retained for lines of communications work and for support of the Hejaz Arabs. As nine regiments of Yeomanry (or three-fourths of the total) had departed, the Yeomanry Mounted Division designation was scrapped, and with the influx of Indian cavalry, two new divisions, the 4th and 5th Cavalry were cast. By June, Chauvel possessed:

Desert Mounted Corps
4th Cavalry Division: 10th, 11th, 12th Cavalry Brigades
5th Cavalry Division: 13th, 14th, 15th (Imperial Service),
Cavalry Brigade
ANZAC Mounted Division (unchanged)
Australian Mounted Division: 5th Light Horse substituted for 5th Mounted

Each brigade of the 4th and 5th Cavalry Divisions retained one Yeomanry and two Indian regiments, excepting the 15th Imperial Service Cavalry Brigade which derived from Indian princely state regiments – namely, the Jodhpore, Mysore, and Hyderabad Lancers. While the Yeomanry, Australian and New Zealand regiments contained three squadrons each of four troops, the Indian regiments had four squadrons each of three troops. Horse artillery used the 13 pounder. By August, the Australians had opted for the sword and were given two weeks training with it. Thus, three of the four divisions of the Desert Mounted Corps rode with the sword or lance, the age-old weapons of the *arme blanche*.

Fortune was otherwise with the infantry. The replacement Indian battalions arrived on such a scattered schedule from February to August that campaign operations were dislocated. Twenty-two of the battalions had seen no service, and one-third had had no riflery practice. Of the 22

battalions with service experience in India and Mesopotamia, each had forefeited one veteran company to the Western Front. A further ten battalions were of technical veterans, but none had been in formation as a battalion. The Indian units were almost entirely devoid of signallers, Lewis gunners, hand bombers, or experienced transport drivers.

▼ General Allenby (right) with General Bailoud of the *Détachment Francais de Palestine et de Syrie*, or DFPS. The DFPS was a token command suggesting Allied solidarity and was obviously representative of French interest during the Last Crusade in the Holy Land. DFPS incorporated two battalions of the *Régiment Mixte de Tirailleurs* and four battalions of Armenians, two of these forming the *Légion d'Orient*, four squadrons of *Spahis* and *Chasseurs d'Afrique*, three batteries and engineer and auxiliary supports.

The junior officers, both British and Indian, were inexperienced, and few British officers spoke Hindustani. Only the 54th (East Anglian) Division was left untouched so that the War Office and the new Chief of the Imperial General Staff, Sir Henry Wilson, could have yet another resource to tap.

One interesting formation was the forerunner of the modern Israeli Army, the Jewish Legion. Since the Balfour Declaration of November, 1917, unnaturalised Jews living in Britain's larger cities had been recruited for service in Palestine. Three battalions were raised by spring, 1918, the 38th and 39th battalions shipping to the Palestine Front, while the 40th battalion went to the Force in Egypt. Their armbands sported a golden Star of David sewn on three bands of red, white and blue, which were themselves sewn diagonally across two larger bands of blue and white.

Summer

From May to October none of Palestine's three topographical regimes receives much cloud or rain to temporise the condition of summer. The seacoast mellows the plains with breezes, bringing a mean August temperature of 80°F. The mean temperature of the Judean–Jerusalem–Summerian hill country is less, with a 20°F variance. In the Jordan Valley temperatures reach 130°F, the averages not being known because, as a contemporary Intelligence manual testified, no one had gone on record as having survived a summer in the southern Jordan Valley.[1]

It was into this 'Valley of Death' Allenby proposed that the troopers of the Desert Mounted Corps should ride, and bivouac for the duration of the season. Tactically, the bridgeheads and EEF right flank would thus be made secure, but the chief reason was strategic and far-seeing. The Turks well knew the rigours of such an encampment, and only such apparent folly could 'convince' them the autumn offensive would fall in the Trans-Jordan onto Dera and Amman and in coordination with the Arabs.

The Jordan Valley Force embodied the four divisions of the Desert Mounted Corps, a brigade of Indian infantry, and two battalions of the British West Indies Regiment. Only half the cavalry was posted in the treacherous valley during a given month. When the month was up, two divisions rotated into the cooler hills at Bethlehem while the rested two divisions came down into the Valley.

Shade temperatures of 100° to 130°F at Ghoraniyeh told only part of the plight of the Jordan Valley Force. Nature had cut the 'Ghor' hundreds of feet into the ground and below sea level so that the great evaporation of moisture from the Dead Sea weighted the atmosphere with an oppressive lassitude. This air pressure was worse on the horses, which would hardly move even to obtain water; on the men, the stagnant aura stifled initiative and confidence.

Underfoot were several feet of salty white marl. Given any movement this flour-fine powder rose in a choking cloud. Even the morning north wind would bring discomfort and occasional gushing dust devils. Before noon the wind would die into a graven silence as if in fear of the day's worst heat. By mid-afternoon a southern wind braced the Ghor till dusk ushered in another breathless night. And so the interminable clockwork hell visited man and beast of the Jordan Valley Force.

Conditions were not inimical to every form of life, however. Scorpions, six-inch centipedes, and great stinging spiders found their homes in the dry areas, and the anopheles mosquito among the marshes. The biggest scourge of the animals was the *surra* fly which had recently killed 42,000 Turkish transport camels so that in 1918 the Valley was littered with acres of bones like some forgotten world in a fantasy novel.[2]

For all this, survival of the Jordan Valley Force was essentially a medical problem and Major-General Sir Richard Luce, Chief Medical Officer, testified to Allenby's unstinting support of this arm. Anti-malarial projects received top billing over all other support services, thousands of the Egyptian Labour Corps being set to work draining or oiling marshes or diverting streams. Consequently, with a reduced breeding base for the mosquitos so malaria was reduced in algebraic ratio. If the Turks had attacked their problem with similar competence EEF contagion would have been even further reduced. The Australian, Sir James Barrett, spoke highly of Allenby's efforts: 'He was, as far as I know, the first Commander in that malarial region in which many armies have perished to understand the risk and to take measures accordingly.'[3]

One pleasant irony was that such a hateful land was blessed with abundance of water. The Jordan could yield water for beast, and the clear streams of the Wadi Nimrin and Auja for man.

True to form, Allenby frequented this thankless portion of his line. Once, during a Turkish raid on the advanced outposts he went forward for a look-see. If Allenby had not known of his nickname before, or of the alert signals and codes which preceded him, he certainly learned, from this visit to the Light Horsemen. 'While the C-in-C was standing there he noticed a man at the post waving his arms frantically and persistently. After a while he asked what this man was doing and was told that he was only signalling to the next post. But the man kept on and at length the C-in-C sent an officer across to enquire what the urgent message was. The answer was given after much hedging, "B.B.L.," and the embarrassed officer had to explain to the C-in-C that "B.B.L." meant "Bull broken loose."'[4]

Few actions deserving the nomenclature of 'battle' took place that summer, for all antagonists were entangled in their own problems and organisational transitions. Raids in force to test and improve the condition of the new Indian formations was EEF policy. One such raid took place in June along the coast at Arsuf and involved the capture of two small hills by the 7th Division.

A larger raid against the Ghuraheh Ridge west of the Jerusalem–Nablus Road was undertaken by a brigade of 10th Division in August. Turkish defenceworks had been reproduced behind EEF lines and assaulting troops rehearsed cutting sections of the wire with Bangalore torpedoes then crossing the cuts with ladders. On the night, the raiders wore special felt-soled boots to silence movement and followed approach routes marked with luminous tapes and boards. Beacons guided returning troops during

egress from a raid which inflicted 700 casualties and prisoners for an exchange of 107.

The Indian cavalry displayed equal acumen south-east of Ghoraniyeh in July when the 15th Imperial Service Cavalry Brigade and the Sherwood Foresters clashed with the Caucasian Cavalry Brigade. The Jodhpore Lancers took the Turkish 11th Regiment in flank, riding down their opponents with the lance and capturing the Turkish commander with his four squadron commanders. Risaldar Shaitan Singh had galloped ahead of his squadron, shooting two Turks with his revolver and clubbing down three more with his loaded stick. Allenby distributed decorations as a show of favour.

Von Sanders conducted the one serious summer affair against the Jordan Valley Force bridgehead and salient between Musallabeh and the Abul Tellul Ridge. Operations were designed to reduce 4th and 7th Army frontage and by threat of superior position prevent any further EEF transgression into the Trans Jordan. The night attack was scheduled for 13/14 July and was commanded by Ali Fuad Pasha of 20th Corps. Involved were elements of 53rd

▲ SE5 As of No. 111 Squadron, Palestine, 1918.

▼ Obstinate Lewis gun pack mules of the 2nd Leicestershire Regiment, 7th Indian Division, in the Arsuf coastal sector, summer, 1918. Mules inspired Cecil Brown's poem below:

The Ass of Palestine

In these days of bitter struggle, there is glory for the brave,
And patriotic ardour takes its terror from the grave,
But the subject of my verses is quite unknown to fame.
He gets all kicks no ha'pence, and still he plays the game,
Beneath a crushing burden, he scales the stony track,
Unflinching struggles onwards with galled and bleeding back,
No respite for his trembling limbs, e'en on the homeward road
He hears his brutal master, who ruthless plies the goad.
For him no extra ration, for him no sick parade,
However lame or weary, the journey must be made.
If there's anywhere a hero who deserves a happy end,
Who's as gentle as he's plucky, a slave and yet a friend,
Who never shirks his duty be it rain or be it shine
Its that tiny pocket Hercules, the ass of Palestine.

Division, Colonel Böhme's 24th Division (now a shell of 1,000 men), two weak regiments of the 3rd Cavalry, the German 702nd and 703rd Battalions, and one German company of the 11th Jäger Battalion. A diversionary probe was arranged by two battalions of 4th Army and part of the German 146th (Masurian) Regiment.

The main attack was launched at 0300 hours against the 1st Light Horse Brigade, spearheaded by the German units in the centre and supported by a Turkish regiment on either flank. The Germans swiftly overran the first posts and began pressing on the second line. The Turkish regiments went forward, then stopped. One Turk carrying incendiary bombs was riddled and his body exploded in a macabre glow. By the light of this human torch the Australians picked off the remnant of his bombing party.

The German dash worked its own undoing. At dawn, Australian reinforcements arrived and the Germans discovered themselves wholly unsupported by their Turkish ally. Still worse, several pockets of Australian posts were yet holding out to the rear. As the Germans retreated they were raked on three sides and for the first time in Palestine, gave away to the natural reaction of panic. The Jäger company was nearly annihilated, and 337 German prisoners were taken before the survivors could shoot a way out. This incident of 14 July poisoned German–Turkish relations and was a stark indication of the deterioration of Turkish martial pursuit.

Behind the Turkish Front

By summer, von Sanders had come to the conclusion that his German troops were the backbone of his tenure in Palestine. These he endeavoured to shuttle to and fro between endangered sectors. In May, the *Asien Korps* had been augmented by the arrival of the 146th (Masurian) Regiment and the 11th Jäger Battalion which von Sanders had earmarked for 7th and 8th Army reserves. They had come from the Balkan Front but, as soon as their last echelon detrained, they were set to be recalled. Enver Pasha appeared to have the support of Berlin in diverting them for escapades in the Black Sea and Caucasus theatres.

The Russian degeneration into violent civil war had left a power vacuum throughout the Caucasus, Trans Caucasus, Georgia, Azerbaijan, and Persia. Pan-Turkish aspirations revived and Enver determined to rush in where angels feared to tread. To von Sanders this was madness. Every Turkish venture into the Caucasus had failed and the dispersion of Turkish strength into a new theatre could only strip badly needed replacements from the vital Palestine Front. By von Sanders' estimate, six strong divisions numbering up to 9,000 men each were propelled into the Caucasian vortex with all their attendant supplies and railroad support.

In like measure, the Germans were expansionist enough on their own account to assist their Turkish ally's vision of conquest in sending minor units. In July, the former 8th Army commander, Kress von Kressenstein, was sent with German officers and officials to Tiflis, Georgia, ostensibly and ironically to guarantee Georgian independence from

▲ Enver Pasha, Minister for War in Turkey and head of the Committee for Union and Progress (Young Turks) with an officer of the German Military Mission.

Russia and Turkey. Von Sanders vehemently protested the withdrawal of his German units to Enver, to Ambassador Count Bernsdorff in Constantinople, to General Ludendorff, and finally by way of resignation of his command to Kaiser Wilhelm on 22 June. Von Sanders cited the inevitable loss of Turkish morale inherent with such a pull-out of German troops from Palestine and of the correspondant lift in insurgent Arab morale. Finally, a compromise was thrashed out whereby the 11th Jäger Battalion was taken from Palestine while the 146th (Masurian) Regiment was retained.

In mid-May von Sanders had been shocked to learn the Turkish High Command intended to broaden his powers to include internal political control within the boundaries of his military jurisdiction. In essence, he was being offered the sort of politico-military satrapy Djemal Pasha had enjoyed in Syria while commanding 4th Army. Von Sanders' memoirs described the civil situation as 'hopeless'. Never a free or open administration, Turkish local government tightened

German officer with walking stick and soldiers of the *Asien Korps* on board a troop train in Palestine, August, 1918. During a halt, local merchants have come up to tout their wares. Travel for Germans of *Yilderim* was becoming dangerous because of attacks from an increasingly hostile population.

▶

A German cavalry officer, with decoration, cane, and double-breasted tunic, and Turkish Caucasian and regular cavalry troopers with horses, crossing the River Jordan by ferry.

▶

German Flying Corps boot inspection, Palestine, June, 1918. Note neckcloths, and boots held in hands.

▶

still further under the strain of war. Government credit was a joke . . . 1917 contracts had been left unpaid and Arab merchants found it lucrative whenever possible to smuggle products and grains for British gold. Corrupt officialdom had provoked universal dissatisfaction and Moslem, Jew, and Syrian Christian were at religious and social odds. Sensibly, von Sanders rejected the dubious honour of civil administration.

Also shocking was Enver's communiqué 'that in agreement with German headquarters he would not renew the contract of the military mission which expired on December 14, 1918.'[5] Despite their rounds of quarrels it is a tribute to von Sanders that Enver Pasha respected him enough to ask him to stay on in the Turkish Army beyond the mission's contract. It was, of course, another offer von Sanders declined. Enver fully expected the Germans to crack the Western Front and win the war. Such a contract termination was undoubtedly to decrease Turkish dependence on Germany in the aftermath, if such a thing were possible. As a British War Office document assessed: 'The Turkish General Staff and War Office are largely in the hands of Germans; Turkish armies and minor units are commanded by German officers; German machine-gun units and artillery are to be found in all Turkish theatres; Germany is the source of Turkish munition supplies; and several thousand German and Austrian troops are in Constantinople, which is at the mercy of German warships, the "Goeben" and the "Breslau," anchored in the Golden Horn.'[6]

The irresponsible result of diversifying wartime commitments rather than the reinforcement and consolidation of existing ones demands vivid condemnation when one analyses conditions on the Palestine Front. The lines of communications, already hampered by a terrible rail situation, were by summer being starved of coal until wood – then out of desperation, vines – were burned to keep any service running, even at reduced efficiency. Rations were cut to the extent soldiers went hungry and artillery and transport animals could only pull half their normal loads. The overextension of 7th and 8th Armies resulted in no furlough relief during the hot season, the consequence of which was physical and mental fatigue in the front lines.

Most of the men and even the officers had no boots but wore wrappings around their feet. The lucky ones wore *tschariks*, or animal skins tied in cord. 'The Turkish soldiers had no summer clothes, but wore their cloth uniforms which might better be called rags. They suffered the most as fully three-fourths of them had not had underclothing for a long time, and wore their clothes next to the body. That, after the many futile attacks, the British or Indian dead left before the Turkish front were promptly robbed and found naked is not to be looked upon as intentional cruelty. It appeared to the Turkish soldiers the only means of procuring clothing, linen or boots.'[7]

Exacerbating these conditions, British Intelligence orchestrated propaganda through agents and by leaflet bundles dropped from aeroplanes. Two consistent messages were hammered home; that Turkey was being exploited by Germany, and (the believable allegation) that Turkish prisoners ate better than Turkish soldiers. A blunder of 4th

Army's Chief of Staff, Major von Papen (of the Zimmerman telegram fame) allowed secret papers to fall into Turkish hands. The papers outlined recommendations for German possession of Turkey's railroads so as to be in a superior economic position over its ally after the war. Such mistakes could only increase the impact of British propaganda. On 3 September the entire 3rd Battalion of the 109th Regiment deserted at Affule Station. By this date, in fact, more soldiers had been posted as deserters than were concurrently soldiering in Palestine.

Lieutenant Heiden reported that 8th Army had to send armed trucks to round up such deserters who often fled with their equipment and that sometimes pitched engagements were fought with deserter bands. The prevalent rumour in 8th Army was that unless peace came before the religious event of Bairam on 18 September, that the soldiers would vote with their feet. Only Arab replacements could be found for Major Würth von Würthenau's 13th Depot Regiment at Nazareth and Major Blell's 17th Depot Regiment at Haifa (the concept of the depot regiment was to attract enough men to become a division). Von Sanders was even refused the reinforcement of the 530 German sailors of the Euphrates Flotilla so that he had to be content to mine the port of Haifa to secure his rear coast.

As Mustapha Kemal prepared to assume command of 7th Army in August, Enver Pasha briefed him with inexplicable optimism. That August, von Sanders wrote Ludendorff that he expected an impending and considerable attack in his coastal sector which he hoped to contain, but he anticipated a dangerous attack in the Jordan sector.

Delaying Work

The Arab Northern Army was also worried about developments in the Trans Jordan. With the tactical frustration of the Trans Jordan Operations and the immobilisation of the EEF through extensive reorganisation, the Turks were theoretically free to mount an offensive for the relief of Maan, even to the recapture of the Arab Northern Army logistical base at Aqaba. Allenby provided assistance to prevent such an eventuality. His Jordan Valley Force kept the Turks alert to another possible raid while the RAF put bombing pressure on 4th Army.

And, closer to the Arab heart, Allenby supplied camels; 2,000 of them from the recently disbanded Imperial Camel Brigade. The camels were taken from Beersheba to Aqaba and set to two months of natural grazing in order to wean them from EEF barley. Feisal kissed Lawrence out of glee. Simultaneously, Allenby's previous gift of transport camels from the Egyptian Camel Transport Corps was reorganised. They had been run so close to EEF regulations that their efficiency in the Arab sphere had been diminished. By sending home their drivers and supervisory staff and by repacking their loads, the camelry's draught was doubled.

A new officer, Young, had been sent out by the Hejaz Operations Staff in the hopes of 'doubling' Lawrence's power with the tribes. The hopes were in the end, futile, for although Young was fluent in Arabic and had cultivated tribal experience in Mesopotamia, he was a 'regular' in mind and unable to doff the uniform and assume the dress and custom of Arab ways. He was, however, indefatigable in transport and quartermaster work and in the planning of demolition raids.

It was not easy for any British officer to be accepted by the Arabs. In the early days advisory officers were treated with resentment, even with scorn. As Sherif Nasir replied to a complaint: 'Don't forget that until a month ago we never had a European in this country; if we had, we should have shot him. You must give us time to get used to it.'[8] This universal prejudice makes Lawrence's achievements all the more remarkable. Feisal, always tactful and politic, set the stage for respect and good treatment of the allied foreigners by his unstinting personal example and verbal discipline of offending tribesmen.

Such prejudice was certainly reciprocated. Lieutenant J. C. Watson, a flyer from 'X' Flight had written a nasty classified appraisal of the entire Arab Revolt in early 1917. Watson, naturally enough for a 'regular officer', saw in the feudalistic aspects of the Arab armies not a latent nationalism, but a simple power-bid of the Sherifial family. He viewed the Revolt even more cynically as kept in place by a generosity of gold and guns. His more laudable views on the short-comings of aerial cooperation with and assistance from the Arab nationals are understandable and clearly illustrate the problems of *regular* thinking when compared with Lawrence's *irregular* flexibility and native understanding.[9]

After the move to Aqaba, Lawrence's influence grew, not only through the depth of his own prestige, but because no Sherif excepting Feisal held the preponderance in the north that he had held in the Hejaz. But primarily, Lawrence's success can be attributed to his cultivated adherence to '27 Articles' of handling Hejaz Arabs which he insisted was 'an art, not a science, with exceptions and no obvious rules'.[10] In *précis*, these were:

1. To make a good start while paying attention to externals until having attained the inner circle.
2. Learn through listening and indirect inquiry.
3. Deal only with the leader and through him.
4. Strengthen this leader in front of others. Be sure to accept, then carefully modify his plans with strong yet indirect pressure until the desired ideas flow from him as if being his own.
5. Drop these ideas in casual situations while living with, or close to, the leader.
6 & 7. Avoid close relations with his subordinates.
8. Be present, but not noticed.
9. Alleviate inter-tribal jealousies whenever possible.
10. Obtain precedence by referring to the leader as 'Sidi', or lord, while referring to others by their names only.
11. Conceal European customs and Christianity behind the name and banner of the leader.
12. Maintain a sense of humour of which tactful repartee and dry irony are the most effective.
13. The greater the even temper the greater the advantage.
14. Lead, do not drive.
15. Don't do overly much; assist to win *through* the Arabs.

16. Be careful in the giving and receiving of gifts.
17. Wear Arab headcloth in tribal situations; hats are considered immoral.
18. Only wear full Arab dress when confident of acting and surviving as a native, for no allowances will then be made.

▲ Lawrence mounted on a camel (note bare feet). His kit was a lump of unleavened bread, some chocolate, a canteen, chlorinated tablets, a toothbrush, and a book of poetry. His pistol was an American Colt 'Wild West' revolver. Before the war, an ambushing Turkoman tried to shoot him point blank with the safety catch on. Lawrence disarmed him and thereafter carried the Colt as a good luck charm. His Lee Enfield rifle had a fairy-tale history. Manufactured by the British, it was taken by the Turks off a British soldier at Gallipoli. Enver Pasha had it inscribed and presented to Feisal as a gift. Feisal gave it to Lawrence who cut notches in it for dead Turks until he grew tired of the accounting. After World War One it returned to England in the King's private collection. Today it is on display in the Imperial War Museum. His most advanced weapon was an 'air Lewis', a Lewis machine gun devoid of radiator, casing and stock, which he transported in a bucket from the side of his camel saddle.

19 & 20. Then dress like a Sherif if the leader agrees.
21. Realise Islam is more than a religion for the tribesmen; it is a pervading part of their nature.
22. Learn the Bedouin method of war, keeping operations small and unorthodox.
23. Openly expressed reasons are not often the real motivations – search for the inner reasons.
24. Don't mix townsmen with tribesmen, or trained men with tribesmen.
25. Avoid free talk about women.
26. One's own servants may also make or break one's respect with the Arabs.
27. Study unremittingly, and hear all.

The proof of the Arab Northern Army's vitality was in the tasting. Twenty-five bridges were knocked out in two weeks of May alone. Disciples among the northern tribes were gaining. Jerdun station fell for the third time into Arab regular hands and the Hejaz Armoured Car battery destroyed a Turkish sortie out of Maan. The Amir Zeid was operating with half of the army north of Uheida.

At Amman, however, a punitive Turkish column was in the making with orders to move as soon as its supply could be collected from Damascus. The RAF was making that a difficult task. Sherif Nasir had been posted in the Wadi Hesa with a 600-strong band of marauders with orders to delay the column. With him were Peake's Egyptian Camel Corps and Hornby as head of demolitions.

Their procedure for raiding the rail stations was always the same because it had always worked. First, the cutting of the rails north and south of the target station in the dark of

▲ A 'tulip' explosive detonating railroad track near Dera.

'Thirty ounces of gun-cotton were planted beneath the centre of the central sleeper of each ten-metre section of the track. The sleepers were steel, and their box-shape left an air chamber, which the gas expansion filled, to blow the middle of the sleeper upward. If the charge was properly laid, the metal did not snap, but bumped itself, bud-like, two feet in the air. The lift of it pulled them six inches together; and, as the chairs gripped the bottom flanges, warped them inward seriously. The triple distortion put them beyond repair. Three or five sleepers would be likewise ruined, and a trench driven across the earthwork; all this with one charge, fired by a fuse, so short that the first, blowing off while the third was being lighted, cast its debris safely overhead.'

T. E. Lawrence, *Seven Pillars of Wisdom*

night; at dawn, the rain of a sharp bombardment from Rasim's old Krupp gun. Then the tribal charge of Howeitat and Beni Sakr. Angered, the Turks bombed them by air in return till Nasir set up camp in a limestone cave north of Tafila. Based there, Hornby and Peake breached a 14-mile section of the railway. A retaliatory Turkish probe was pinned by Nasir's machine guns while Auda's abu Tayi cavalry swept down rodeo-fashion and whisked away the expedition's camelry and horses. Lawrence judged that Nasir's *travail* had worked enough mischief to last until the opening moves of Allenby's offensive.

Meanwhile the southern armies of Ali and Abdullah were still at work against the Hejaz Expeditionary Force which included the Medina Garrison, and since the 80-mile long demolition in April – the former 2nd Composite Force as well. These troops, after illness and casualties, could still muster 12,000 men. Counting the 5,500 Turkish killed and wounded, the thousands of prisoners and the drain of sickness, the combined Arab contribution had already put 25,000 Turks *hors de combat*.

The southern armies never attained the drive necessary to extinguish the Hejaz Expeditionary Force. Regular officers did not go forward with their men, and ex-Turkish gunners could only be made to fire against the Turks under pain of death. The simple conclusion from this disappointment was that the southern armies lacked a Feisal or a Lawrence, and though true enough, the reasons were more complex. British influence was never significant near the Holy Cities and the more inaccessible nature of operations hurt any close cooperation such as was experienced with the Arab Northern Army. In the south, the Turks exhibited an unusual knack for counter propaganda. Allegations that Germany was winning the war were widespread. Bolshevik Russia had also revealed the diplomatically damaging clauses of the Sykes-Picot Agreement and the Balfour Declaration which made Hussein, King of Hejaz, even more suspicious of Allied intentions.

Hussein had his own court troubles. Among these was a growing jealousy of Feisal and the victorious Arab Northern Army, and increasing mistrust of their close coordination with the EEF in northern lands. Hussein's problems were magnified by enmity with the potent prince of central Arabia, Ibn Saud who, fortunately, was himself pitted against the pro-Turkish Amir of Hail.

But, clearly, Hussein preferred the British to the Turks for whom he expressed 'only the sword lies between us.'[11] These words were in remonstrance to Feisal's negotiations with the Turks – an incredible piece of news Lawrence discovered and kept from EEF ears. Foremost a politician and lover of the concept of Arab nationalism, Feisal had learned through secret channels that the British had met with the Young Turk leader, Talaat, in Switzerland so that when the Turks made overtures to Feisal, Feisal listened. Displaying his usual acumen, Lawrence had Feisal turn his discovered negotiations into a game of harmless diversion, while never letting on he knew the game had been played at least as seriously as the British talks in Switzerland. The diplomats of Britain and Arabia had thus in part been dealing each other a double hand.

PREPARING THE SEVENTH SEAL

'And the number of the army of the horsemen were two hundred thousand thousand:
and I heard the number of them.' – Revelation 9:16

THROUGHOUT 1918 one of military history's master-strokes was germinating in the mind of General Sir Edmund H. H. Allenby. On 11 July Lawrence had been informed of the Arab role, while at Allenby's GHQ on 1 August Allenby presented his three corps commanders, Chauvel, Bulfin, and Chetwode his secret orders.

In general, plans are influenced by the personality and the sum of the commander's experiences. Allenby was widely read in the historical and Biblical campaigns in the Holy Land. Many of the topographical, meteorological and intangible military factors and lessons were as valid in 1918 as they had been during the Jewish Kingdom. Other components, particularly in the past six months, could only be appreciated through contemporary Intelligence reports and from personal contact with the enemy.

Allenby was foremost a cavalryman. He had an immense qualitative and quantitative superiority in cavalry which could only be given a free run in the plains. That was obvious enough in a textbook sense and also witnessed in the hill fighting for Jerusalem. This meant his weight of cavalry would have to be massed in readiness for a breakthrough in the Plains of Sharon and Esdraelon. In order to achieve surprise this concentration had to be undetected, and opposed by as few enemy troops as possible at the point of attack. Fortunately Allenby was directly aided by Turkish and German psychological fear for their communications centre and main artery of retreat through Dera on the opposite flank. Allenby had fine-tuned that fear through the Arabs and the Trans Jordan Operations so that enemy assets had been transferred from the *real* point of his attack to the *imagined* object of his attack. Further, weather dictated the time frame of operations, which had to commence after the hot season, and culminate before the advent of the seasonal rains. The attack matrix was thus mid-September.

Early in July, Sir Henry Wilson had mooted the idea of presenting Allenby with an additional four divisions as an autumn loan returnable for the anticipated spring, 1919 operations on the Western Front. The War Cabinet quickly dropped the idea, however, informing Allenby he would have to make do with in-theatre resources and cautiously encouraging him to maintain an active defence. Yet, Allenby's mood was one of offense. Three weeks into August Allenby came off a morning ride and strode into his GHQ planning offices with daring modifications to his previously doctrinaire if substantive plans. He would attempt no local victory, but a crushing campaign.

His initial punch would come on 19 September in the eight-mile long coastal plain from the Mediterranean Sea to the railway. The 3rd and 7th Indian Divisions and the 54th, 60th, and 75th Divisions of Bulfin's 21st Corps would conduct the northeast axis attack against the Turkish 8th

▲ Allenby maintained constant touch with his front lines via touring car. Allenby is in the rear seat on the viewer's left side. Note Union Jack pennant, and lettering, foreground. Photo taken in Damascus, 1918.

▲ French DFPS soldier of the *Régiment Mixte de Tirailleurs* or the *Légion d'Orient.*

▲ Major-General Chaytor, commanding the ANZAC Mounted Division at Richon, Syria, 1918.

Army, opening a wide breach or 'gate'. The Desert Mounted Corps, consisting of the 4th and 5th Cavalry Divisions and the Australian Mounted Division, having been secretly concentrated as close to the projected 'gate' as possible, would now have the cavalryman's 'G' in 'Gap' which had proved so frustratingly elusive on the Western Front. The Desert Mounted Corps would push through the gap up the road and rail through the Plain of Sharon to 8th Army headquarters at Tul-Karm. From there the cavalry would cross a narrow spur of hills through two passes, entering the Plain of Esdraelon (or Megiddo, the biblical place of Armageddon) to the Turkish communications nerve at El Affule. El Affule was situated 40 miles from the start and 25 miles from Tul Karm. As a force was detailed to deal with von Sanders' GHQ at Nazareth, the Desert Mounted Corps would split, one division forking to Haifa on the coast, another division thrusting south-east to Beisan. As the infantry thus opened the gate, the cavalry would effect an enormous incursion across the rear of Turkish 7th and 8th Armies. The result was meant to be catastrophic.

Chetwode's reduced 20th Corps would contain only the 10th and 53rd Divisions, and their mission would be to advance on both sides of the Jerusalem–Nablus road and 'pin' 7th Army, till it was too late to assist 8th Army. Chaytor's Jordan Valley Force would simultaneously demonstrate versus 4th Army while the Arabs menaced 4th Army's hinterland.

Such a bold conception with its attendant risks to the cavalry was believed acceptable by Allenby who had analysed two factors; the deterioration of Turkish morale, and the failure of its government to supply it with meaningful reinforcement. In the words of Chetwode's Chief of Staff, Brigadier (later Field-Marshal, Viscount) A. P. Wavell: 'It was a daring plan, even against an enemy so inferior in numbers and morale. It would involve a continuous ride of over fifty miles for the majority of the horsemen, and over sixty for some, in the course of which they would have to cross a range of hills in the enemy's possession, passable only by two difficult tracks. There is no parallel in military history to so deep an adventure by such a mass of cavalry against a yet unbroken enemy.'[1]

Camouflage and Concentration

In the weeks prior to his greatest military action, Allenby was headquartered near Ramle at Bir Salem, a small town ten miles from Jaffa and 25 from Jerusalem. The General's quarters were in a two-storey stone house, ironically once a German school. To the north he could see the Moslem minarets of Ramle, to the south the fruit-laden groves of the native Jewish colonies, to the west the sparkling blue waves of the Mediterranean, and to the east the spine of the Judean Hills. Topographically speaking, it was a portrait of Palestine in miniature.

Allenby maintained his presence at the front, leaving only for a brief and necessary official function in Egypt. During his tenure in the EEF the soldiers knew his efforts in the areas of medical and supply were for their benefit even if he had what many considered annoying insistence on details such as 'no shorts'. They could trust that their lives would be risked in boldness, not rashness. The Headquarters branches were themselves mere basic mat houses framed in wood, and supplemented by square tents. 'A Spartan life was the rule at GHQ. Work has the order of the day every day. Continually with his troops, it can be said with absolute truth that no commander-in-chief was better known by his soldiers, and none possessed in a higher degree the affection and confidence of his men'.[2]

Certainly, the ruses, camouflage, and disinformation employed by Allenby and staff to achieve the mandatory decisive concentration of force should remain legendary in history. In the first instance the secret plans were intentionally revealed to only a few key staff, corps and division commanders and to certain select individuals. The plans did not even reach brigade or regimental commanders until 48-72 hours before 'H' hour on 19 September. At this time he personally toured his front by car to brief the assembled divisional staffs. This severe limitation on a 'need to know' basis – so often the vital element in secrecy – was only possible because of his seasoned and veteran upper echelons of commanders and staff which had fortunately not been affected by the crisis transfers and reorganisation.

During the September period of concentration, the Desert Mounted Corps left the Jordan sector at night, moving west toward the coast only at night, while lying low by day. Upon arrival, the units sheltered in designated orange groves surrounding Jaffa. The Corps tents had been left standing in the Jordan Valley and Allenby permitted no new erection of tents outside the Valley. Camps in 21st Corps sector had initially been constructed along expansive lines so that when the moment of concentration came the camps and complementary orange groves could hide double the usual number of Corps troops.

Chaytor also took extensive pains to mask the absence of the Desert Mounted Corps by marching his West Indian Battalions east by day, then secretly returning them by night only to march east the next day. Mules dragged sleighs across the Valley floors so that the clouds of dust gave the illusion of cavalry formations. Reinforcing this impression, 15,000 'dummy' horses constructed of four sticks for legs under superimposed army blankets were set up as mock horse lines. From the air this ruse was utterly believable! Classified documents dated 17 September were later captured from *Yilderim* headquarters professing that far from *transferring* cavalry from the Jordan Valley, Chaytor's Force had been *supplemented* by 23 squadrons!

Twentieth and 21st Corps areas were tasked under similar west by night, east by day marching orders and stringent bivouac rules were in force in 21st Corps from 0430 hours to 1800 hours, backed by special 'police' patrolling with binoculars.

'All ration dumps were kept in the bivouac areas and no fires were lighted, all cooking being done by solidified alcohol to prevent smoke issuing from field kitchens. Horses were generally watered by bucket, but where animals had to be taken from their hiding places for this purpose strict rule prescribed that this should be done between noon and two o'clock, when the Royal Air Force arranged to have fighting patrols in the air to keep away enemy aircraft. Special roads were made into and out of each bivouac area and no other could be used. No enemy aeroplanes could be fired at from concealed bivouacs, no lights were to be shown at night, and the visits of staff officers and despatch riders were kept down to a minimum.'[3]

Nor did Allenby permit increased use of telephone or telegraph communications which was usually a give-away indication of an impending offensive. While being briefed at Allenby's GHQ in July Lawrence cast an interesting insight on EEF procedures: 'Allenby every morning for breakfast had a log of Turkish signals over the preceding 24 hours: and we read their every message – and I presumed they read all ours. To keep our moves secret we used air-mail or word of mouth. To keep the Turks' public, one of my cares was to distribute wire-cutters over their rear, and cut their telegraph at least daily.'[4]

Other techniques were equally resourceful. The Fast Hotel in Jerusalem was turned into a duplicate GHQ and the rumour disseminated Allenby was coming. City buildings were put on alert they would soon be turned out for military occupation. Meanwhile, Arab agents commissioned by Lawrence were sent throughout the Trans Jordan to barter for forage and sheep. Near Madeba he scouted two possible airfields, marked them with smoke signals and landing signs, and hired dubious Arabs to 'guard' them. Lawrence also leaked news of a large cooperative EEF drive on Amman to Arab staff officers in Turkish 4th Army. Naturally, these tidings reached intended Turkish spies.

In 21st Corps sector where pontoon bridges would be needed from the first minute of the offensive, a bridging school had been established that summer. The Turks were thus used to seeing the assembly and disassembly of

▲ Eight German staff of 4th Army Headquarters at Es Salt, August, 1918, with Turkish liaison officer (far right) and probable Turkish officer (seated left) in Turkish cork helmet.

▲ A German AEG CIV two-seat reconnaissance aircraft in Palestine. The engine is a Mercedes 175 horsepower. A camera is attached to the rear cockpit.

bridges over the Nahr el Auja. On 19 September, the extra bridges were simply not taken down . . .

Few of these activities could have been successful without the air support of the Palestine Brigade, Royal Air Force (the name had been changed from Royal Flying Corps in 1918). In June, *Yilderim* aircraft crossed EEF lines 100 times. By the last week of August increased counter-air reduced crossings to 18. During the critical three weeks of deployments in September, only four enemy aircraft sortied over EEF skies.

In October, 1917, *Yilderim* had fielded 56 aeroplanes in four squadrons (301st, 302nd, 303rd, 304th)[5] to augment the 300th Flight Detachment of Pasha I. As a whole, these aircraft were inferior in climb and speed to the newer British models. Spares and replacements arrived so damaged they were worthless. Since spring, the *Yilderim* air arm lost 59 pilots and observers and only five aeroplanes were in action in 7th and 8th Armies on the day of the big offensive. *Yilderim* had been effectively swept from the skies.

The EEF possessed another ace card up its sleeve – the Training Brigade of the Middle East command. Not only did this school create a reserve of pilots and observers, but it left a valuable bank of trained personnel who could be farmed out on special duties. These air service officers were attached to staffs in advisory liaison capacity, and their assistance in ground to air cooperation was invaluable.

▲ A camel patrol of the Arab Northern Army lead by Jafaar Pasha's *aide-de-camp*, and flying the Sherifian standard of red, black, green, and white.

One testimony to the secrecy and professionalism of the concentration was that of W. T. Massey, the official correspondent of the London newspapers. Always in search of a story, he could find nothing unusual, no hint of a major offensive. Not even the gossiping civil populace was aware. As he went to locate the 60th Division which was being transferred from 20th to 21st Corps, he motored by the division, lost, while thousands of the men lay just off the road in their daytime position.

Readying the Right

Lawrence and Alan Dawnay left Allenby's GHQ in July with a scheduled agenda. From 15–17 September they were to commence hostilities in the Trans Jordan with the Arab Northern Army. Such an opening on the opposite flank of the real attack would confirm *Yilderim* still deeper into its misconceptions of Allenby's plan.

After sharp quarrels over logistics, Lawrence's 'irregularities' of march won out over Young's textbook 'regularities'. Lawrence decided to dispatch a thousand-man camel column to Azraq by 13 September where they would be

a bridge south of Amman, and finally, returning to EEF lines at Beersheba.

The operations would therefore assume the mantle of a spoiling raid by Buxton's companies followed by a raid in force by a nucleus of Feisal's Arab Northern Army. Nuri Said Pasha was selected as column commander with, of course, Lawrence as his advisor.

August was a busy month of preparation. Buxton's men had to be escorted, Nuri es Shalaan and the northern tribes alerted to the rising, a route pioneered over which the armoured cars could navigate, and potential landing strips located for 'X' Flight's accompanying aircraft.

Fortunately, Buxton spoke Arabic, and with fair Sudanese experience to his credit had acquired a temperament suitable for cooperation with his new allies. Lawrence briefed the companies in Aqaba and ensured the loyalty of their escorts before setting out northeast for Guweira with 60 of his bodyguard.

At Guweira was based 'X' Flight which had assisted Arab raids on Jerdun, Mudauwara, and Maan. 'X' Flight now flew Lawrence, resplendent in white silk, to Jefer in the second week of August. There he and Feisal worked on the Rualla headmen in tandem, a charismatic team stirring memories of historic Arab glory. Nuri es Shalaan gave assurance for his tribal rebellion.

Buxton, meanwhile, had finally succeeded in the capture of Mudauwara Station. The camelry had marked the intended approaches with white tape. Then, just before dawn three bombing parties attacked the main redoubts and station. These were followed by the second wave which was supported by Lewis guns, some artillery pieces, and a brief aerial bombardment. Fourteen camel troopers fell for

situated to envelop Dera on the 16th. The column would contain 500 regulars, the French Algerian battery of .65 mountain guns, proportionate machine guns, two aircraft, two armoured cars, engineers, scouts, the 2,000 former EEF camel transport, and bare base supplies for three weeks. From Abu el Lissan to Dera was reckoned at two weeks of maneuver, with one week figured for the destruction of Dera's three-line convergence of railroads. On 18 September, the column was to retreat southeast on Azraq to await the success of Allenby's offensive and fresh orders. Nuri es Shalaan's Rualla warriors and the Serdiyeh, Serahin tribes, and the Haurani peasants under the famed Talal el Hareidhin would meanwhile have collected to Feisal's call.

Allenby loaned the British detachment in Aqaba Numbers 5 and 7 (British) companies of the former Imperial Camel Brigade. This body of 300 troopers, under Major R. V. Buxton, marched across the Sinai to arrive in Aqaba on 30 July. In addition to raising the ante for the Trans Jordan distraction, it was to assist Jafaar's regulars in besieging Maan. Turkish counterattacks had driven Sherif Nasir's partisans out of the Wadi Hesa, and wishful Turkish eyes were sizing up the Arab base at Abu el Lissan with its rich springs outside Maan. Buxton's camelry were first to strike the eternally surviving Mudauwara Station, thence through Bair northeast of Maan to Azraq, and from Azraq to blowing

▲ Lewis gunners of the Imperial Camel Corps with captured Turkish heavy machine gun inside Mudauwara Station during Buxton's raid on the Hejaz Railway, August, 1918.

an exchange of 171 Turkish casualties and prisoners. Next stop Jefer.

Joyce and Lawrence motored by car on reconnaissance to meet Buxton in Jefer, then drove two marches ahead to Bair to secure Buxton a welcome with Auda abu Tayi's kinsmen. At the old castle and oasis of Azraq they located a mud flat suitable for an airstrip. The land at Azraq was too barren of forage to support the camelry for the Dera operation. Therefore, barley and supplies would have to be pre-positioned. When they returned through Bair they dis-covered to their dismay a good 40 per cent of Buxton's supplies had been pilfered and this necessitated an unfortu-nate reduction of his technical force. Here Lawrence passed his 30th birthday reorganising Buxton's supply system and loading 6,000 pounds of gun-cotton onto 30 Egyptian camels.

When Buxton's troopers came in their experiences of Bedouin ways were apparent. Gone was the formal two company line of march for the native style of clotted clumps, merging together or diverging as tactics dictated. Loads were lightened and rehung from the conventional pattern in order to increase the camels' pace and range. Instead of halts, the troopers learned to let their animals stale en route and EEF grooming standards were relaxed. The only blight on these improvements was in the mounting by numbers after a stop. The 300 male camels inevitably roared when rising in formation, which betrayed their position for miles around.

Buxton's mission was cancelled one march short of the bridge south of Amman. Turkish aerial observers had picked them up then quickly lost them. The ground troops, however, were fully alerted in anticipation of a raid. It was 20 August and Allenby had ordered Turkish attention to be distracted from a counteroffensive till 30 August. Settling for a clever hoax, Lawrence and Buxton drove a patchwork of armoured car tracks and spread opened tins all over Muagger, south of Amman. Friendly tribesmen spread disinformation that this was a reconnaissance before Feisal's army hit Amman. This left the Turks scanning the horizon for a week as Lawrence buried demolition muni-tions in waiting at Azraq and while Buxton's cameliers returned to Beersheba having traversed 920 miles in 41 days.

When Joyce and Lawrence arrived back in Abu el Lissan, a stunning blow threatened the entire preparation. Hussein, King of Hejaz, forwarded a proclamation to Feisal insulting the officer corps of the Arab Northern Army. This thunder-clap pointed out that there was no Hejaz rank above captain nor decorations such as had been received from the English. Jafaar Pasha and most of the senior staff resigned in dishonour. Feisal protested and Hussein branded him an outlaw.

Hussein's jealousy of Feisal's power and his knowledge that most of the Arab Northern Army was fighting for its own concept of Arab nationalism rather than for the dignity of the King of Hejaz had finally boiled over. Desperately, Lawrence faced down a mutiny of the rank and file by proving that Feisal had not left them, then set about restoring the morale of soldier and officer and ensuring

Feisal's supremacy was left undamaged. Allenby directed all possible diplomatic pressures on Hussein for a written retraction. Only at the last possible moment in which to start the three week campaign did a partial and obstinately veiled 'regret' issue from Hussein. This paper arrived in the middle of a council convened to decide the fate of the campaign. Fortunately, Lawrence grasped the cipher and using full command of Arabic innuendo and with much poetic licence manipulated the wording to a message of apology and reinstatement. Only Feisal had guessed the alteration of this historic communiqué. The Arab campaign was on.

▲ ANZACs bringing in a cleverly camouflaged Turkish sniper, Palestine. Natural 'bush' foliage has been attached to his uniform.

▲ Austrian howitzer on limber with Austrian gunners, Palestine. Some Germans and Turks are included in the personnel.

ARMAGEDDON

'And he gathered them together into a place, called in the Hebrew tongue Armageddon.' — Revelation 16:16

IN early September Colonel von Oppen requested that von Sanders call off further attempts at aerial observance in 8th Army sector. Royal Air Force counter air missions had become so fierce and the struggle so unequal, that the aerial duels were having a disheartening impact on morale. *Yilderim* was like an ostrich sticking its head in the sand.

Official records and Allenby's own account report the EEF with 12,000 cavalry, 57,000 infantry, 540 guns and 350 machine guns in the main battle line. A secret, recently declassified War Office document indicates that an additional 30,000 combat troops were in direct support or reserve.[1] *Yilderim* opposed Allenby with only 3,000 cavalry, 23,000 infantry, 340 guns and 600 machine guns. The enemy general reserve consisted of 3,000 depot troops with 30 guns, while 6,000 infantry with some cavalry and 30 guns lay under Arab siege at Maan or along the rail to Dera. The overall main battle line ratio of EEF to *Yilderim* was 2.15 to 1, while considering the War Office document the ratio of supporting reserves seems to have been 10 to 1. The EEF enjoyed a quantitative differential in cavalry of 4 to 1.

The decisive *qualitative* differential was in the morale of opposing personnel. Colonel Trevor Dupuy has used statistical analysis to express the human combat effectiveness of the British trained to Turkish soldier as 1.98 to 1.00 and reflected his calculations as similar to the moral and technical superiority enjoyed by the Israeli's over their Arab opponents in 1967 and 1973.[2]

These facts were only part of the story, for the genius of Allenby's secret concentration becomes clear when analysing the 15 mile coastal sector which was the butt of his prime attack:

	Cavalry	Infantry	Guns
EEF	9,000	35,000	383
Yilderim		8,000	130

At his selected point of attack Allenby achieved an overall battle line advantage of 5.5 to 1. His infantry would begin the battle with a ratio of nearly 4.4 to 1, supported by an artillery advantage of approximately 3 to 1. When the infantry opened the gate, the 9,000 cavalry of the Desert Mounted Corps would dash through, theoretically or relatively unopposed.

East, over the 45 miles of three-quarters of his remaining front Allenby had balanced in main battle line:

	Cavalry	Infantry	Guns
EEF	3,000	22,000	157
Yilderim	3,000	21,000	270

As Allenby could count on Arab support to destabilise the rear flank of this Turkish force, the seriousness of *Yilderim's* position becomes clear.

Captured Turkish Quartermaster returns revealed *Yilderim* and attached ration strength south of Damascus:

4th Army	21,899
7th Army	28,575
8th Army	39,783
Jordan Group	5,223
Palestine (LOC)	4,958

Including 2nd Army, the Hejaz Expeditionary Force, and labourers, the returns reached 247,000.

Allenby's own EEF ration returns were considerable. Including the 140,000 in his three front-line corps, lines of communications detachments, the Force in Egypt, and 80,000 men of the Egyptian Labour and Camel Transport Corps, the EEF ration strength was 340,000. Adding all on the Egyptian payroll in every menial capacity, the aggregate totalled 450,000.

If *Yilderim* was in the dark concerning EEF strengths and whereabouts Allenby had conversely acquired an accurate picture of his enemy's order of battle. In the month before his offensive 1,100 Turkish deserters took to their heels, while soldiers representing 16 different regiments, three batteries, and a cavalry and machine gun unit went over to the EEF with information. Shortly before the offensive a British-trained Indian NCO did desert to the Turks revealing such incredible (but true) facts and positions, that he was considered by *Yilderim* Intelligence to be a 'plant'.

Abbreviated orders of battle are listed here, detailed orders of battle are recorded in the appendices.

EEF ORDER OF BATTLE, SEPTEMBER, 1918

Commander-in-Chief: General Sir Edmund H. H. Allenby
Chief of Staff: Major-General Sir L. J. Bols

Desert Mounted Corps Lieutenant-General Sir H. G. Chauvel
4th (Indian) Cavalry Division
5th (Indian) Cavalry Division
Australian Mounted Division

20th Corps Lieutenant-General Sir Philip W. Chetwode
10th Division
53rd Division

21st Corps Lieutenant-General Sir E. S. Bulfin
3rd (Lahore) Division
7th (Meerut) Division
54th (East Anglian) Division
60th Division
75th Division

Palestine Brigade, Royal Air Force
Commander Brigadier-General A. E. Borton

*The 4th and 5th Cavalry had one British per two Indian regiments. All infantry divisions had one British per three Indian regiments, excepting the 54th (East Anglian).

5th Wing
Nos. 14, 113, 142 Squadrons

40th Wing
Nos. 1 (Australian), 11, 144, 145 Squadrons

YILDERIM ORDER OF BATTLE, AUGUST, 1918

Commander-in-Chief: Marshal Liman von Sanders
Chief of Staff: General Kiazim Pasha

8th Army General Djevad Pasha
22nd Corps Colonel Refet Bey
7th, 20th Divisions
Asia Corps Colonel von Oppen
16th, 19th Divisions, *Asien Korps* Brigade
Army Troops
46th Division

7th Army General Mustapha Kemal Pasha
3rd Corps Colonel Ismet Bey
1st, 11th Divisions
20th Corps Major-General Ali Fuad Pasha
24th, 26th, 53rd Divisions

4th Army General Mohammed Djemal Kuchuk Pasha
8th Corps Colonel Ali Fuad Bey
2nd Caucasian Cavalry Brigade, 48th and Composite
Divisions, Mule Mounted Infantry Regiment
2nd Corps
Hauran and Maan Detachment, 25th Amman Division
Army Troops
3rd Cavalry Division, 146th (German Masurian) Regiment,
63rd Regiment
Yilderim Flying Command
1st Pursuit Detachment, 302nd, 303rd, 304th Reconnaissance Detachments
Yilderim GHQ Troops
109th, 110th Regiments, 13th, 17th Depot Regiments

The Arab Northern Army Opens

Lawrence had promised Allenby to envelop and destroy the Dera railroads on 16th September, three days before the grand offensive. The disinformation concerning the attack on Amman was an excellent play of cards, a double bluff. It not only drew Turkish attention away from Allenby's real attack, but rivetted its attention away from that of the Arab Northern Army. Dera was north of Amman on the Hejaz Rail (*see* map on *page 130*) and the column of Lawrence and Sherif Nasir was to march to Azraq – but instead of striking west on Amman – would ride north and base out of Umtaiye, then surround Dera, the one Yilderim major communications centre Allenby's cavalry could not reach.

Lawrence conceived his bluff not from an empty hand. Hornby, with Sherif Zeid was armed with guns, money, explosives, part of Lawrence's bodyguard, and the Zebn tribesmen with instructions to attack Madeba southwest of Amman. 'I had put all my influence behind Hornby's push, personally attaching to him all the Beni Sakhr sheikhs, and telling them that he would roll up Moab from the south while I cut it off from the north and east. I had also given

him Dhiab of Tafileh, an old wind-bag, and two of the Majalli sheikhs of Kerak, who notably had a foot in each camp.'[3]

Beyond the bluff and diversion lay a variability. As Hornby and Zeid were about to begin north, the Turks again flailed in counterattack toward Tafila. Lawrence knew that as soon as he reached Dera this Tafila force would likely be quickly withdrawn, thus reviving Hornby's push on Madeba. And, should the Arab Northern Army fail at Dera, they might still fall on Amman as consolation, in conjunction with Hornby. In the end, the Turkish reoccupation of the Arab base at Tafila only dispersed their assets farther south as Sherif Nasir and Lawrence marched north. Meanwhile, Jafaar Pasha with the bulk of the Arab Northern Army regulars poised in siege of Maan ready to occupy or destroy it should the Turks divert their forces northward.

By 14 September, the mobile Arab column reached the old Roman fort at Azraq with its palms and pools of pure water. Though due east of Amman, their safety was assured because of the paucity of Turkish cavalry, and because of the friendliness of the local tribes. Sherif Nasir's 450 regular Sherifial Camel Corps with 20 Hotchkiss machine guns, the French mountain battery under Captain Pisani, two armoured cars, a party of Egyptian Camel Corps for demolitions, and a detachment of Gurkhas with four machine guns were soon joined by Nuri es Shalaan's Rualla, Auda abu Tayi's Howeitat, and Talal el Hareidhin's Hauran villagers. It was a merry band of 5,000 with imminent promise of a full scale rising behind the Turkish lines.

The roads from Azraq led to Dera and Amman, and finally, Damascus, the cherished Arab dream. The opening move, early on 15 September, was for Peake's Camel Corps and Scott-Higgins' Gurkhas, with two armoured cars, to cut the Hejaz rail north of Amman and south of Dera. This would confirm the Amman garrison's belief they were the target of attack while fulfilling one of Allenby's three Dera objectives. Allenby ordered Dera, the rail centre of the Hauran, to be knocked out for a week so that 4th Army would be delayed for its piecemeal destruction.

On the morning of 15 September the main column set out for the old Roman border town of Umtaiye with its huge well, situated 15 miles southeast of Dera. Gone was the solitary expanse of Arabia for the closer, developed confines of Syria and Trans Jordan with their traffic of men. The column now marched with a crew of 1,000 regulars and 300 of Nuri es Shalaan's personal sheikhs, servants, and retainers. Feisal had moved up and encamped at Azraq where an airstrip had been demarcated for two cooperating RAF planes. Two thousand of the Rualla tribal camel corps lay in wait in the Wadi Sirhan.

On 16 September, Lawrence learned Peake's party had failed, so he and Joyce set out in two armoured cars and blew the four-span 80-foot long bridge themselves. This demolition secured the Arab rear from Turkish rapid rail movement. As Hornby had settled in Shobek, with Zeid at Abu el Lissan, it was believed this cut would also remove Turkish pressure from them. Half the column's air support was lost that day when one of their pilots, Murphy, in a Bristol Fighter, downed a Turk but received such structural damage that he was forced to return to Palestine.

▲ Two officers of the Sherifian Regular Army. Their uniforms are British khaki with Sam Browne belt, their hats a peculiar khaki helmet with khaki neck-cloth. Three gold cords with silver vertical bands are joined in sections by clumps of larger purple threads around the helmet's circumference – in the *agal* and *kaffiyeh* tradition of the *Bedouin*. A long purple tassle is connected to the cords on the reverse of the helmet, and a red rounded cone is on top, crowned with a gilt emblem. Rank is denoted on the collar patches. Note cigarette and riding crop.

By 0800 hours on 17 September, the main column approached Dera's northern side and bore down on the redoubt of Tel Arar. Pisani's guns hurled shells while the regular infantry and Rualla horse charged the Turkish defences. An hour later the southernmost ten miles of the Damascus–Dera rail were in Arab hands, the most vital of the hub of rails. The promise to Allenby was technically satisfied. A 'permanent' break, however, would be exceptionally damaging and 600 tulip charges were employed to take out over four miles of rail.

As the column posted machine guns on the head of the Tel, the Turks grew restive. Nine aircraft lined up on the Dera aerodrome as Turkish artillery fired futile bursts from four miles away. Locomotives in Dera fiercely puffed steam, loaded with troops. A Pfalz reconnaissance aircraft flew over to observe the extent of damage as eight more aeroplanes, one a yellow-bellied Albatros, followed in echelon. An aerial circus of bombing and strafing ensued, the Arabs replying with Hotchkiss automatic rifles. Pisani elevated the trajectory of his mountain guns, spitting upward a hopeful barrage of shrapnel. With respect, the Turkish–German aeroplanes climbed, then circled at higher altitude, their effectiveness degraded.

The remainder of the column's air force came to the rescue, piloted by Junor in a BE 12 based out of Azraq. Incredibly, as he dashed into the fray, all of the enemy aircraft pulled off in pursuit. Lawrence took advantage of this

fracas to direct a third of the regulars, half the artillery, and most of the village peasantry who had collected in support of the revolt, west in direction of the Palestine–Yarmuk railway line. This left Colonel Joyce, the Rualla horse, the Gurkhas, armoured cars, and the regulars as a covering on Tel Arur. Meanwhile, like some cartoon caricature, Junor came roaring back, riddled by the enemy flying circus, and crashlanded. Within minutes, Junor had escaped from the fiery wreck, and dashing up to Colonel Joyce, grabbed a Ford car and raced south where he began setting explosives under the nose of the Turkish Dera artillery.

Meanwhile, Lawrence's group watered at Mezerib where they were bombed from the air; Lawrence receiving a metal splinter elbow-wound in the process. Lawrence's bodyguard, led by Abdullah, secured the Mezerib suburban approaches while Sherif Nasir, Nuri Said, and the regulars caught them up. Pisani's guns, supported by 20 machine guns, then set up point blank suppression fire as Nuri Said theatrically walked forward sword in hand and smoking his pipe, accepted the Turkish post's surrender. Lawrence and Young then destroyed the main and trunk telegraph lines into Palestine. Mezerib was left burning as a torch, an advertisement the rebellion was under way.

Insurgent support now followed them in increasing swarms. Adherents had learned that Sherif Nasir was with the column and that he was planning to take Dera that night. Once again, with chagrin, the British advisors had to control the effervescence of their would-be irregular allies. Not till the success of Allenby's offensive was assured could the general rising be called and this would be known in scarcely 60 hours.

Still on the 16th of September, Lawrence set off with a war band down the Yarmuk Valley for the critical bridge at Tel el Shehab. Once again, Lawrence espied the bridge which had eluded him during the Jerusalem campaign. Silently, the bridge was shrouded in the grey mist of the Yarmuk River. Just below the gorge lay a somnolent German troop train bringing reinforcements from El Affule bound for Dera. Warily, Lawrence's party retreated east and blew more rails on the western approach into Dera. If they had failed against the bridge, the surgery of explosive had amputated all three rail trunks into Dera. At the same time, the German train was assurance that the Arab Northern Army distraction was working. From the point of his greatest unrealised peril, von Sanders was dispatching men to the quiet sector of his line.

Early on 17 September, the main column was reunited at Mezerib when Joyce brought in his covering force from Tel Arar. Together, they circumvented Dera on the western and southern approaches, sheltering back at Umtaiye on the next day. Logistically, the regular column could not afford to provision the horde of rebel peasantry so they were sent home to await the call. A clever moment was chosen to disband them – while enemy observer aircraft were overhead. From the air, 8–9,000 dispersing tribesmen alarmingly appeared as though the Arabs were fanning out to attack in all directions!

Late on 17 September, the Arab column had again struck the rail south of Dera, taking out Nasib Station. Lawrence enjoined the additional opportunity of blowing his 79th bridge, each of the multi piers being five feet thick and twenty-five feet high. This covered the western flank of the Arab Umtaiye encampment. It was now time for Allenby to unleash the dogs of war.

The Stroke of Armageddon

Over the ten mile width of the plains of Sharon from Tul Karm to the sea, the Turks had constructed two systems of defence. The first ran along a sandy ridge covering 14,000 yards in length, extending 3,000 yards to the rear (see map). These were a series of redoubts supported by continuous fire trenches. The second, or Et Tireh defence was a weaker line 3,000 yards further to the rear, itself even weaker near the coast where there were inherent natural defences provided by marshy ground.

Bulfin's orders were to break these defences from the railway to the sea, seize the foothills east of the rail, and pivotting on the right, advance northeast as a large gate opening the gap for Chauvel's Desert Mounted Corps. Allenby had allotted Bulfin's 21st Corps the 3rd, 7th, 54th, 60th, 75th Divisions, the French DFPS, the 5th Australian Light Horse Brigade, two brigades of mountain artillery, and 18 batteries of heavy and siege artillery.

Having achieved strategic surprise Allenby now opted for tactical suprise. In the early dark hours of 19 September, Captain Smith's Handley Page bombed *Yilderim's* central telegraphic and telephonic exchange at El Affule. Within a few hours, five DH9s of No. 144 Squadron attacked again while, just before noon, eight more aircraft heightened the confusion at von Sander's GHQ. Simultaneously, No. 142 Squadron bombed 8th Army headquarters at Tul Karm and No. 144 Squadron hit 7th Army headquarters at Nablus.

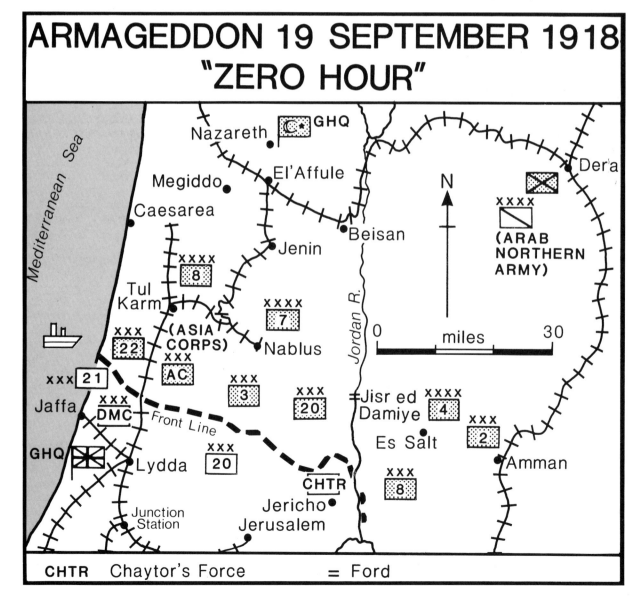

ARMAGEDDON 19 SEPTEMBER 1918 "ZERO HOUR"

CHTR Chaytor's Force   = Ford

No. 14 Squadron additionally struck three smaller Turkish headquarters. RAF counter air kept the main *Yilderim* aerodrome pinned down from dawn to dusk. From the opening shot *Yilderim* thus lost communication with 8th Army which was never effectively restored. Command and control functions were seriously degraded throughout *Yilderim*.

What transpired on the Sharon Front can only be viewed as a precursor to the modern *blitzkrieg*. Zero-hour came at 0430 hours in the gloom before dawn. At one gun per 50 yards average the opening 15 minutes of preparatory bombardment was the heaviest of the Palestine–Arabian campaigns. Rear Admiral Jackson's destroyers *Druid* and *Forester* joined in offshore and a thousand shells per minute exploded into the Turkish lines, churning the earth into a dust-clouded inferno. To the soldiers stumbling out of bivouac the unexpected bombardment followed by the surprise assault of five EEF divisions must have seemed like the crack of doom.

As the thick waves of 21st Corps infantry advanced through the protective pall of smoky haze a creeping barrage carpeted their van. What Turkish guns fired back were searched out by the angry wrath of the heavy EEF guns – which, having premapped 8th Army artillery positions, put down an accurate and devastating counter battery fire. The battle quickly assumed the proportions of an overrun attack. In places the infantry had to pause to avoid running into its own barrage. The offensive's centre of gravity – 3rd, 75th, and 7th Divisions – carried its objectives at the first rush. The 'latch of the gate' – 60th Division – covered four miles along the coast in two and a half hours. In historical repetition, Shea's 60th trod the very ground where Richard the Lionheart defeated the Saracens on a similar September day in AD 1191.

Cooperating on the 60th left flank, as insurance for the necessary pressure to open the 'latch', was the 5th Light Horse Brigade which rapidly moved to the north and rear of Tul Karm. By late afternoon, the 22nd Corps and 8th Army headquarters at Tul Karm fell to the combined arms of infantry, cavalry, and aerial assault. In the first few hours, 7,000 Turkish prisoners and 100 guns had fallen into 21st Corps hands: 22nd Corps ceased to exist. (One escapee from 22nd Corps' destruction was its commander, Refet Bey, an efficient and gallant officer destined to be one of Mustapha Kemal's best generals in the 1919–1922 war with Greece. Wandering behind British lines on horseback for a week, Refet Bey eventually reached the Turkish army near Tyre.)

Only against 21st Corps' right, that is east of the rail, was there any delay. Here the 54th and French DFPS encountered initial difficulties against the Turkish strongpoints nestled into the foothills. The front was for a while stoutly held by the Asia Corps, 8th Army's second corps component (the Corps named should not be confused with the *Asien Korps* Pasha II Brigade), but here also ground was given.

Chetwode's 20th Corps operations were dependent upon and subordinate to those of Bulfin's 21st Corps. His mission was to advance against 7th Army with his 10th and 53rd Divisions, clearing opposition through the hill country up to Nablus, and to block the critical escape routes east across the Jordan. At noon Allenby sent him the go-ahead with news of 21st Corps' success. Chetwode had long since planned such an advance must be made on the 'flanks' of his Corps boundary – the 10th on the left, the 53rd on the right. In between would be left a lightly screened seven mile gap. He had effected some forward adjustments the night before the offensive to capitalise on water sources and to improve terrain postures.

Chetwode's conception of attack had also been formulated on deception. Opposite 10th Division, the Turks were positioned on northeast to southeast standing ridges. For weeks raids and reconnaissance aimed at convincing the Turks of a future attack from the south when Chetwode's intention all along had been to attack from the west. Both Chetwode's divisions thus advanced to outflank the dug-in 7th Army hill positions. Both divisions received proportionately heavy casualties. That evening resistance eased and 20th Corps surged forward until dawn of 20th September. Communication between Nablus and Tul Karm had been sporadic throughout the day until afternoon, when it had ceased altogether. Seventh Army had some physical contact with elements of the Asia Corps through its own adjacent 3rd Corps. Surviving units of the Asia Corps had only imprecise impressions of the fate of 22nd Corps and the rest of 8th Army, so that 7th Army could only logically fall back by stages to the rear in hopes of an eventual *Yilderim* front realignment.

Von Sanders was himself caught in the throes of a 'news blackout'. What few orders he could get through his damaged El Affule communications centre usually had to be routed through 7th Army headquarters in Nablus and forwarded on to 4th Army. Not even 7th Army units adjacent to 8th Army had a clear picture of what had happened to the right flank. Intermittently, a signal came through that Colonel von Oppen's *Asien Korps* Brigade was still under some coherent formation and was attempting to claw its way out of the cauldron.

Irruption

El Affule, Beisan and Dera were the escape exits for *Yilderim* and by Allenby's grand design the severance of these rear arteries was now the mission of his mobile forces. The Arab Northern Army had already disrupted Dera and was poised for attack upon Allenby's signal. Allenby ordered Chauvel (Desert Mounted Corps less the ANZAC Mounted Division) to: 'advance along the coast, directly the infantry had broken through and had secured the crossings over the Nahr Falik. On reaching the line Jelameh–Hudeira, he was to turn northeast, cross the hills of Samaria, and enter the Plain of Esdraelon at El Lejjun and Abu Shusheh. Riding along the plain, the Desert Mounted Corps was to seize El Affule, sending a detachment to Nazareth, the site of the Yilderim General Headquarters. Sufficient troops were to be left at El Affule to intercept the Turkish retreat there. The remainder of the Corps was to ride down the Valley of Jezreel and seize Beisan.'[4]

After dark on 18 September the cavalry had crowded in behind the assaulting infantry. Allenby and his cavalry generals – MacAndrew, Barrow and Hodgson were bound and determined that, this time, the cavalry would make use of its 'G in Gap'. As El Affule was 45 miles away and Beisan a good 60, time was of the essence. Crossing the narrow seven-mile wide spur of Samarian hills, dividing the Plains of Sharon and Esdraelon, before *Yilderim* infantry could block the passes was in fact critical.

Major-General MacAndrew's 5th Cavalry commenced its march at 0700 hours as the 60th Division cleared the way ahead. Hugging the coast, they had covered an impressive 25 miles by noon. Major-General Barrow had personally gone forward to Fane's 7th (Indian) Division headquarters so as to be personally informed of the precise moment his 4th Cavalry could be launched. That moment came at 0840 hours. For the cavalry, textbook opportunities had begun to unfold. The divisions were experiencing the unique situation of marching parallel to the new 8th Army 'front', as the 21st Corps infantry swung the gate and prised the Turks away from the coast on a northeast axis. Resistance to the cavalry was slight to nonexistent. After 12 miles the 4th Cavalry paused for an hour in the early afternoon, then overran the primitive third 'line' of Turkish defences and panicked an 8th Army depot regiment. Hodgson's Australian Mounted Division started north mid-morning.

The 4th Cavalry's three brigades halted for water between 1630 and 2030 hours on the first day. Barrow urged them on again an hour before midnight, dispatching the 2nd Lancers of the leading 10th Brigade into the Musmus Pass. The low hills and narrow opening, however, made the entrance to the Pass obscure in the darkened hours and 10th Brigade marched past, inflicting a touchy delay of two hours. Then, Barrow's car broke down and he had to attempt to sort his cavalry out on horseback and alone. Pragmatically, Barrow maneuvered the 12th Brigade into the Pass after the 2nd Lancers. With light armoured cars in the van the lancers traversed the Musmus Pass and mounted the *tel*, below which lay the ancient ruins of Meggido, or Armageddon. It was 0330 hours on 20 September. The 6th Lancers were following as quickly as possible, trotting for five minutes, walking for 20 minutes, then resting for five minutes, in cyclical repetition which

▲ Aerial bombing of El Affule, 19 September 1918. El Affule handled the telephonic and telegraph communications of von Sanders' GHQ. From the start of Allenby's offensive the RAF paralysed *Yilderim* command and control functions through continual pre-planned bombing.

▼ German Albatros DVs captured intact at El Affule. One aircraft sports a pre-Nazi swastika. Mount Tabor is in the background overlooking the plain of Esdraelon, the Biblical place of Armageddon. What few German aeroplanes were still flyable were kept grounded by a very aggressive RAF bombing and counter air strategy.

maximised speed while preserving of the horses' stamina.

Four hundred feet below the Tel of Meggido, the Plain of Esdraelon lay like a carpet of green cloth smooth against the backdrop of the Galilean Hills. Ten miles away were the whitewashed houses of Nazareth, the *Yilderim* GHQ, and in the centre of the plain, Tel Affule, all clearly illuminated by the fingerlet rays of dawn. Scarcely had the 2nd Lancers fed and watered than the Turkish 13th Depot Regiment was spotted moving toward the Tel. This discovery highlighted the importance of the speed Allenby had demanded and Barrow had striven so hard to deliver, for von Sanders had ordered the regiment to block the pass.

Immediately, the acting commander of the 2nd Lancers, Captain Davison, took action. While the section of armoured cars and one squadron held the deploying Turks frontally, two squadrons charged with levelled lances at both the right and left Turkish flanks. The blow was so swift that the Turks fired high, working their rifle bolts with nervous urgency. Forty-six Turks were ridden down with the lance before the remaining 470 surrendered. One lancer and 12 horses were casualties!

At 0800 hours, the 4th Cavalry rode into El Affule to discover the 5th Cavalry was already inside and winding down opposition. The aerodrome was caught with three intact German aeroplanes. Within minutes of the airfield capture, another German aircraft touched down, discovered its mistake, then began to taxi and shoot its way out. Before taking off, the pilot and observer were shot down. Barrow's 4th Cavalry left that afternoon heading southeast to close off Beisan by early evening: in 34 hours they had ridden 70 miles.

MacAndrew's 5th Cavalry had meanwhile halted near refreshing wells at mid-day then returned to the advance at 1815 hours. Brigadier Kelly's leading 13th Brigade entered the Abu Shushe Pass at 0215 hours on 20 September and in less than an hour debouched from the Pass and demolished a stretch of the railway to Haifa. Detaching squadrons to deal with demoralised Turkish-held villages, Kelly launched the Gloucester Hussars in a bid to capture *Yilderim* GHQ at Nazareth.

Nazareth, a town of 15,000 inhabitants, resided 'at the bottom and on the sides of a cup-like depression in the hills, three sides being so steep that in places the roofs of the homes seem to form a giant stairway'.[5] Nazareth had won the reputation of being the best constructed town in Palestine, and was of course the scene of Jesus Christ's childhood. With swords drawn, the Gloucester Hussars rode into town shortly before dawn. They were not far into Nazareth when rifle and machine gun fire erupted from the balconies and darkly mute windows. German clerks and GHQ staff boldly counter-attacked and a running gun battle developed in the streets. The tactics of street fighting put any cavalry at disadvantage. Von Sanders' housekeeper later testified that when the cavalry entered Nazareth that to avoid capture, von Sanders scampered to his car in pyjamas. Soon, after surveying the battle situation, he returned to direct the defence. Having disrupted *Yilderim* GHQ the cavalry was forced to withdraw. Unfortunately for history, the Germans had taken the precaution of burning their classified campaign records.

Hodgson's Australian Mounted Division had commenced its northern ride in the mid-morning of 19 September and had ridden 28 miles before its first bivouac. Several hours in transit behind Barrow's 4th Cavalry, the Australians exited the Musmus Pass late morning of 20 September; the Desert Mounted Corps headquarters following closely in their wake. At Megiddo, Chauvel established his new corps headquarters in contact with his three attached divisions and Allenby's GHQ.

The 3rd Light Horse Brigade was next ordered southeast on Jenin which was located at the northern end of the Dothan Pass. Through the Dothan, retreating elements of 8th Army from Tul Karm and 7th Army from Nablus, had to transit. Again, speed was the critical factor. At one point the Light Horse travelled 11 miles in 70 minutes. A subaltern with his leading troop rear-flanked 1,800 Turks in a grove, taking them prisoner. Inside Jenin, a skirmish flushed out further prisoners until the Light Horse were encumbered with 3,000. The Arab population had already risen in revolt, the rebellion being chiefly aimed at the Turkish supply depot. Screaming 'Arab! Arab', as if some understood allied password for the Australians not to shoot, the villagers burned and pillaged. Warning shots were fired in order to establish some semblance of shaky order. A brisk wrestling match broke out between the Light Horse and their new irregular friends over a government gold bullion wagon and 120 cases of quality German champagne. It appears that later accounting for the strict tally of champagne cases was done tongue-in-cheek.

Some indication of the breadth of their success and of the success yet to be was experienced by Lieutenant Patterson's 23-man troop of the 10th Light Horse Regiment which had pushed into the Dothan Pass. In the late darkness hours the tiny troop jostled into a large Turkish formation retreating out of the plain. Putting out machine guns, Patterson and Lance-Corporal George met the Turkish van with an extraordinary ruse. Using a German nurse as interpreter, the Turks were informed that they were surrounded in the head of the pass by a huge body of dismounted cavalry demanding their capitulation. At the correct moment of indecision, Patterson signalled for the machine guns to rattle over the heads of the Turks in parlez. The Turks in front laid down their arms and the gesture rippled backward infectiously. Four pieces of artillery and 2,800 soldiers were taken!

By the evening of 20 September, 36 hours into the first phase of Allenby's offensive, the Desert Mounted Corps cavalry had drawn a wide net over the hinterland of 7th and 8th Armies. Metaphorically, the EEF infantry were like beaters in a hunt driving the quarry into the net. Allenby's two infantry corps were positioned in the shape of a large 'L', the Turks having been completely herded away from the coastal plains. Chetwode's 20th Corps formed the base of the 'L' with the French and 54th Division the hinge: from hinge to top were respectively the 3rd, 7th, and 60th infantry divisions. This behemoth 'L' bore down on the right and front of the slowly crumbling 7th Army. As a coherent entity 8th Army had ceased to exist.

THE SWORD OF HIM THAT SAT UPON THE HORSE

'And the remnant were slain with the sword of him that sat upon the horse.' – Revelation 19:21

ON 18 September the northern column of the Arab Northern Army had awakened to the 'clump' reverbation, the whistle, then explosion of artillery shooting long range into its encampment at Umtaiye. A Turkish train mounting a gun on a flat car was standing off lobbing shells under the direction of spotting aircraft based out of Dera. The enemy, however, was forward staging its aeroplanes out of a valley five miles distant. Joyce sent Lawrence and Junor out in armoured cars to convince the three observer aircraft to move on. The cars managed to ambush the aeroplanes when grounded, driving straight on them firing machine guns. Two escaped airborne.

The message, though, was certain. Bivouaced 12 miles from the Dera aerodrome the Arabs were sitting ducks while the enemy enjoyed unrestricted local air superiority. Umtaiye, situated in the open desert, was nevertheless the only sufficient source of water for the horses and camelry of the mobile Arab force. In order to confuse the Turks, the column temporarily relocated to the old Roman frontier town of Um el Surab on 19 September. From there, small raiding parties under British advisors kept demolition activity alive.

Lawrence, meanwhile, rode south to Feisal's headquarters at Azraq where he conferred with Feisal and Nuri es Shalaan. Joyce passed through on 21 September in transit to assist Amir Zeid and Jafaar Pasha in their siege of Maan. Northwest of Maan, Hornby was out raiding with the Beni Sakr tribesmen. The 'news' aircraft from Allenby's GHQ at Ramle landed with the intelligence the Turks were in rout. Lawrence hopped the return flight to Palestine and drove by car to meet Allenby and to request air support. Lawrence

found Allenby possessed of a great calm with the only hint of his resounding victory betrayed by a faint glint of light about his eyes.

That same day of 21 September witnessed the last

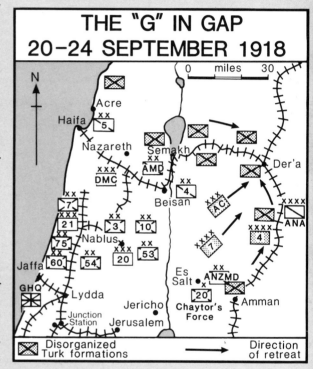

THE "G" IN GAP
20–24 SEPTEMBER 1918

Disorganized Turk formations

Direction of retreat

serious infantry fighting of the campaign. Colonel von Oppen reorganised his *Asien Korps* Brigade, merging the stricken German 702nd and 703rd into one battalion while retaining the individuality of the 701st and one cavalry squadron. Rallying part of the 16th and 19th Divisions for a total of 2,000 men, the body pushed east in the hopes of escaping over the Jordan fords. With 8th Army destroyed, the gathering weight on the front, and right flank of 7th Army was unbearable. At noon, Chetwode's 10th Division and Bulfin's attached 5th Light Horse Brigade took Nablus, the headquarters of 7th Army.

With the Desert Mounted Corps ensconced across the *Yilderim* rear, retreat had become something of a luxury. In most areas the difficult terrain restricted Turkish escape under any recognisable formation to five routes; Tul Karm to Samaria, Samaria to Jenin, Anebta to Jenin, Nablus through the Wadi Fara to Jisr ed Damiye on the Jordan, and Balata through the Wadi Fara to Beisan. Before the offensive, the RAF took photographs of the passes and had analysed at what chokepoints bombing could inflict maximum damage. Bristol Fighters of No. 1 Squadron, Australian Flying Corps, conducted a steady watch over these routes and reported back data via long-range wireless sets.

September 21 was a landmark in the history of the Palestine Brigade. Masses of Turks from Nablus and Balata in 7th Army sector were choking the gorge of the Wadi Fara in a desperate bid to escape over the Jordan. 'The chief attacks fell to the Bristol Fighters of No. 1 Squadron, Australian Flying Corps, each carrying eight 20lb bombs, to the D.H.9's of No. 144 Squadron, each carrying one 112lb and eight 20lb bombs, and to the S.E.5a's of Nos. 111 and 145 Squadrons (four 20lb bombs), but the three corps squadrons (14, 113, and 142) also took a part in the attacks.'[1]

Just after 0600 hours, the aerial bombardments began, increasing in tempo until nine-and-a-quarter tons of bombs and 56,000 machine gun rounds were expended among the Turks crowding the Wadi Fara. Reports were laconic, but to their bloody point: 'I dived and fired continually on the thickest part of column. They were literally sprayed and I succeeded in inflicting heavy casualties.'

And another: '4 direct hits, one in a body of cavalry roughly 50 strong: the bomb appeared to have practically demolished them as less than 6 got up and ran away. All the rest fell and remained stationary. 3 bombs direct hits on large lorries. One lorry blown off road into valley by direct hit; the other two bombs fell among transport on road causing wreckage. The road must be impassable for transport.'[2]

The 88 bombing sorties and 88 strafing passes so devastated the column heads that the Wadi became a dam behind which a swollen reservoir of life died. Man and animal panicked. Drivers jumped from moving lorry and wagon. Along the defile of death 100 guns, 55 lorries, 4 cars, 912 wagons, and 20 water carts and field kitchens

▲ Liman von Sanders, *Yilderim* commander-in-chief, emerges pointing from his staff car in Haifa, 1918. Turkish and Austrian officers are in attendance.

▼ The fruits of war: 3,000 Turkish prisoners driven into the net in the plain of Esdraelon, Armageddon.

Left: The Jodhpore and Mysore Lancers of the 15th Imperial Service Cavalry Brigade entring Haifa, 23 September 1918.

Right: Arab horse patrol coming in. In times of greeting or exuberance it was usual for them to discharge their rifles while galloping to and fro in *razzia* fashion.

reposed in immobile tribute to the gods of war. Tactfully, the official records are silent on the cost of life.

Other retreating columns, unaware of the preponderance of enemy behind them walked straight into the nets of the EEF cavalry. *Yilderim* GHQ at Nazareth was occupied by MacAndrew's 5th Cavalry on 21 September and the next day he dispatched his 15th (Imperial Service) Brigade toward the Mediterranean port of Haifa while his 13th Brigade rode on Acre a few miles north along the coast. Acre, the scene of so much misery and bloodshed during the Crusades, fell in 1918 as an anti-climax. Haifa was a different matter.

The road's entry into Haifa from the Plain of Esdraelon is commanded from the south by Mt. Carmel and to the north by the treacherous marshes of the Kishon River. In fact, the Mysore Lancers lost their first reconnaissance patrol of horses who waded into a treacherous bog. Two scouts of the Jodhpore Lancers were also sucked down in quicksand. Against these tricky approaches a Turkish depot regiment had placed a battery of guns on Mt. Carmel with machine guns at the foot.

Fifteenth Brigade's handling of the obstacle was both innovative and gallant. Two squadrons of Mysores and a squadron of Sherwood Foresters (from 14th Brigade) negotiated their way up winding tracks to take the guns while a battery of artillery provided counter battery fire. Simultaneously, the Jodhpores and remaining Mysores charged the defile under Mt. Carmel, lances extended. As the machine guns rattled, the first squadron of Mysores went down in rows. The charge was irresistible and the fifteen

troopers still in the saddle speared the Turkish gunners as even mortally wounded horses added their weight to the momentum before falling dead. The lancers continued on into the town, encountering minor skirmishing. For a tally of 37 men and 143 horses, 689 Turks, 16 guns and 25 machine guns were bagged and Haifa opened to receive EEF supplies by sea.

Allenby sent the 7th Infantry Division up the coast to take over the port areas and free the cavalry for their next strategic assignment – Beirut and Damascus. The 5th Cavalry and Australian Mounted Division were to be given orders taking them west of the Sea of Galilee then northeast via the Quneitra Road to Damascus. The 4th Cavalry would strike east from Beisan on Dera to assist the Arab Northern Army in capturing the town and its strategic environs. Then the Arabs and 4th Cavalry would push north on Damascus together.

Allenby had given Chaytor's Jordan Valley Force instructions to move on Amman. Between Chaytor, the 4th Cavalry, and the Arab Northern Army, Turkish 4th Army was to be destroyed, along with whatever shattered 7th and 8th Army elements had managed to escape over the Jordan. Such an escape was, in fact, becoming real and its potentiality demonstrated the only fault in Allenby's master plan. Chaytor had been ordered on the Jisr ed Damiye crossing but that was not enough. From there to Beisan was a 25 mile long gap constituting a serious hole in the hunter's net. On the morning of 23 September, Chauvel ordered Barrow's (11th Brigade) 4th Cavalry to ride due south down both banks of the Jordan to intercept the crossings. Barrow

was in an exposed position and encumbered with prisoners, but it had to be done. The day before, the RAF had put four tons of bombs and 30,000 rounds into the fords, and spied several white flags of surrender. Dash could pay off.

The 11th Brigade encountered the rearguard of the Asia Corps at Makhadet abu Naji and, after a brief engagement, killed the commander of 19th Division and captured the 16th Division commander along with 800 personnel. Von Oppen's German *Asien Korps* had already crossed and were making their escape on Dera. A mile south, the cavalry became enmeshed in a spirited fight where guns of 4th Army out-duelled a horse artillery battery. Then, once again, the cavalry redressed the balance through a bold charge which sealed off both entrance and exit to the ford. The haul was 4,000 prisoners. On the morning of 24 September, the 11th Brigade completed its mission of closing the Jordan fords at Makhadet el Masudi where another cast of the net garnered 5,000 prisoners. The cavalry operations had been a model pattern of performance against the flank of a beaten and disconsolate foe.

Yilderim had been surprised, battered, demoralised, then hustled between irresistible force to the fore and immovable object to the rear. Heavy equipment, guns, machine guns, supplies which could not readily be at hand, even rifles, had been discarded in the turmoil. All who were destined to escape the net cast over 7th and 8th Army had already done so. At the end of 20 September, Chauvel had proudly remarked to Allenby that he had 13,000 prisoners and received a laughing retort: 'No bloody good to me! I want 30,000 from you before you've done.'[3] At the close of 24 September, Allenby had nearer 40,000! It was time to cast the net over the Trans Jordan.

Attempting a Rally

Von Sanders had left Nazareth on 20 September, the day of the cavalry's first attack on his GHQ. A battleground makes a poor headquarters, and his relocation was just as well, for Nazareth fell the next day. Von Sanders' picture of his own front was none too clear. In Tiberius that afternoon he learned what he must have already suspected – that Major Frey and the 13th Depot Regiment had failed to reach and hold the Musmus Pass. His primary strategy was to hold a line from Lake Hula down the Jordan to the Sea of Galilee while his retreating forces made for the Yarmuk Valley and thence by rail into Dera.

At Tiberius and Semakh he commissioned Major Frey with 260 men to begin establishing a defensive line. Von Sanders also issued orders for Colonel von Oppen to bring any men he could muster to break through to Beisan and reinforce the mouth of the Yarmuk. Whether or not these orders were realistic is a subject for controversy, but von Oppen's staff persuaded him instead to the Jordan crossing where, as it was, only half his force managed to elude the 4th Cavalry. The subject remained one of acrimony and was another blow to von Sanders' reformation of a front.

The commander-in-chief next rode one of the last trains into Dera over the just repaired track and there to learn Dera had been reattacked by the Arabs on 20 September. Major

Plate from the *Illustrated London News.*
◄

Willner, who had gallantly fought at Gallipoli, had organised the town as best he could and as a temporary measure von Sanders placed him in command of the new front. In the meantime, thousands of the Druses tribe were riding the town streets discharging their rifles as if in a fantasia. Inimical to Feisal, the sheikhs offered their loyalty to the Turks in exchange for support which, of course, von Sanders was quite unable to give. Unhappily, he watched his would-be irregular allies ride off . . . at least in neutrality. One of the first telegrams he opened was from a bureaucratic idiot in Constantinople asking him to nominate a prize for a local sack race! Feeling himself to be swept up in a difficult sack race of his own, von Sanders testified he was more interested in finding his army![4]

On 22 September von Sanders instructed Djemal Pasha Kuchuk to withdraw his 4th Army without delay. Djemal had already – if nobly – waited too long in order to hold open the door for his 2nd Corps which was trying to fight its way through the Arabs along the Hejaz rail. Von Sanders then entrained for the new *Yilderim* headquarters to be set up in Damascus, at times riding, at times dismounting to circumvent demolished sections of the rail on foot. Upon his arrival in Damascus, late on the 23rd, he wired 2nd Army, which was headquartered north at Aleppo, to send any possible reinforcements south. The answer was that only a few 'Arab' battalions could be spared.

Von Sanders' plan for the Hula-Jordan-Galilee line came to consummate grief at Semakh the morning of 25 September. Semakh was situated on the Sea of Galilee, facing over an open plain and flanked by small hills. Barely west of the town the River Jordan flowed south out of the sea. The Palestine Railway tracked north of Beisan for 12 miles, entered Semakh, then ran east through the Yarmuk Valley and tunnel system to Dera, 30 miles away. Captain von Keyserling had gathered 461 soldiers and stragglers, a third of them German, to hold the position into the Yarmuk.

At Desert Mounted Corps headquarters at Meggido, Chauvel examined his assets. MacAndrew's 5th Cavalry was along the coast and moving inland, Barrow's 4th

Cavalry was at Beisan and east of the Jordan harrying Turkish rearguards. The Australian Mounted Division's brigades were stretched over the rough triangle of Jenin, Beisan, and El Affule. Chauvel set Brigadier General Grant (of Beersheba fame) with his 4th Light Horse Brigade the task of breaking Semakh.

Grant moved on the town in the dark before the dawn on 25 September. At 0430 hours, as the 11th Light Horse Regiment came under machine gun fire, a squadron officer shouted 'What orders, Colonel?' – to which was replied – 'Form line and charge the guns!'[5] Lieutenant-Colonel Parsons rapidly ordered the machine gun squadron to place six pieces on both sides of the railway and lay down suppression fire at the flashes of light hammering from the town. The Light Horse galloped across the darkened plain yelling in the dark to locate each other and to warn their own marksmen of their whereabouts.

As they bore down on the eastern access to Semakh 'A' and 'B' Squadron troopers began falling into pits which had been prepared with Teutonic thoroughness. Dismounting on both sides of the train station the Light Horse shot its way in on foot while 'C' Squadron stood in reserve on a knoll to the right rear. One squadron from the assembling 12th Light Horse rode into the town from the west side and the garrison surrendered. One hundred dead Germans testified to the ferociousness of the street fighting but it was revealed over half of the Turks had not expended a single cartridge. The cavalry had reacted quickly, covered its ground protected by darkness and supporting fire, and dismounting, had again won the day. A few hours afterward, Tiberius – scene of the great Crusader defeat at the Horns of Hattin – was found evacuated. *Yilderim*'s new line was out of luck.

Von Sanders now had to consider some inkling of a new line approximately 30 miles south of Damascus, from southwest of Riyaq eastward to the Dera-to-Damascus Railway. As Damascus was a seething hotbed of civil unrest he decided to relocate *Yilderim* headquarters north at Baalbek. Who was to man his new front was becoming a matter of increasing anxiety. Djemal Pasha Kuchuk was ordered urgently to send any units with formation or morale on from Dera. Among the first of these to leave was von Oppen's *Asien Korps* Brigade, depleted to 70 per cent of its original men, and the 146th (Masurian) Regiment. Von Sanders was particularly concerned to deploy these in echelon southwest of Damascus along the Meissner Pasha Road. Should the Desert Mounted Corps break through toward Baalbek and Homs, 4th Army, Damascus, and northern Syria would be doomed. Recognising the loss of his 7th and 8th Armies, von Sanders instructed on 26 September the demolition of the seven Yarmuk Valley tunnels and the multi-span iron bridges, some of which were 150 feet long.

Recasting the Net

The contribution of Chaytor's Jordan Valley Force to Allenby's offensive was significant in itself. Until the first guns crashed out their surprise, *Yilderim* had believed the threat was to come from the Jordan Valley. Chaytor anchored the EEF right flank from 20th Corps zone through Jericho and protected the Ghoraniyeh and Auja bridgeheads. More than this, he maintained the illusion of threat by active probes against 4th Army during the first critical phase Allenby needed to destroy 8th Army. These demonstrations lasted from 17–19 September then intensified during 20–21 September as the Desert Mounted Corps spread across Turkish rear areas.

Chaytor's own offensive began on the 22nd when he advanced north to seal the Jisr ed Damiye crossing over the Jordan which was a major exit of 7th and 8th Armies. The action of his New Zealand Mounted Rifle Brigade also resulted in historical irony – for the second time the Wellington Regiment captured a commander of the Turkish 53rd Division (the first time at Gaza, March, 1917)! Es Salt fell next day and for the third time that year to the ANZAC Mounted Division.

Allenby now pressed Chaytor to cut off Amman in the hopes of helping the Arabs destroy Turkish 2nd Corps which had evacuated the Maan district and was fighting its way up the Hejaz rail in the hopes of rejoining its parent 4th Army. Chaytor found the road from Es Salt to Amman had been damaged by Turkish engineers, sections of which caused delay, but fortunately it had been a hurried job. Once more the citadel of Amman presented a stubborn bastion, but there seemed less fight this time and no counterattack. The dismounted Canterbury Regiment took the fort with the bayonet on the afternoon of 25 September. Ten guns, 300 horses and 2,563 Turks were taken, adding to the Jordan Valley Force's growing list. Paradoxically, Chaytor's two Jewish battalions which had been expected to perform well behaved badly, and his two West Indian battalions – of which little had been expected – did splendidly, and took the highest proportion of casualties of the command.

To Chaytor's ledger, therefore, was a closing of the southern Jordan, the pressing of 4th Army, the capture of Amman and the cutting off of 2nd Corps. Gullet, in his *The Australian Imperial Force in Sinai and Palestine* wrote: 'Chaytor was a mounted infantryman of the highest order,

▲ Plumed and spurred Light Horse officers of the Australian Mounted Division receive first-hand field intelligence from the pilot and observer of a BE 2e. Aircraft acted as an express reconnaissance service which reported significant battle developments directly to requesting formations. Allenby's air and cavalry superiority gave him a crushing advantage.

one of those rare soldiers who did everything in this prolonged campaign so surely, thoroughly, and yet so quietly that it might be said no task set him between the Canal and Amman was big enough to test his full capacity.'[6]

Lawrence had returned from Allenby's GHQ on 22 September with his requested air support: two Bristol Fighters, a DH9, and Palestine's only Handley Page. Carrying their own petrol and supplies, they were perhaps the world's first air-contained fighting unit. The Arabs were astonished at the size of the Handley Page and they spread rumours over the Hauran that matters were clearly weighted in Feisal's favour. 'Indeed and at last they have sent us *the* aeroplane, of which these things were foals.'[7]

The Arabs were encamped at Um el Surab for safety and twice daily sent patrols to Umtaiye to fetch water. Remarkably, the enemy pilots were still bombing Umtaiye in ignorance of the Arab relocation! That same day the RAF downed two of the Germans then flew Lawrence on to Azraq to meet Feisal. The two of them drove in Feisal's green Vauxhall, in company with Nuri es Shalaan, to view the lauded Handley which went on a bombing mission over Mafrak and Dera that night. The Arab leaders then drove back to Azraq to rally the tribes.

The Arab column raided for the next two days to give the revolt time to grow. A wooden makeshift bridge was demolished at Jabir, and Mafrak Station was unsuccessfully attacked due to the accuracy of German machine gunners. Out of revenge the RAF again bombed Mafrak Station on the night of 24 September.

When Chaytor marched into Amman the next day, the Beni Hassan tribe reported the Turks were falling back like a gypsy exodus. Clearly the moment had come. From the west, southwest and south the Turks were rushing with

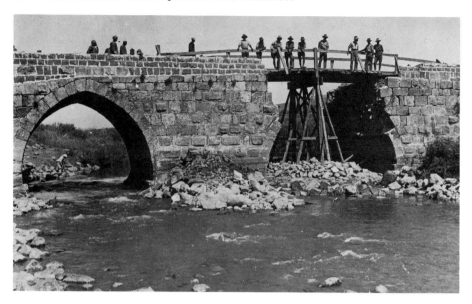

Jisr Benat Yakub or the 'Bridge of Jacob's Daughters' being repaired by the 2nd Field Squadron, Australian Engineers on 25 September 1918. A German demolition party had thus caused a delay on the road during the pursuit to Damascus. The bridge was a selected Jordan crossing just south of Lake Hula and north of the Sea of Galilee.

◀

mad determination to reach the supposed safety of Dera. The question was whether the Arab Northern Army could cling to 4th Army long enough to cause its eventual destruction, or if 4th Army could shake free, rally *Yilderim* forces, and retreat on Damascus ahead of Allenby's cavalry.

On 26 September the main Arab column of 4,000 marched out of bivouac north of Dera. Pausing at the rail the Turks had just put back in restricted working order, hundreds of the Arabs descended on the track like a plague of locusts to a sheaf of wheat. Every sort of unsophisticated explosive and hand tool ripped at miles of the railway. The body then shifted to Sheikh Saad, 15 miles north-northwest of Dera by dawn of the 27th, taking the surrender of 2,000 Turks en route. Sheikh Saad lay on the Pilgrim's Road on the flank of the Damascus rail; observation and water supply were excellent and access to retreat good on at least two sides. Here, the northern column of the Arab Northern Army was planted like an island awash with 4th Army's recoiling tide.

Barrow's 4th Cavalry and an Indian brigade from the 3rd Division had moved out of Beisan but they would first have to reach Irbid before they could begin to influence events nearer Dera. Overhead a British aeroplane circled and dropped a message on Sheikh Saad that 2,000 Turks were coming northeast from Mezerib and 4,000 moving north from Dera, both columns heading for Sheikh Saad.

It needed a split decision, and such was made. Part of the mobile Rualla with Tallal ed Hareidhin's peasant footmen shifted against the larger column to harry its progress while Auda abu Tayi, Lawrence and his bodyguard, half the regulars with artillery and a large augmentation of irregulars, set off to intercept the smaller column. Even numbers of one's own allies were becoming indistinct because everywhere they set foot their numbers waxed and waned as hordes of enthusiastic supporters tagged along or returned home at leisure. The role of these local enthusiasts in spreading anti-Turkish disinformation and in verifying outside events to a spiderweb of locales was of incalculable propaganda value. The Turks found the countryside rising against them.

The Turkish column of 2,000 marched in good order through the villages of Miskin and Tafas – the latter place being the personal home of the chief, Tallal ed Hareidhin. The van and rear of the Turkish march was covered by a lancer regiment with infantry on both side flanks supplemented by machine guns. Transport accompanied in the centre.

The Arabs opened with Pisani's mountain guns blasting high-explosive and with Hotchkiss automatic rifles raking the line. The Turks answered with over-fused shrapnel which, as usual, exploded high. The mobile Arabs maneuvered into Tafas village behind the Turkish march. There they witnessed ugly scenes of torture and despoliation which had been perpetrated upon the populace, neither age nor sex being spared in a savage catalog of hurt and mutilation. Lawrence admonished his bodyguard, 'The best of you brings me the most Turkish dead.'[8]

These had been Tallal ed Hareidhin's own people and extended family group. Quietly, he rode to the hill overlooking the flat where the Turks were trying to march away. Grieved beyond comprehension the chieftain charged. Sword raised, Tallal crossed the dead ground at the gallop in the evening air. Arab and Turk watched dumbstruck as this solitary and quixotic gesture of Arab chivalry thundered across the silent gap between the two armies. At the last moment Tallal pierced the hush with his enduring war cry and a hundred rifles heralded his passing among the points of the Turkish lances.

This victory purchased no honour or respite. Auda abu Tayi's comment to Lawrence was brief if deadly acidic: 'God give him mercy; we will take his price.'[9] Auda's wrath and force of personality then asserted a lion-like control over the Arab column. Boldly, the Arab mass charged behind Tallal's example, striking the Turks in the rear as the Haurani peasants closed from the hills on all flanks, mad for revenge. Even Lawrence had shouted 'no prisoners' but it was wasted voice, for no quarter would have been given.

By dark the Turkish column had fallen in an orgy of massacre, the wounded being dispatched where they lay. None but a cluster of German and Austrian machine gunners with three motor cars escaped and these only through superior formation and fire discipline and not a little courage in dispersing the Arab assaults.

Into Dera

The Arab hilltop position at Sheikh Saad certainly exerted the intended leverage. For the Turk nowhere was safe, and night ambushes exaggerated rumours into a fantastic perception of Arab strength. Dera was ordered to be evacuated and the Turks burned their six surviving aircraft. Six trains, for want of track, were left standing useless as units straggled out on foot. By 27 September many of the formations, rather those who were to escape at all, had left Dera while overhead smoke curled from destroyed munitions.

After the massacre of the smaller column at Tafas, Lawrence set about supporting the Rualla and peasantry, harassing the larger Dera column of 4,000. Throughout the night of 27/28 September the butchery continued, the Turks finding no sleep as village after village turned out against them and the mounted Arabs grew emboldened by the grip of night. As men fell out from fatigue, each to await his personal fate, Arab and Turk became intermingled and the trunk column staggered on in slivers chipped at from every side.

Before midnight Lawrence rallied several hundred tribesmen and directed them south toward Dera. Now nearly defenceless, only a skeletal Turkish garrison had been left behind. Shortly after sunset the powerful Anazeh tribe had ridden into Dera on its own strength and was engaged in the arts of booty and reprisal. Another 500 Turks were taken. Not having slept in four nights and having worn out two camels, Lawrence mounted a third and entered Dera alone at dawn. At the Mayor's house he met Sherif Nasir who had already set up police, a military governor, and a court of inquiry. Lawrence supplemented these actions by posting guards over what stores and public utilities remained.

Barrow's column of 4th Cavalry had not marched from Beisan till 26 September. At Irbid, about half way to Dera, the front brigade had been turned back by an unexpectedly strong Turkish rearguard. The next day was slow going so that only on the 28th was he in sight of Dera. Unfortunately, Barrow's RAF support bombed the Arab welcoming party as his Indian machine gunners opened up on them from below. To Lawrence fell the onerous lot of traversing 'no man's land' and convincing Barrow the gunfire coming from Dera was mere joy-riding and that the town was indeed in Allied hands.

Relations were off to a bad start, made worse as Barrow expected Dera to be handed over to regular EEF administration and Lawrence treated the column as Arab guests. As a favour, Allenby's Chief of Intelligence, Brigadier Clayton, had seen to it Barrow had no specific instructions for such an administration and Lawrence's demeanor thus presented

him with a *fait accompli*. Finally, taking it with good nature, Barrow saluted Sherif Nasir's silk banner on the balcony of the government buildings. It was a gallant gesture and the moral effect of it rippled through the Arab Northern Army.

On 28–30 September occurred a ludicrous incident of war. Chaytor's 2nd Light Horse Brigade rode down the Hejaz Railway south of Amman in the hope of intercepting the remnants of Turkish 2nd Corps. Jafaar Pasha and Amir Zeid had taken possession of Maan on 23 September after a very long siege which had begun that April. Hornby's tribesmen had clung to 2nd Corps' retreat north out of Maan like a plague so that: 'On the hills east and west of the railway station hundreds of men, mounted on horses and camels, could be seen: their patient, watchful attitude suggesting the spectacle of vultures attending on a dying man.'[10]

The Light Horse encountered the Turks below El Qastal near Ziza. On 28 September the RAF dropped a note that all water points were in EEF hands and that 2nd Corps had until the morrow to surrender or face bombing. The commander, Colonel Ali Bey, was very much of that frame of mind but sent word he feared the Australians were not strong enough to fend off an Arab massacre of his men (those Turkish soldiers not of ethnic Arab stock who had already deserted had been tortured). A night of macabre comedy followed with the Australians camping next to the beleagured Turks to protect them while the Turks, having given their parole to surrender when able, nervously shot into the dark at the marauding Arabs, the Australians' allies.

The next day, Lieutenant-Colonel Cameron, commanding the 5th Light Horse, found himself in a pickle. His own Australian reinforcements were due to arrive but the RAF bombing was due even sooner. It was not certain whether his request for bombing cancellation had been received. 'With great presence of mind he sent into the Turkish position the ground-sign employed to indicate the position of his regimental report-centre to aircraft, and had it spread out behind the trenches. The Turkish commander was informed of the situation and advised to put his men under cover. Colonel Ali Bey was, deeply grateful for this chivalrous action, but did not blench at the prospect of the raid. If it came, he said resignedly, it would be the will of God.'[11]

The air attack did not come, but neither did Cameron's reinforcements. Chaytor had sent down Brigadier-General Ryrie to lend extra weight to the proceedings. Night was falling and the Arabs were demanding Turkish heads and rifles. Ryrie was inspired to controversial action. This involved a hostage exchange of senior Turkish officers for Arab sheikhs which he demanded from both sides to guarantee the peace.

On the morning of 30 September, Ryrie ordered the majority of the Turks to pile the disassembled bolts of their rifles, except for two select battalions of Anatolians who were allowed to retain their assembled rifles to assist in escort duty! This procession made an extraordinary impression marching into Dera. By this novel method, Ryrie saved 4,068 soldiers and 534 wounded. In total, Chaytor's men had seized 10,322 Turks and 57 guns for the miraculous price of 139 casualties!

20

CAVALCADE

DURING the unfolding offensive Allenby had spent as much time with the fighting troops as possible. His open-top touring car was a common enough sight – on opening day he had been at Bulfin's 21st Corps headquarters, on 21 September with Chetwode's 20th Corps, and the same day with Chauvel's Desert Mounted Corps headquarters at Meggido. These first-hand impressions of friend and foe gave him the confidence to order an immediate advance on Damascus.

On 26 September Allenby called a corps commander conference at Jenin. In one week all of Palestine had fallen with a bag of 50,000 prisoners. About 40,000 Turks were still estimated at large between EEF lines and Damascus. Most of these were trudging in ragged columns seeking some rearward consolidation, or perhaps just security in numbers on the road home. It was always Allenby's maxim to press hard on a rout and prevent the comeback of a beaten foe. But there was a pressing motivation from his own soldiers; the medical corps had warned that two weeks after entering the malaria-infested Turkish lines that his own men would begin dropping. Chaytor's Force was already falling sick.

Allenby had kept secret his Damascus plans until three days after the offensive was underway. This was both pragmatic and psychological. This second bound was entirely dependent upon the crushing blow of the opening move and he desired his staff emotionally concentrated on the task at hand. Then, as victory was apparent, he sought to translate the height of morale into another phase of concrete operations.

Bulfin was to set a division marching up the coast for Beirut while the main tasking fell on the three divisions attached to the Desert Mounted Corps and to the Arabs. Barrow's 4th Cavalry was to link with the Arab Northern Army and march by the Pilgrim's road on Damascus, while Hodgson's Australian Mounted Division, followed by MacAndrew's 5th Cavalry Division, were to take the more direct route, north of the Sea of Galilee and south of Lake Hula, across the Jordan by road to Quneitra. This assigned Barrow a march of about 140 miles and that of the Australians and 5th Cavalry approximately 100 miles. Barrow was to begin one day before the other column and a junction was planned for 30 September. From these figures one calculates Allenby expected them to ride about 35 miles a day while potentially grappling with Turkish rearguards. Allenby obviously knew his men.

The Australian Mounted Division kicked off the morning of 27 September. Their ride encountered only one hitch at Jisr Benat Yakub, the Biblical bridge of Jacob's daughters. It was the crossing of the Jordan north of the Sea of Galilee and the Germans had posted rearguard machine gunners as well as engineers to demolish its fourteenth-century stone

structure. During the spirited little action the Australians sent out two flanking brigades while the colourful French colonial *Spahis* skirmished over the steep banks. The rearguard drew off by the damaged bridge during the night causing the cavalry to cross at dangerously swift fords.

By early afternoon the Australians found at Quneitra enough water to bivouac the entire division while one brigade was detached northeast up the Damascus road. Quneitra was a Circassian village, a subject race loyal to Turkish administration. To protect the lines of communications, therefore, two regiments from the 5th Cavalry were attached and put under Grant's brigade.

On the morning of 29 September Hodgson's Australians found themselves held up by machine guns on the road at Sasa. In the daylight no impression against the 1,500 Turks (including 300 Germans) could be made either mounted or dismounted. But at night, infiltration told a different story and the enemy was forced to escape in lorries after losing six machine guns. This rearguard action delayed the cavalry till dawn the next day when the advance resumed.

Soon after, 350 Turks and Germans were rounded up along with four pieces of artillery which they had not known how to use. Hodgson now asked for speed to Damascus and the entire division deployed 'in column of squadrons in lines of troop columns'. It was one of the final cavalry spectacles in history, the picturesque *Spahis* and *Chasseurs d'Afrique* standing out against the Australian khaki. Ahead, Kaukab, ten miles southwest of Damascus, which was defended by nearly 5,000 Turks. Bourchier's regiments were on the right, the 5th Light Horse Brigade to the left, and the 3rd Light Horse behind. Fortunately, the Turks possessed no artillery and there seemed a good chance of turning their right flank.

Two EEF horse artillery batteries moved to within 2,500 yards and pounded the Turks over open sights while much of the division swung wide behind their right flank. The shelling caused the Turks to waver and encouraged Bourchier to risk a frontal charge with his two regiments over the rough ground. It was a risk well taken, for almost immediately, as the cavalry thundered up the slope leading to Kakaub, the Turks broke, running toward the shelter of the gardens leading to Damascus. A squadron of the once vaunted Turkish 3rd Cavalry led the rout in shame.

Fifth Brigade then spread across the western and northern approaches to Damascus and blocked the escape routes to Beirut and Baalbek. In the Barada Gorge 4,000 Turks were surrounded, fired on from the heights, and induced to surrender arms. The 3rd Light Horse had a similar experience while intercepting the road to Homs. Four hundred Turks were killed, the rest driven back to Damascus.

At Kiswe, nine miles south of Damascus, MacAndrew's 5th Cavalry Division split a Turkish column and isolated

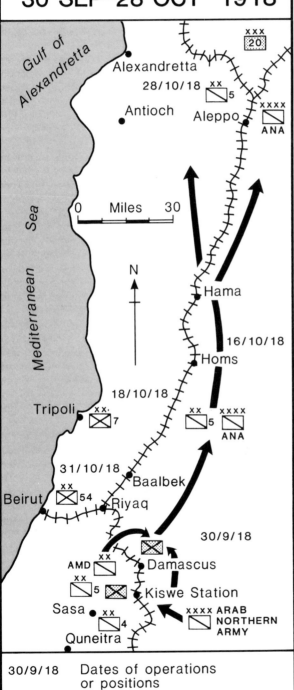

THE FALL OF DAMASCUS AND THE ALEPPO ADVANCE

30 SEP–28 OCT 1918

Gulf of Alexandretta

Alexandretta

28/10/18

XX 5

Antioch

Aleppo

XXXX ANA

Mediterranean Sea

0   Miles   30

N

Hama

16/10/18

Homs

18/10/18

Tripoli   XX 7

XX 5   XXXX ANA

31/10/18

Baalbek

Beirut   XX 54

Riyaq

30/9/18

AMD   XX

Damascus

XX 5   Kiswe Station

Sasa   XX 4

Quneitra

XXXX ARAB NORTHERN ARMY

XXX 20

30/9/18   Dates of operations or positions

2,000 in the village. Skirmishing produced a further 500 prisoners, but the cavalry was unable to close. By nightfall of 30 September elements of the Desert Mounted Corps had isolated the southern, western, and northern exits of Damascus. Only a German battalion and several hundred stragglers had escaped the cavalry for the temporary shelter of the doomed city.

Simultaneously, 4th Cavalry and the Arab Northern Army had cooperated in the joint mission of surrounding Damascus. At Dera, Feisal had motored in from Azraq to ensure the new Arab government was on a secure foundation. The prisoners in the Dera environs numbered thousands. Some of these were handed over to the EEF but most were farmed out to the local villages where they were set to work in the fields in exchange for food and board. To Lawrence, Dera had been but a thread in a tapestry of sacked towns. To Barrow's regulars, virgin to the excess of irregular war, the town was a ghastly spectacle of burned images and of wounded stripped and humiliated.

On 29 September, Barrow's division happily moved north on Damascus, its right flank secured by the Arab Northern Army led by Colonel Nuri Bey, Feisal's chief of staff. Sherif Nasir, Nuri es Shalaan, and Auda abu Tayi were already far ahead of Nuri Bey with 1,200 irregulars. The original Dera column of 4,000 Turks had become a river swollen nearly double from the tributaries of Turkish refugees and these the irregulars had harried night and day. For the 6–7,000 escaping in column, the 75 miles from Dera to Damascus seemed forever. For most, it was; at each step they were sniped, cut-out, subjected to night ambushes, and even to cooperative bombing by the RAF.

In the Rolls-Royce tender *Blue Mist* Lawrence and Stirling with two drivers drove ahead of Barrow's force and kept between it and the retreating Turks, dropping back reconnaissance messages. To guerrillas accustomed to the chance and exigencies of irregular warfare Barrow moved maddeningly slow. Every position was scouted and picqueted in regular textbook fashion, despite a perhaps logical consideration the Turks would attempt no stand until Kiswe – where road and railway intersected south of Damascus.

Barrow's men began to come down with malaria and influenza, even hunger, and food and forage was acquired along the way by bartering Turkish equipment with Arab traders. Early on 30 September, divisional progress was still 30 miles south of Kiswe and Brigadier-General Gregory's 11th Brigade was sent ahead. Late afternoon, the advanced guard discovered the Arabs engaging the rearguard of 4th Army. The Arab irregulars had greatly worn down the Turkish column to perhaps 2,000 men but had been unable to win a direct confrontation. As Sherif Nasir maneuvered to delay the column for an hour, Lawrence asked Gregory for assistance and received the Hampshire Battery and Middlesex Yeomanry. While Nuri es Shalaan's Rualla gripped the flanks, Auda abu Tayi led the Walud Ali tribe to the Turkish rear and arranged them in ambush along the twin peaks of Jebel Mania. The EEF artillery pushed to the front, shooting over open sights until dark while receiving return fire from the Turkish mountain screw-guns. Then the Yeomanry and Arabs charged against the reversed face of the Turkish column, crumbling its crust, and channelling the stream of humanity directly into Auda's trap. 'In that night of his last battle the old man killed and killed, plundered and captured, till dawn showed him the end.'[1]

It was the signal passing of 4th Army.

Damascus

Damascus was and is possibly the oldest inhabited city in the world. It is not walled, nor was its position founded on defence but on trade. Millennia of conquerors had decided its fate in the open plain on its many-rivered plateau, set between the Anti-Lebanon Mountains and the Arabian sea of sand. With historical repetition so again had its fate been settled by the forces camped in 1918 about its suburbs. MacAndrew and Barrow's divisions had linked hands at Kiswe, and several hundred allied Rualla had already infiltrated the city for the morrow's entry which no hand could now stay.

The Turkish commandant of Damascus was in fact having an early breakfast with Major-General Barrow just after midnight on 1 October. Ali Riza Pasha, an ethnic Arab with 40 years of Turkish service, had long been chairman of a secret anti-Turk society pledged to seize control of Damascus at the earliest opportunity. It had been with great and tragic irony that von Sanders had appointed him commander of the Turk's last defensive line. That evening and early morning – the last of several hundred years of Ottoman rule over the city, Ali Riza Pasha laughed so heartily over his premeditated acts of sabotage that he upset the breakfast table.

Hung as a stage backdrop, the Damascene silhouette was bathed in reddened glare and explosions rocked the ancient streets. To Lawrence it sounded as though the highwater of Arab victory would be cloaked in ruin. Yet at dawn Damascus lived, its beautiful gardens were intact and a river mist inspired the city to shiver in the radiance of the sunlight morn. The Citadel stood, and with it the Ommayyad Mosque, resting place of the great Saladin. Only above Kadem Station did the sky twist in angry black spirals at the burnt offering below.

Controversy between the EEF and Arabs leaves to interpretation which of the city's new masters first entered. The Arab irregulars – up to 4,000 Rualla – had certainly already slipped in, but the first regular formation was the 3rd Light Horse Brigade at about 0630 hours on 1 October. Shortly after, Sherif Nasir, veteran of 50 battles, and Nuri es Shalaan came in on horse and Lawrence motored in in the *Blue Mist* at 0730 hours. The Australians found themselves showered with perfumes, flowers and confetti and the city was set to hold its wildest celebrations in 600 years.

For the footsore, demoralised and beleagured soldiers of *Yilderim* Damascus had been a chimeric haven. As they had tried to march out on 30 September supplies could not be bought, even for gold. The Arabs had ridden wild in the street waylaying the stragglers and sniping at exiting units. The Sherifian standard had been unfurled above the townhall and no one had possessed the temerity to tear it down. Characteristically, the 146th (Masurian) Regiment

had been the last intact formation (1,500 men) to leave and it held up well against the Australians in rearguard action north to Homs. Other German units had demolished what munitions they were able.

But for the rest of the hodge-podge broken *Yilderim* troops it was disintegration. The 10th Light Horse Regiment discovered a train loaded with Turks awaiting an engine which never came. In hospital, 1,800 of the enemy lay in filth and despair, the living interspersed with the dead. And 11,000 Turks had waited at their barracks to surrender. The pursuit to Damascus, its encirclement, and subsequent fall had since 26 September inflicted a further 20,000 Turkish–German prisoners. Von Sanders was estimated to own no more than a ration strength of 17,000, with probably no more than a 4,000 effective combat strength.

Damascus was in high revelry until 2 October when Chauvel's Desert Mounted Corps paraded up the Pilgrim's Road and returned business as usual. Unlike Barrow at Dera, Chauvel refused to salute the Sherifian flag. Like Barrow, Chavel acquiesced at least for the moment in an Arab administration. Again, Allenby and General Clayton had given no specific instructions and Lawrence's assertion of certain control, acceptance of responsibility, assurance of his assets, and confidence of a larger numerical following combined to win Damascus for the Arabs.

The Arabs had gone a long way to ensure this for themselves. For months Feisal had cultivated a shadow Damascene government whose purpose was a takeover once the Turkish administration collapsed. Feisal's program of political preaching had aided Chauvel's corps advance. His Allied link made the passage of convoys and EEF administration of 'occupied' or 'liberated' territory a fact of common consent rather than the common dissent which had attended the Turks in flight. The Rualla, in fact, had infiltrated Damascus' quarter of a million inhabitants not only to support the new government but to prepare the population, by their presence, for an EEF-Arab occupation. Incident-free cooperation was the joint aim.

Sadly, it was not the goal of certain dissident factions. Two Algerian expatriate brothers, Abd el Kader and Mohammed Said (the former was the Turkish spy who had betrayed Lawrence's Yarmuk raid), had gained considerable political influence in Damascus through supporting the Turks. As the sun shone at last on Arab nationalism, the brothers changed their complexion overnight, and by dint of a powerful guard of retainers had forced themselves on the popular Damascene political figure Shukri el Ayubi and were ensconced in the Town Hall. Suddenly Arab national-ists, they were nevertheless inimical to Feisal, and Lawrence determined to oust them.

At the first session of the new government on 2 October, Lawrence came prepared. Nuri es Shalaan's Rualla and Nuri Said's regulars were posted outside the Town Hall. Inside were Lawrence's veteran bodyguard along with the leaders and chief supporters of the new government. On behalf of Feisal, Lawrence deposed the shadow government with the mercenary Algerians, and named Shukri Pasha as acting military governor, Nuri Said as commandant, Azmi as adjutant general and Djemil as chief of public security.

The Algerian brothers had come to the session with murderous intent and were not amused by their deposition. Backed by his own guardsmen, Abd el Kader railled against Lawrence then tried to knife him, but Auda abu Tayi leaped first, wrestling Kader into submission. Then, publicly, Nuri es Shalaan pledged, unconditionally, his Rualla host to support Feisal and Lawrence. Outside as well as inside, the guns bristled and by force of arms the new government was born.

Other trouble threatened. Auda had set to fists with the chief of the strong Druses tribe who had been somewhat tardy in cutting his Turkish umbilical cord. Within hours the Druses had joined forces with the Algerians (Lawrence had interceded for their release as an example of mercy) in an abortive coup d'état. But most trying was merely the establishment of a semi-efficient administration out of the internal chaos. This need ironically returned to their areas of expertise many of the bureaucrats who had proved so useful to the Turks.

Rapidly, the trappings of 'civilised' government were restored: the police, a fire brigade, relief work, the water supply, the power house lighting, sanitation, a labour corps. As a gesture of the new solidarity, the transport of the Arab Northern Army was turned over to the city. Currency was a problem, for the only paper was Turkish and the Australians had captured so much of it that when they dumped it on Damascus, the value bottomed out. Chauvel's corps, with over 25,000 horses to feed, put a stiff requisition on the city.

Within a few days the first Arab government had

▼ In his younger days as a camel-driver, the Prophet Mohammed reflected on the distant beauty of Damascus and refused to enter, declaring Paradise could only once be crossed. Its position at the hub of rivers situated between the mountains and the desert assured its perpetual value as a merchant city. In the foreground is an Arab cemetery on the outskirts of the world-famous grove and walled gardens. In the centre background can be seen the Citadel and slightly behind, the Ommayyid Mosque, resting place of the great Saladin.

collapsed then quickly renewed when Ali Riza Pasha assumed the reins of military governor. 'Our aim was a façade rather than a fitted building. It was run up so furiously well that when I left Damascus on October the fourth the Syrians had their *de facto* Government, which endured for two years, without foreign advice, in an occupied country wasted by war, and against the will of important elements among the Allies.'[2]

Allenby met Feisal in Damascus on 3 October, Allenby in a grey Rolls-Royce and Feisal up from Dera by special train. 'They were a striking contrast — the burly confident Englishman, accustomed to command and to dominate by sheer force of personality, and the slight, ascetic Arab with his princely bearing, to whom the arts of the politician were more natural than the vigour of a soldier.'[3]

The meeting was cordial but the official harbinger of bad news. The invocation of the Sykes-Picot Treaty had arrived and Feisal was informed of what rumour had already whispered.

In brief, and with generalisation, Britain was to hold a mandate over Palestine and a protectorate over the Trans Jordan while France was to possess a mandate over Lebanon and a protectorate over Syria. Feisal was enjoined to formulate an Arab administration in the protectorate areas from Aqaba to Damascus, and to bear the attachment of Anglo-French advisors. Feisal could do little but wait for the 1919 Peace Conference when he could try to redress the status quo. For Lawrence, who had acted as interpreter throughout, it seemed the confirmation of his own unintended treachery. When Feisal had gone Lawrence asked from Allenby and finally received what had been his keenest wish for a year . . . permission to leave the Middle Eastern theatre.

Aleppo

During Allenby's offensive the Allies made strident gains on the Western front, and in the Balkans one of the Central

Powers, Bulgaria, was knocked out of the war. The War Cabinet was pressing Allenby for a raid in force on Aleppo, which, 200 miles from Damascus, would create the greatest political effect. Distance, supply, and disease were Allenby's main obstacles; the predicted malaria was striking with escalating vengeance, and influenza – the dreaded 'Spanish Flu' which was sweeping the world – was putting the 4th Cavalry out of action.

Allenby resisted the War Cabinet's urgency and built the last advance of his campaigns along solid lines. While the Australian Mounted Division occupied Damascus, the 4th Cavalry rode northwest to the Beirut–Homs–Damascus railway junction at Riyaq. There they remained in indirect support and to recover from illness. Meanwhile, the 7th (Meerut) Division had marched up the coast from Haifa to Beirut then to Tripoli by mid-October. Beirut was a very small port in 1918, but important as a handy stores-base for the northern bound to Aleppo.

MacAndrew's 5th Cavalry proceeded up the railway past Baalbek (von Sander's recent headquarters) to Homs, where stood the glorious Crusader castle *Krak des Chevaliers* in guard of the Homs Gap. At Homs MacAndrew was joined, on 16 October, by Sherif Nasir and 1,500 Sherifial regulars of the Arab Northern Army who had ridden up the desert side of the rail from Damascus. Nasir had counted on and received irregular support from the Anazeh Tribe in passage.

MacAndrew's fighting strength was no greater than that of Sherif Nasir – a mere 1,500 sabres but he at least had the additional support of two RHA batteries and a squadron of RAF. Combined, it was a small column very strong in firepower and mobility (in fact the strongest armoured car support of the campaigns) and with the aeroplanes and Arab scouts, strong in reconnaissance.

It was just as well, for their advance was deep into former Turkish territory and Aleppo was a risky 120 miles north of Homs. Intelligence knew that von Oppen's *Asien Korps* of about 700, the 146th Regiment of Lieutenant-Colonel Freiherr von Hammerstein-Gesmold consisting of 1,500 and about 300 Germans and Austrians from Haifa, had escaped relatively intact and that the corps rifle strength of reliable troops ahead of MacAndrew in retreat was 4,000. The energetic Turkish General, Mustapha Kemal, was known to be assembling the defence of Anatolian Turkey at Aleppo with an estimated inclusive ration strength of 20,000. With headquarters at Katma and working with his old 7th Army staff, Mustapha Kemal was assigned to forge a new 7th Army in cooperative line with Nehad Pasha's 2nd Army.

Allenby, on 20 October, was at Baalbek with Chauvel on one of his touring inspections of the front lines. Chauvel thought the situation deserved caution and he received Allenby's luke warm concurrence to halt the Aleppo advance. MacAndrew, however, would have none of it and replied in 'Nelsonesque' fashion, curtly detailing his confidence in his men and in local conditions under the caveat 'Not understood'. It was, of course, a polite way of refusing orders. Allenby appreciated a 'thruster' and his memories of his own Boer War conclusions were not so dim. It was

characteristic of his generalship that having set his objectives and picked his men he gave them free rein. Winking at Bols, his chief of staff, Allenby had MacAndrew signalled that he wanted Aleppo secured as early as possible.

The country through which the column passed was the most beautiful of the Palestine–Arabian Campaigns. The Lebanon and Anti-Lebanon Mountains starkly rose from 3–10,000 feet. Decked with vines and cedar trees, theirs was an unrivalled grandeur. By 23 October, MacAndrew and Sherif Nasir were within a few miles of Aleppo where the Turks had elected to take their stand. The Turks had viewed the advance with trepidation. Most of the coastal towns had exchanged loyalties and Feisal was falsely thought to be arriving with a levy of 20,000. Inside their lines, Arab agents were at work in Aleppo preaching to a receptive population. The presence of MacAndrew's column alone was disturbing, for its self-contained lorry transport (mistakenly thought to be packed with infantry), and strength of armoured car attachments seemed to presage an invasion and probably an Allied amphibious landing in the Gulf of Alexandretta.

The Turk's own situation was in a high state of flux. General Kiazam, von Sanders' chief of staff came down with pneumonia, Colonel von Oppen – whose decisive gallantry had guided the *Asien Korps* out of Armageddon – died of cholera. The German units were transferred west to Tarsus with the 23rd and 47th Divisions to help guard the coastline, and as a closer step to eventual repatriation. At Alexandretta was the 41st Division and in the Gulf, the 44th. Mustapha Kemal was reconstituting the 24th and 43rd Divisions, but it must be noted that all these divisions were so seriously understrength that it would have been less a misnomer to term them regiments, if not battalions. Only Kemal's 20th Corps composed of the 1st and 11th Divisions, with 2–3,000 rifles apiece, could demand even the credible pretence of a brigade.

On 19 October the first whispers of Armistice wafted in from Constantinople. Finally, on 24 October the civil unrest in Aleppo forced a declaration of a state of siege. EEF forces had contacted the defensive line three miles south of the city and were knocking at the gates.

The battle for Aleppo by plan was to take place on the 26th, but Colonel Nuri Bey slipped his Arab regulars into the city the night before, entering the Citadel and government buildings. Pockets of citizenry joined the insurrection and, finding their communications untenable with the Arabs to the rear and MacAndrew in the front, the 3,000 Turks withdrew out of the Aleppo vicinity.

That day, the last official engagement transpired at Haritan when the Indian lancers of 15th Brigade were checked while attempting to turn 3,000 Turks out of a position selected by Mustapha Kemal. On 29 October Nasir's Arabs and MacAndrew's 1/1st Sherwood Foresters occupied Muslimiié Station, the meeting terminal of the Syrian–Mesopotamian rails, and thus ruptured Turkish 6th Army's communications. It was the highwater of the campaigns.

Armistice came into effect on 31 October, 1918. Within 11 days Germany sued for peace. The war was over.

21

EPILOGUE

ALLENBY'S crushing of the Turkish southwest flank was total; in the event of a renewed offensive, Mustapha Kemal's tragically weakened line in the Gulf of Alexandretta could not have held. From 19 September to 31 October Allenby's EEF took 75,000 prisoners (including 3,700 Germans and Austrians). This figure is exclusive of enemy killed outright, some of the wounded, and obviously whatever deserters managed to escape the clutches of both sides . . . and these subtractions from a ration strength of 104,000! Additionally, the EEF captured 360 pieces of artillery, 800 machine guns, 210 lorries, 89 train engines with 468 rail trucks — all in *functional* capacity — destroyed equipment not being counted. Army Group 'F' or *Yilderim* and 4th Army had been obliterated.

In exchange, the EEF took 5,666 casualties (only 853 killed) with two-thirds occurring in the Desert Mounted Corps.[1] (From January, 1915 to October, 1918 the EEF lost a total of 51,451 battle casualties, or comparable to America's *killed* in Viet Nam). During Allenby's final offensive alone the EEF pushed the general front back 350 miles, the 5th Cavalry covering nearly 600 miles over 38 days with only a 21 per cent loss in horses. The Desert Mounted Corps advance over a three-day period from 19–21 September averaged 56 kilometres per day, while during the 1967 Arab–Israeli War the Israelis advanced 55 kilometres per day over a four-day period – and this with modern armour, not cavalry! In fact, from an analysis of 15 campaigns noted for speed or distance selected over the past two centuries, Allenby's Meggido Campaign stands premier in statistical success and is *the* 'quick win' of the First World War.[2]

The policy of the Palestine campaigns had been directly effected by events on the Western Front. British policy began with a concern for the Suez Canal throughout both the Maxwell and Murray administrations. Under Murray, a hesitant advance began by stages solely to push back the Turks to better protect the Canal. The outbreak of the Arab Revolt in June, 1916 was supported, but only considered a

Above: No. 12 Light Armoured Motor Battery and No. 7 Light Car Patrol, north of Aleppo, shortly before the Armistice. In the background is the military barracks of Mohammed Ali. The advance to Aleppo was supported by the strongest contingent of armoured cars in the campaigns: Nos. 2, 11, 12 Light Armoured Motor Batteries and No. 1 (Australian), 2, 7 Light Car Patrols.

Right: Sherifian Camel Corps regulars with the Sherwood Foresters, 14th Cavalry Brigade, at Muslimie Station, 28 October 1918. Muslimie was the junction of the Syrian–Mesopotamian Railways and its occupation cut off 6th Army as well as marking the highwater of the campaigns.

convenient thorn in the Turkish side. Not until after First Gaza in March 1917 did the War Cabinet seriously deliberate on an invasion of Palestine. Before Allenby arrived in Palestine he was assured he would receive reinforcements sufficient to plan for Jerusalem; his EEF at Third Gaza was double the size of Murray's force at Second Gaza. The Arab capture of Aqaba coincided with Allenby's assumption of command so that from June 1917 the Arab Northern Army became a fully cooperative and coordinated arm of the EEF. The Government's policy, thence forward, consistently aimed at the elimination of Turkey from the war, it was only the emphasis of their commitment which differed. Thus, the stripping of the EEF to help counter the German spring 1918 offensives delayed Allenby's final campaign.

In Allenby's 28 June 1919 summation of theatre events he accurately portrayed the parallel between the Western Front and events in Palestine: '. . . the first period, the defence of the Canal, corresponded to the first check of the enemy's onrush in France and Belgium; the period of the advance through the Sinai desert, to the general develop-ment of the Allied strength and building up of a secure battle line along the whole front; the 1917 advance to the period of increased Allied pressure which exhausted the enemy's reserves; while the last advance coincided with the final Allied counteroffensive.'[3]

That this victory was largely purchased through the spending of the mounted arm sparked a controversy over the future utility of the arme blanche. Antagonists argued that it was a one-off circumstances and indicated the limiting possibilities of cavalry against a force in depth with no flanks, such as was the case on the Western Front. Proponents countered that seldom had armies marched to war with a smaller proportion of cavalry with the result that when an opportunity for the cavalry knocked, no cavalry was there to open.

One lesson established by the cavalry action in Palestine was that of its tremendous psychological impact upon even 'modern' infantry in the open and against shaken infantry even in positions – especially without barbed wire. Repeti-tiously, a bold charge delivered at speed in fluid or extended order, after a proper reconnaissance and attended with sufficient fire support, struck home. These were the same lessons which were being demonstrated by Cossack and White Russian cavalry in the contemporary Russian Civil War.

Turks captured after such a charge revealed the psycho-logical disadvantage felt when opposed by such mounted momentum at close quarters with cold steel. The lance of the EEF Indian cavalry was feared all the more. As further proof there was yet life in the arme blanche, three of the five Austrian Light Horse Brigades applied to be equipped with the sword after the 1917 campaigns, and it is believed the remaining two brigades so applied at the end of 1918.[4]

The value of cavalry in reconnaissance, both alone and in cooperation with aircraft, is obvious. Additionally, terrain was not ultimately the deciding factor in the utility of the mounted arm. As Allenby commented: 'We used to hear, especially in peace maneuvers that such and such a tract of country was suited to cavalry action. The truth is that cavalry

can, and will, fit its tactics to any country. This has been shown repeatedly during the war just ended; in the rocky hills of Judea . . . and the mountains of Moab.'[5]

Taking the balance of military history, of course, the tremendous success of the cavalry in Palestine–Syria can not be taken as absolute or universal, and progress has proved this so in the development of light and heavy armour and by the discontinuance of cavalry as a mainline force. Equally, the direct relationships of cavalry and armour in the questions of speed, reconnaissance, and soldier psychology should be recognised.

It is more truth than sensationalism to assert that Allenby's tactics in the 19–21 September 1918 offensive were a precursor of the modern blitzkrieg. The elements are unmistakable. First, concentration of force (21st and Desert Mounted Corps) at the decisive point, surprise and intense moving barrage (massed EEF artillery, even naval guns) while the infantry engaged the enemy, overcoming or sectionalising his forces. Overhead, meanwhile, aircraft (RAF) destroyed or degraded command and control and communications centres (von Sanders experienced a virtual news blackout and for several days did not know the full extent of Armageddon's maw). Then, the penetration and exploitation of the mobile forces (cavalry of the Desert Mounted Corps) driving for maximum irruption and bypassing local pockets of resistance . . . followed by clean-up or a hauling in of the prisoners as aircraft interdicted all major avenues of escape. Simultaneously, diversionary attacks (the reduced 20th Corps, Chaytor's Force, the Arab Northern Army) pinned enemy troops and prevented the transfer of reinforcements to the main danger. As Lawrence adulised: 'the perfection of this man who could use infantry, and cavalry, artillery and Air Force, Navy and armoured cars, deceptions and irregulars, each in its best fashion!'[6]

Surprise, mobility, and concentration were the keynotes of Allenby's victories, backed by relentless determination in the pursuit. While taking care to minimise the needs for risk, he was quite willing to take risks to succeed. Underlying these techniques was a solidity of administration and attention to health, communication and logistical details, so vital at the trunk core if the branches are to bend under the strain of war. Allenby always meticulously developed communications and supply along his strategic axis of advance. That he achieved a near perfection is evident in the rapid moves on Damascus and Aleppo. At GHQ before the offensive, Lawrence complimented Allenby's approved staff distribution of corps transport. No longer by textbook slide rule, the practical logistics allowed freedom of movement to fit the varying roles of mobility and even a pragmatic living off the land at the completion of the advance.

Allenby started his men full, then, when the pressure was on, drove them through half rations and twice the planned speed when necessary. By nurturing and honing his troops and by reestablishing the age-old importance of general-to-soldier contact at the front line, his troops were in a fit physical and moral condition to give their best – and perhaps beyond – when he so required. Personally, Allenby was served by a solid background. 'On active service he had commanded a troop in Zululand and Bechuanaland; a squadron, a regiment, a column (the equivalent of a brigade), in the South African War; a division, a Corps, an Army, and finally an independent Expeditionary Force in the Great War. In peace he had led and trained a troop, a squadron, a regiment, a brigade, a division — not for a season or so, in the intervals of staff employment, but each for several years. In addition to all this practical experience, he had studied the theory of his profession seriously; he had passed the course of the Staff College, and had held a staff appointment most efficiently.'[7]

Throughout, his character was courageous, loyal, and direct. His size, bearing, inner strength, and forsaking of field luxury at GHQ and during tours at the front made a positive impression, on even the independent ANZACs. Whatever the gripe concerning enforced details, such as no wearing of khaki shorts, or the insistence on the wearing of helmet and chinstrap in France, the troops knew they were being led and that their best interests were at heart. They could see and feel this evidence in their daily routine.

Allenby has received bad press during his tenure in France, despite the fact that his record equalled that of any British commander, and exceeded that of many. Allenby had difficulty coming across to personnel on a one-to-one basis, except for those who knew him best, and he was not a ready debater in the staff room. Yet his knowledge and competence was immense. Lawrence said of him: 'His mind is like the prow of the *Mauretania*. There is so much weight behind it that it does not need to be sharp like a razor.'[8] Obviously, the independence and opportunity to apply his strategic concepts in Palestine suited him.

Allenby's cavalry victory was also aided by the acquired EEF mastery of the skies, the absence of massed artillery as on the Western Front, and, in the end, the inherent morale factor between the opposing armies.

From autumn 1917, the impact of successive defeat compounded by degenerative internal conditions within the Turkish Army produced an inferior soldier by the autumn of 1918. This state of being increased the *extent* of Allenby's final triumph. This is apparent from von Sanders' surprise when whole divisions collapsed or melted away under the weight of Allenby's carefully prepared assault. Previously, von Sanders had witnessed such an act only once, in the summer of 1918 in the attack, and never when on the defence.[9] Thus, his entire positional logic of static shoulder-to-shoulder defence was in a few hours undermined. But the factor of morale should not be played as the decisive card in the cavalry's victory. During Allenby's 1917 campaigns the cavalry had achieved only one wide flank around Beersheba and the Turks were flush from their victories at First and Second Gaza. The cavalry won through by the bold and skillful handling of its mission.

Nor is the calibre of the Turk to be denigrated. Drained in the Balkan Wars, at Gallipoli, and in Caucasia his suffering under generally poor leadership and under sad conditions of service was terrible. Lieutenant-Colonel R. M. P. Preston, who fought in the Desert Mounted Corps against the Turks, has written that the Anatolian — 'nearly always fought splendidly, and that not alone in defense, but in the attack also. Indeed, some of their counterattacks were simply

▲ Count Raymond of Toulouse's Twelfth century Crusader castle above the Kadisha River, Tripoli, October, 1918.

heroic. Out-numbered, out-gunned, out-maneuvered, doomed to defeat before even the attack was launched, they yet advanced with the most reckless courage, shouting their war cry, Allah! Allah! Allah!'[10]

It was not the soldier who lost his war but his leadership. In 1914 Turkish resources were sufficient to protect Constantinople from the European approach and perhaps to affect the outcome of one of its other fronts. Turkey was not equipped for the multi-front scenarios to which Enver Pasha and his supporters committed her. The result, of course, was the over-taxing of the soldier, the ignorance of his need, and the absence of any decisive theatre or national strategy. And in the field the German–Turkish commanders were simply outgeneralled. Von Kressenstein was duped by Allenby and his planning staff in October, 1917 into thinking the offensive would begin against the opposite flank for which he was prepared and Allenby repeated the same trick against von Sanders on the reverse flank in September, 1918. Von Falkenhayn, from whom only the most brilliant might be expected, arrived at a bad moment and could never regain his equilibrium, nor could he grasp during his allotted time the differentials in the slower and less precise Turkish command and control as applied across the terrain and conditions of the Palestine Front.

The contribution of the Arab Revolt to the Allies and to the EEF was marked. As Keeper of the Holy Cities, Sherif Hussein's non-endorsement of the Turkish Caliph's call to Holy War acted as a powerful suppressant. The mere outbreak of the Arab Revolt in 1916 taxed Turkish supply and manpower and split their psychological will. The Arabs were co-religionists in a sense little understood by the varied Christian sects of the West, so that the Revolt can be argued to have been at least in part as much a civil war as an insurrection against an occupying power. To the bitter end Djemal Pasha sought reconciliation.

Further, the ideal of Arab nationalism as inherently projected in the Revolt offered a potentially attractive optional allegiance to the tens of thousands of ethnic Arab soldiers serving the Turks. Those who did not desert or 'betray' the Turks in other capacities were nevertheless

▲ Allenby and Feisal in Damascus. 'They were a striking contrast; Feisal, large eyed, colourless and worn, like a fine dagger; Allenby, gigantic and red and merry, fit representative of the Power which had thrown a girdle of humour and strong dealing round the world'. T. E. Lawrence, *Seven Pillars of Wisdom*.

treated as suspect. Arabs on the flanks and rear became the insecure, the intangible factor, even among the indigenous Arab population, for Turkish logistics and communications to the Palestine Front lay superimposed over Arab lands.

Militarily, the Arab Revolt was a masterpiece chapter in guerrilla war. A corps of 3–4,000 Arab Northern Army regulars, scarcely capable of containing a Turkish brigade in the open field, became the nucleus which, through irregular augmentation, tied down the equivalent of divisions. This disproportionate dispersion of Turkish strength is ultimately expressed in that nearly half of *Yilderim*'s ration strength and combat troops in September, 1918 were poised against the Arabs and away from Allenby's main offensive thrust. A testimony to the Arab threat came from the enemy commander-in-chief, von Sanders: 'At the beginning of September, I pondered the idea of a voluntary retirement to a position with the right abreast the Lake of Tiberias, center

and left in the Yarmuk valley. Aside from Enver's instructions to hold Palestine, I gave up the idea, because we would have had to relinquish the Hedjas railroad and the East Jordan section, and because we no longer could have stopped the progress of the Arab insurrection in rear of our army.'[11]

The successful use of the mounted arm is of course the hallmark of the Palestine–Arabian Campaigns. The strategic lesson is not, however, so much the vindication of *cavalry* as it is the attestation of *mobility*, however accomplished. Mobility is itself dependent upon supply and the driving force of its leader. Certainly, the Arab irregulars under Lawrence expressed the highest form of mobility. Their camel raids bit off 250 miles between waterings, and this in a three day march. Each man carried a six-week ration in a 45 pound camel sack . . . they struck with relative impunity, spied, preached revolt, and hopelessly outmaneuvered the Turk with his small complement of cavalry and with his semi-industrialised reliance on the civilised arteries of his occupied lands. As for leadership, Lawrence set a maddening pace which was, even in Arabia, legend.

Lawrence from the start of the Revolt conceived its necessary blueprint to victory. In Feisal he found the 'Armed Prophet' or political architect of rebellion. From Lawrence's advent as the 'man on the scene' he used his liaison role to direct – as far as one great man could direct – the Revolt along the guidelines of this blueprint. It was an enormous undertaking set over a thousand miles among multi-tribal scenarios.

Lawrence's supreme art was in converting the Turk's advantage into their disadvantage and in translating Arab weakness into their strength. In concrete terms, Turkish strength was in its weaponry and regular supply. These Lawrence undermined through a guerrilla war against Turkish material and the rail link which was necessary to supply it. His formula for Medina was particularly ingenious; he kept it running, but 'only just'. This maximised its expenditure yet minimised its effectiveness. Through the stratgegic and psychological application of guerrilla force he reduced the Turks to an ineffective defensive along a ribbon of territory which they could neither expand, nor even protect.

Whereas Allenby's regular game was *concentration* of force, Lawrence's irregular game was *dispersion*. Much of his strategic success lay in the preliminary *distraction* of enemy forces, then an execution of plan variants – a main plan with alternatives, each of which might be capitalised as the fluid situation warranted. Through this equation small mobile Arab bands unable to face regulars in pitched battles were made into a deadly unbiquitous foe . . . 'pressing everywhere yet assailable nowhere'.[12] Surely, for his appreciation of the material dependency of 'industrial' nations Lawrence must stand as a founding forefather of 'modern' insurgents.

After the Armistice came the occupation and enforcement of the provisional clauses. It is ironical that it took longer to conclude peace with Turkey than it had to defeat her in war. The Treaty of Lausanne was not signed until 1923. The

ANZAC and Australian Mounted Divisions helped suppress the Egyptian nationalist rising in 1919 before sailing home by the end of that summer, and the Desert Mounted Corps was broken up. Barrow took over 'Northforce', an occupational concept over the conquered territory, consisting of the 4th and 5th Cavalry and two infantry divisions. In November 'Syria' was handed over to the French.

In 1918 the Young Turk leaders Enver, Talaat, and Djavid fled by German ship across the Black Sea, leaving Izzet Bey to negotiate the Armistice. Turkey was soon at war again, this time with Greece. Mustapha Kemal became Turkey's first President, and became known as 'Ataturk', the father of his country, and the Sultanate was naturally abolished. Fakhri Pasha, the Turkish 'Tiger of Medina' wound up as ambassador to Afghanistan. Von Falkenhayn had been transferred to a quiet army command on the Eastern Front in 1918, then died of a mysterious illness in 1922. The German contingent was expatriated after a circuitous routing, and von Sanders spent six months interned in Malta before returning home.

From Damascus, Feisal tried to work within his joint Anglo–French advisory framework, but his agents so alarmed the French with agitation for an independent Syria that the French marched into the city in July 1920 and deposed him. Through the intervention of Lawrence and Winston Churchill, Feisal received a compensatory (elected) kingdom in the new Iraq. Lawrence had remained Feisal's interpreter during the Paris Peace Conference wherein the Arab statesman at least won the debate over France's Crusading *rights* to Syria by reminding M. Pichon who had in fact won the Crusading *wars*!

Feisal's father, the King of Hejaz, continued in receipt of subsidy from H. M. Government for the purpose of maintaining a friendly Arabia. The relationship did not prosper over the issue of Palestine and gradually the British subsidy was withdrawn. Ibn Saud, the powerful desert prince of the fanatical Wahabis in central Arabia, took his cue and defeated 4,000 regulars of the Sherifial Army. Hussein abdicated in favour of his eldest son, Ali, who was soon deposed in turn by Ibn Saud. Out of it grew the modern 'Saudi' Arabia. Hussein was exiled to Cyprus where he died in 1931.[13] Hussein's son, Abdullah, became ruler of Jordan till his assassination in 1951. Jafaar Pasha, chief of staff and 'trainer' of the Arab Northern Army, became Feisal's ambassador to London, then Prime Minister of Iraq, until he too was assassinated. Auda abu Tayi returned to his desert to build a modest castle.

From 1919–1922 Lawrence helped the Arab cause as best he could, first as liaison to Feisal at the 1919 Paris Peace Conference, then as Political Advisor to the Middle East Department of the Colonial Office under Winston Churchill. Here, the post-war British aerial and armoured car tactics successfully adopted to preserve British influence in the Middle East were attributable to Lawrence. Under great pressure to publish for profit and granted a fellowship to All Souls College, Oxford, Lawrence's life might have taken a far different course than it did.

Such publishing profit he deliberately dodged and Lawrence passed the rest of his life trying to hide from the public eye. His self-critical awareness was too strong for him to bask in the glory others were so willing to bestow. It has been said that he shied clear of a promotion to brigadier-general, the award of a Victoria Cross (for Aqaba) and even a knighthood. Instead, he chose the life of a common soldier, enlisting under assumed names in the RAF and the Tank Corps throughout the 1920s. Some said it was to expunge his 'sins', others that having fulfilled his dreams, little else remained. It was for these reasons, and more, for the body, mind, and soul of this sensitive scholar had entered the supreme tournament of life, death, war, and peace and emerged scarred from its pillars of wisdom.

After surviving a thousand Turkish bullets, and seven write-off aeroplane wrecks, Lawrence died six days after a motorcycle accident which occurred on Egdon Heath on 13 May 1935. Even his death was shrouded in controversy, for there were conflicting eyewitness reports of a mysterious 'black car' in the accident vicinity. Feisal, also a young man, had died shortly before Lawrence.

In a sense, Allenby had also fulfilled a dream with his independent command in the East, for he was never to campaign again. From 1919–1925 he remained in Egypt as Special High Commissioner. Allenby's rewards were swift and heady. In 1919 he was thanked by both houses of Parliament and enlarged with a £50,000 sterling grant. By 1920 he had been elevated to Field Marshal Viscount E. H. H. Allenby of Meggido and Felixstowe, GCB, GCMG, Colonel of the Life Guards, with Court appointment of 'Gold Stick in Waiting' and 'Freedom of the City of London' (a civic honour given only to Allenby, Haig, French, Beatty, and Jellicoe). Allenby died a year to the week after Lawrence.

Overall, the Palestine–Arabian Campaigns had no direct military bearing on the European Theatre either in negative expenditure of resource or in outcome. The Campaigns did create a positive boost in Allied morale, contribute heavily toward the defeat of Turkey, and to the great moral and material enhancement of Britain's post-war prestige throughout the Middle East. As a direct result of the victorious campaigns the Balfour Declaration was honoured, out of which eventually grew the state of Israel and the contention with Palestine. As a consequence of territorial 'liberation', Syria, Iraq, Jordan, Lebanon, and even (indirectly) 'Saudi' Arabia were born. Yemen and Aden were freed from Turkish rule. The Middle East had been redrawn.

The Allied effort was clearly fortunate to possess in Lawrence one of history's great captains of irregular warfare, and in Allenby one of history's great generals of regular war. Together, in their respective spheres and fighting in co-operation, they wrought prodigies of skill and valor. Field-Marshal Viscount Wavell, himself a veteran of the Palestine Campaigns and, during World War Two, against the *Afrika Korps*, regarded Allenby as 'the best British general of the Great War'.[14] As for Lawrence, perhaps the simple epitaph of the renowned Bedouin Robin Hood, Auda abu Tayi, is most expressive:

'I have never seen anyone with such a capacity for work, and he is one of the finest camel riders that ever trekked across the desert. By the beard of the Prophet, he seems more than a man!'[15]

APPENDICES

A. EEF Order of Battle, October, 1917

Commander-in-Chief: General Sir Edmund H. H. Allenby
Chief of the General Staff: Major-General L. J. Bols

Desert Mounted Corps Lieutenant-General Sir Henry G. Chauvel

ANZAC Mounted Division Major-General E. W. C. Chaytor
1st Light Horse Brigade: 1st, 2nd, 3rd Regiments
2nd Light Horse Brigade: 5th, 6th, 7th Regiments
New Zealand Mounted Rifles Brigade: Auckland, Canterbury, Wellington Mounted Rifles Regiments

Australian Mounted Division Major-General H. W. Hodgson
3rd Light Horse Brigade: 8th, 9th, 10th Regiments
4th Light Horse Brigade: 4th, 11th, 12th Regiments
5th Mounted Brigade: 1/1st Warwick, 1/1st Gloucester, 1/1st Worcester Yeomanry Regiments

Yeomanry Mounted Division Major General G. de S. Barrow
4th Mounted Brigade: 1/1st Bucks, 1/1st Berks, 1/1st Dorset Yeomanry Regiments
8th Mounted Brigade: 1/1st City of London Yeomanry, 1/1st County of London (Middlesex) Yeomanry, 1/3rd County of London Yeomanry
22nd Mounted Brigade: 1/1st Lincs. Yeomanry, 1/1st Staffs. Yeomanry, 1/1st East Riding Yeomanry

Corps Troops
Nos. 2, 3, 11, and 12 Light Armoured Motor Batteries
Nos. 1 and 7 Light Car Patrols

Attached
7th Mounted Brigade: 1/1st Sherwood Foresters, 1/1st South Nottinghamshire Hussars
Imperial Camel Corps Brigade: 2nd Imperial Battalion, 3rd ANZAC Battalion, 4th ANZAC Battalion

20th Corps Lieutenant-General Sir Philip W. Chetwode

53rd (Welsh) Division Major-General S. F. Mott
158th Brigade: 1/5th, 1/6th, 1/7th Royal Welch Fusiliers, 1/1st Herefordshire Regiment
159th Brigade: 1/4th, 1/7th Cheshire Regiments, 1/4th, 1/5th Welch Regiments
160th Brigade: 1/4th Royal Sussex Regiment, 2/4th Royal West Surrey Regiment, 2/4th Royal West Kent Regiment, 2/10th Middlesex Regiment

60th (London) Division Major-General J. S. M. Shea
179th Brigade: 2/13th, 2/14th, 2/15th, 2/16th London Regiments
180th Brigade: 2/17th, 2/18th, 2/19th, 2/20th London Regiments
181st Brigade: 2/21st, 2/22nd, 2/23rd, 2/24th London Regiments

74th (Yeomanry) Division Major-General E. S. Girdwood
229th Brigade: 16/Devonshire Regiment, 12/Somerset Light Infantry, 14/Royal Highlanders, 12/Royal Scots Fusiliers
230th Brigade: 10/East Kent Regiment, 16/Royal Sussex Regiment, 15/Suffolk Regiment, 12/Norfolk Regiment.
231st Brigade: 10/Shropshire Light Infantry, 24/Royal Welch Fusiliers, 25/Royal Welch Fusiliers, 24/Welch Regiment

Corps Troops
1/2nd County of London Yeomanry

Attached: 10th (Irish) Division Major-General J. R. Longley
29th Brigade: 6/Royal Irish Rifles, 5/Connaught Rangers, 1/Leinster Regiment, 6/Leinster Regiment

30th Brigade: 1/Royal Irish Regiment, 6/Royal Munster Fusiliers, 6/Royal Dublin Fusiliers, 7/Royal Dublin Fusiliers

31st Brigade: 5/Royal Inniskilling Fusiliers, 6/Royal Inniskilling Fusiliers, 2/Royal Irish Fusiliers, 5/Royal Irish Fusiliers

21st Corps Lieutenant-General E. S. Bulfin

52nd (Lowland) Division Major-General J. Hill
155th Brigade: 1/4th Royal Scots Fusiliers, 1/5th Royal Scots Fusiliers, 1/4th King's Own Scottish Borderers, 1/5th K.O.S.B.
156th Brigade: 1/4th Royal Scots, 1/7th Royal Scots, 1/7th Scottish Rifles, 1/8th Scottish Rifles
157th Brigade: 1/5th Highland Light Infantry, 1/6th Highland Light Infantry, 1/7th Highland Light Infantry, 1/5th Argyll and Sutherland Highlanders

54th (East Anglian) Division Major-General S. W. Hare
161st Brigade: 1/4th, 1/5th, 1/6th, 1/7th Essex Regiments
162nd Brigade: 1/5th Bedfordshire Regiment, 1/4th Northamptonshire Regiment, 1/10th London Regiment, 1/11th London Regiment
163rd Brigade: 1/4th Norfolk Regiment, 1/5th Norfolk Regiment, 1/5th Suffolk Regiment, 1/8th Hampshire Regiment

75th Division Major-General P. C. Palin
232nd Brigade: 1/5th Devonshire Regiment, 2/5th Hampshire Regiment, 2/4th Somerset Light Infantry, 2/3rd Gurkhas
233rd Brigade: 1/5th Somerset Light Infantry, 1/4th Wiltshire Regiment, 2/4th Hampshire Regiment, 3/3rd Gurkhas
234th Brigade: 1/4th Duke of Cornwall's Light Infantry, 2/4th Dorset Regiment, 123rd Outram's Rifles, 58th Vaughan's Rifles (Field Force)

Corps Troops
Composite Mounted Regiment
'E' Company, Tank Corps

GHQ Troops: Palestine Brigade Lieutenant-Colonel A. E.
Borton
5th (Corps Artillery) Wing (Nos. 14, 113 Squadrons)
40th (Army) Wing (No. 67 Squadron. Australian FC, No. 11
Squadron RFC)
No. 21 Balloon Company

B. EEF Order of Battle, September, 1918

Commander-in-Chief: General Sir Edmund H. H. Allenby
Chief of the General Staff: Major-General Sir L. J. Bols

Desert Mounted Corps Lieutenant-General Sir Henry G.
Chauvel

4th Cavalry Division Major-General Sir G. de S. Barrow
10th Cavalry Brigade: 1/1st Dorset Yeomanry, 2nd Lancers,
38th Central India Horse
11th Cavalry Brigade: 1/1st County of London (Middlesex)
Yeomanry, 29th Lancers, 36th Jacob's Horse
12th Cavalry Brigade: 1/1st Staffordshire Yeomanry, 6th
Cavalry, 19th Lancers

5th Cavalry Division Major-General H. J. MacAndrew
13th Cavalry Brigade: 1/1st Gloucestershire Yeomanry,
9th Hodson's Horse, 18th Lancers
14th Cavalry Brigade: 1/1st Sherwood Foresters, 20th
Deccan Horse, 34th Poona Horse
15th Imperial Service Cavalry Brigade: Jodhpore Lancers,
Mysore Lancers, 1st Hyderabad Lancers

Australian and New Zealand Mounted Division (see
Chaytor's Force)

Australian Mounted Division Major-General H. W. Hodgson
3rd Light Horse Brigade: 8th, 9th, 10th Regiments
4th Light Horse Brigade: 4th, 11th, 12th Regiments
5th Light Horse Brigade: 14th, 15th Regiments and the
(French) Régiment Mixte de Marche de Cavalerie

Corps Troops
Nos. 11 and 12 Light Armoured Motor Batteries
Nos. 1 and 7 Light Car Patrols

20th Corps Lieutenant-General Sir Philip W. Chetwode*

10th Division Major-General J. R. Longley
29th Brigade: 1/Leinster Regiment, 1/101st Grenadiers, 1/
54th Sikhs (F.F.), 2/151st Indian Infantry
30th Brigade: 1/Royal Irish Regiment, 1/Kashmir I.S.
Infantry, 46th Punjabis, 38th Dogras
31st Brigade: 2/Royal Irish Fusiliers, 2/101st Grenadiers,
74th Punjabis, 2/42nd Deoli Regiment

53rd Division Major-General S. F. Mott
158th Brigade: 5/6th Royal Welch Fusiliers, 4/11th Gurkha
Rifles, 3/53rd Indian Infantry, 3/154th Indian Infantry

*Chief of Staff: Brigadier-General A. P. Wavell.

159th Brigade: 4/5th Welch Regiment, 3/152nd, 1/153rd, 2/
153rd Indian Infantry
160th Brigade: 1/7th Royal Welch Fusiliers, 1/17th Infantry,
1/21st Punjabis, 1st Cape Corps

21st Corps Lieutenant-General Sir E. S. Bulfin

3rd (Lahore) Division Major-General A. R. Hoskins
7th Brigade: 1/Connaught Rangers, 2/7th Gurkha Rifles,
27th Punjabis, 91st Punjabis
8th Brigade: 1/Manchester Regiment, 47th Sikhs, 59th
Scinde Rifles, 2/124th Baluchistan Infantry
9th Brigade: 2/Dorsetshire Regiment, 1/1st Gurkha Rifles,
93rd Infantry, 105th Mahratta Light Infantry

7th (Meerut) Division Major-General Sir V. B. Fane
19th Brigade: 1/Seaforth Highlanders, 28th Punjabis, 92nd
Punjabis, 125th Napier Rifles
21st Brigade: 2/Royal Highlanders, 1st Guides Infantry, 20th
Punjabis, 1/8th Gurkha Rifles
28th Brigade: 2/Leicestershire Regiment, 51st Sikhs (F.F.),
53rd Sikhs (F.F.), 56th Punjabi Rifles (F.F.)

54th (E. Anglian) Division Major-General S. W. Hare
161st Brigade: 1/4th Essex R., 1/5th Essex R., 1/6th Essex
R., 1/7th Essex R.
162nd Brigade: 1/5th Bedfordshire R., 1/4th
Northamptonshire R., 1/10th London R., 1/11th London
R.
163rd Brigade: 1/4th Norfolk R., 1/5th Norfolk R., 1/5th
Suffolk R., 1/8th Hampshire R., Détachement Français de
Palestine et Syrie

60th Division Major-General J. S. M. Shea
179th Brigade: 2/13th London R., 3/151st Punjabi Rifles, 2/
19th Punjabis, 2/127th Baluch Light Infantry
180th Brigade: 2/19th London R., 2nd Guides Infantry, 2/
30th Punjabis, 1/50th Kumaon Rifles
181st Brigage: 2/22nd London R., 130th Baluchis, 2/9th
Deccan Infantry 2/152nd Indian Infantry

75th Division Major-General P. C. Palin
232nd Brigade: 1/4th Wiltshire, 72nd Punjabis, 2/3rd
Gurkha Rifles, 3rd Kashmir I.S. Infantry
233rd Brigade: 1/5th Somerset Light Infantry, 29th Punjabis,
3/3rd Gurkha Rifles, 2/154th Indian Infantry
234th Brigade: 1/4th Duke of Cornwall's Light Infantry,
123rd Outram's Rifles, 58th Vaughan's Rifles (F.F.), 1/
152nd Indian Infantry

Chaytor's Force Major-General Sir E. W. C. Chaytor

ANZAC Mounted Division
1st Light Horse Brigade: 1st, 2nd, 3rd Regiments
2nd Light Horse Brigade: 5th, 6th, 7th Regiments
New Zealand Mounted Rifles Brigade: Auckland,
Canterbury, Wellington Mounted Rifles Regiments
29th Indian Brigade: Alwar, Patiala and Gwalior Imperial
Service Infantry Regiments, 110th Mahratta Light Infantry,
38th, 39th Royal Fusiliers (Jewish Legion), 1st, 2nd British
West Indies Regiment

C. Palestine Brigade Air Order of Battle, September, 1918

Commander, Palestine Brigade, RAF: Brigadier-General
A. E. Borton GHQ Troops: headquarters at Bir Salem*

Fifth (Corps) Wing Lieutenant-Colonel C. S. Burnett at Er
Ramle

14 Squadron (at Junction Station)
16 RE 8s
3 Nieuports

113 Squadron (at Sarona)
16 RE 8s
5 Nieuports

142 Squadron (at Sarona, less one flight)
7 Armstrong-Whitworths (160hp) and one flight of 5 RE 8s
at Jerusalem

*Advanced stores and motor transport were established at Er Ramle;
Advanced Aircraft Park 'X' remained at Qantara.

Fortieth (Army) Wing Lieutenant-Colonel R. Williams at
Er Ramle

1 Squadron Australian Flying Corps (at Er Ramle)
18 Bristol Fighters
1 Handley Page

111 Squadron (at Er Ramle)
15 SE 5as

144 Squadron (at Junction Station)
13 DH 9s

145 Squadron (headquarters and one flight at Er Ramle)
6 SE 5as

No. 21 Balloon Company (headquarters at Sarona)
49 Section near Kh. Hadra
50 Section near Sh. Muwannis
57 Section near Et Tire

One of the Rolls Royce tenders (Corporal McKechnie driving) of the Hejaz Armoured Car Battery which travelled from Aqaba to Damascus. ◀

Light horsemen of the Australian Mounted Division at rest outside Damascus. ◀

NOTES

PART 1

Chapter 1
1. Aspinall-Oglander, *Military Operations Gallipoli*
2. Wavell, *Palestine Campaigns*, pp. 20–21

Chapter 2
1. Jones, vol. 5, p. 160
2. Djemal, p. 150
3. Powles, p. 39

PART 2

Chapter 3
1. Wavell, *Palestine Campaigns*, p. 32
2. Powles, p. 47
3. Jones, vol. 5, p. 178
4. *Cavalry Journal*, vol. XI, January 1921, p. 10
5. Teichman, p. 58
6. *Cavalry Journal*, vol. XI, January, 1921, p. 10
7. Thompson, p. 301
8. Hogue, pp. 41–42

Chapter 4
1. *Cavalry Journal*, vol. XI, January 1921, p. 17

Chapter 5
1. Thomas, pp. 54–55
2. Falls, *Military Operations, Egypt and Palestine*, to June, 1917, p. 226
3. Lawrence, *Revolt in the Desert*, p. 33
4. Ibid., p. 34

Chapter 6
1. Reid, p. 146
2. Teichman, pp. 124–125

Chapter 7
1. WO 158/602
2. WO 196/715
3. WO 158/627
4. Lawrence, *Revolt in the Desert*, p. 59
5. Lawrence, *Seven Pillars of Wisdom*, p. 246
6. Ibid., p. 283
7. WO 158/605
8. Lawrence, *Seven Pillars of Wisdom*, p. 181

PART 3

Chapter 8
1. Wavell, *Allenby*, p. 48

2. Falls, *Military Operations, Belgium and France*, p. 73

Chapter 9
1. Wavell, *Allenby*, p. 158
2. Fall, *Military Operations, Egypt and Palestine*, from June, 1917, p. 16
3. *Journal of the R.U.S.I.* (von Kressenstein), p. 508
4. Von Sanders, p. 191

Chapter 10
1. Wavell, *Allenby*, p. 165
2. Arab Bureau, *Military Handbook on Palestine*, p. 34
3. Falls, *Military Operations, Egypt and Palestine*, from June, 1917, p. 77

Chapter 11
1. Falls, *Military Operations, Egypt and Palestine*, from June, 1917, p. 107
2. Wavell, *Allenby*, p. 183
3. Falls, *Military Operations, Egypt and Palestine*, from June, 1917, p. 136
4. Teichman, p. 184
5. Preston, pp. 53–54
6. *Journal of the R.U.S.I.* (von Kressenstein), p. 511
7. Wavell, *Palestine Campaigns*, pp. 154–155
8. Falls, *Military Operations, Egypt and Palestine*, from June, 1917, p. 150

Chapter 12
1. Lawrence, *Seven Pillars of Wisdom*, p. 166
2. Lawrence, *Revolt in the Desert*, p. 168
3. Ibid., p. 169
4. Thomas, p. 209
5. WO 158/634
6. Lawrence, *Seven Pillars of Wisdom*, p. 389

Chapter 13
1. Preston, pp. 94–95
2. Thompson, p. 471
3. Falls, *Military Operations, Egypt and Palestine*, from June, 1917, pp. 260–261
4. Ibid., p. 262
5. Ibid., p. 262
6. Von Sanders, p. 177

PART 4

Chapter 14
1. WO 106/729
2. Ibid.
3. WO 106/378
4. WO 158/634
5. Hart, *Lawrence in Arabia and After*, p. 261
6. Ibid., p. 361
7. Lawrence, *Seven Pillars of Wisdom*, p. 490
8. Falls, *Military Operations, Egypt and Palestine*, from June, 1917, p. 315
9. WO 158/616
10. WO 158/634

Chapter 15
1. Lawrence, *Seven Pillars of Wisdom*, p. 527
2. Cox, p. 288
3. Von Sanders, p. 204
4. Falls, *Military Operations, Egypt and Palestine*, from June, 1917, p. 393

Chapter 16
1. Arab Bureau, p. 111
2. Powles, p. 229
3. Wavell, *Allenby*, p. 216
4. Powles, p. 223
5. Von Sanders, p. 237
6. WO 106/378
7. Von Sanders, p. 226
8. Hart, *Lawrence in Arabia and After*, p. 141
9. WO 158/605
10. Hart, *Lawrence in Arabia and After*, p. 142
11. Ibid., p. 317

Chapter 17
1. Wavell, *Allenby*, p. 224
2. Massey, p. 8
3. Ibid., p. 98
4. Hart, *Lawrence in Arabia and After*, p. 312
5. Jones, vol. 6, p. 208

Chapter 18
1. WO 106/718
2. Dupuy, pp. 162–164
3. Hart, *Lawrence in Arabia and After*, pp. 331–332
4. *Advance of the Egyptian Expeditionary Force*, p. 26
5. Falls, *Military Operations, Egypt and Palestine*, from

June, 1917, p. 525

Chapter 19
1. Jones, vol. 6, p. 225
2. Ibid., p. 226
3. Falls, *Armageddon 1918*, p. 102
4. Von Sanders, p. 290
5. Falls, *Armageddon, 1918*, p. 108
6. Gullett, The Australian Imperial Force in Sinai and Palestine, 1914–1918, p. 354
7. Lawrence, *Seven Pillars of Wisdom*, p. 640
8. Ibid., p. 652
9. Ibid., p. 653
10. Falls, *Military Operations, Egypt and Palestine*, from June, 1917, p. 556
11. Ibid., pp. 556–557

Chapter 20
1. Lawrence, *Seven Pillars of Wisdom*, pp. 661–662
2. Lawrence, *Revolt in the Dessert*, p. 434
3. Wavell, *Allenby*, p. 242

Chapter 21
1. Falls, *Military Operations, Egypt and Palestine*, from June, 1917, p. 618
2. Dupuy, pp. 13, 16
3. Falls, *Military Operations, Egypt and Palestine*, from June, 1917, pp. 632–633
4. *Cavalry Journal*, vol X, July, 1920, p. 327
5. Ibid., vol. XII, July, 1922, p. 134
6. Lawrence, *Seven Pillars of Wisdom*, p. 636
7. Wavell, *Allenby*, p. 248
8. Ibid., p. 254
9. Von Sanders, p. 274
10. Preston, p. 68
11. Von Sanders, p. 273
12. Thomas, p. 469
13. Hennessy, p. 12
14. Wavell, *Allenby*, p. 254
15. Thomas, p. 292

BIBLIOGRAPHY

Official Records and Sources

Public Records Office, London, War Office

WO 106: Numbers 14, 43, 715, 716, 717, 718, 721, 725, 728, 729, 1569

WO 158: Numbers 602, 604, 605, 615, 616, 617, 624, 625, 627, 628, 629, 630, 632, 634, 637

Advance of the Egyptian Expeditionary Force, July 1917–October 1918. Cairo: published by the Palestine News, 1919.

Arab Bureau, *Military Handbook on Palestine*. Third Edition. Cairo: Government Press, 1917.

Aspinall-Oglander, Br.-General C.F., *Military Operations: Gallipolli*, vol. 1 '*Inception of the Campaign to 1915*', London: William Heinemann Ltd, 1929.

Edmonds, James E. editor, *Official History of the War: Military Operations, France and Belgium*. London : H.M. Stationery Office, 1948.

Falls, Captain Cyril, *Military Operations: Egypt and Palestine*. To June, 1917, and from June, 1917. London: H.M. Stationery Office, c.1920s.

Falls, Captain Cyril, *Military Operations: France and Belgium*, 'The German Retreat to the Hindenburg Line and the Battles of Arras.' London: MacMillan and Co., Ltd, 1940.

Gullet, H. S. *The Australian Imperial Force in Sinai and Palestine, 1914–1918*. Sydney: Angus & Robertson Ltd., 1944.

Jones, H. A., *The War in the Air*, vols. 5 and 6, *Official History of the War*. Oxford: Clarendon Press, 1935.

The Palestine News. Cairo: 1917–1918.

Powles, Lieutenant-Colonel C. Guy, *The New Zealanders in Sinai and Palestine*. Auckland, New Zealand: Whitcombe and Tombs, Ltd, 1922.

Thompson, Lieutenant-Colonel R. R., *The 52nd Lowland Division*. Glasgow: Maclehose, Jackson and Co., 1923.

Primary Sources and Sources by Veterans

Aaronsohn, Alexander, *With the Turks in Palestine*. London: Constable and Co., Ltd, 1917.

The Army Quarterly, volume III, number 2. 'General Liman von Sanders on His Experiences in Palestine', by C. T. Atkinson, January, 1922.

Djemal Pasha, *Memories of a Turkish Statesman, 1913–1919*. London: Hutchinson and Co., 1922.

Hogue, Oliver. *The Cameliers*. London: Andrew Melrose, Ltd, 1919.

Inchbald, Captain Geoffrey, *Camels and Others*. London: Johnson Publications, Ltd, 1968.

Inchbald, Captain Geoffrey, *Imperial Camel Corps*. London: Morrison and Gibb, Ltd, 1970.

Journal of the Royal United Service Institution, volume 67. Translation of von Kressenstein's 'Between Caucasus and Sinai', entitled 'The Campaign in Palestine from the Enemy Side.' London: Whitehall, February 1922

Lawrence, T. E. *Revolt in the Desert*. London: Jonathan Cape, 1927.

Lawrence, T. E. *Seven Pillars of Wisdom*. London: Jonathan Cape, 1946, privately printed 1926.

Massey, W. T. *Allenby's Final Triumph*. London: Constable and Co., Ltd, 1920.

Preston, Lieutenant-Colonel R. M. P., *The Desert Mounted Corps*. Introduction by Sir H. G. Chauvel. London: Constable and Co., Ltd, 1921.

Reid, Frank, *The Fighting Cameliers*. Sydney: Angus and Robertson, Ltd, 1934.

Sanders, Liman von, *Five Years in Turkey*. Annapolis: U. S. Naval Institute (translation), 1927.

Teichman, Captain O. *The Diary of a Yeomanry Mounted Officer*. London: F. Fisher Unwin, Ltd., 1921.

Thomas, Lowell, *With Lawrence in Arabia*. London: Hutchinson and Co., Ltd, c.1921.

Wavell, Colonel A. P. *The Palestine Campaigns*. London: Constable and Co., Ltd, 1928.

Secondary Sources

The Cavalry Journal. Royal United Services Institute. London: Whitehall.

Volume X, number 37, July 1920, '4th Cavalry in Palestine'.

Volume X, number 37, July 1920, 'A Defence of the *Arme Blanche*'.

Volume X, number 38, October 1920, Some Critics of Cavalry and the Palestine Campaign'.

Volume XI, January, April 1921 'Operations of the Mounted Troops of the EEF'.

Volume XII, April, July, October 1922 'Egyptian Expeditionary Force'.

Cox, Harold, editor, *The Edinburgh Review*, volume 250. 'Falkenhayn in Syria', by Captain Cyril Falls, October, 1929.

Dupuy, Colonel T. N., *Numbers, Predictions and War*. Fairfax, Virginia: Hero Books, 1985 (revised).

Falls, Cyril, *Armageddon 1918*. London: Weidenfeld and Nicholson, 1964.

Falls, Cyril, *The First World War*. London: Longmans.

Hart, Liddell, T. E. *Lawrence in Arabia and After*, London: Jonathan Cape, 1934.

Hart, Liddell, *T. E. Lawrence to His Biographer*. London: Faber and Faber Ltd, 1938.

Hennessy, Peter. *The Times (newspaper)*. London: February 11, 1980.

Wavell, Field Marshal Viscount A. P., *Allenby: Soldier and Statesman*. London: Harrap and Co., Ltd, 1946.

Young, Brigadier Peter, Editor in Chief, *Marshall Cavendish Illustrated Encyclopedia of World War One*. New York: Marshall Cavendish, Ltd, 1984.

INDEX